# REPENT or PERISH!

Selected Sermons & Essays of

Archie Word

# REPENT or PERISH!

## Selected Sermons & Essays of Archie Word

Edited by

Victor Knowles

All Scripture quotations used in this book
are from the *American Standard Version,* A.D. 1901

International Standard Book Number: 0-89900-445-8

# DEDICATION

**In Loving Memory Of**
**The People Who Shaped Archie Word's Life**

J. Willis Hale
Garland Hay
V. E. "Daddy" Hoven
Howard Hutchins
Bill Jessup
Harold E. Knott
W. S. Lemmon
Teddy Leavitt
Roy Shaw
Florence Procter Word
Maggie Kenny Word

# Table of Contents

# Foreword

He stepped into the pulpit of our little basement church building on the side of a hill in Sweet Home, Oregon. He looked like he had just come from a fine men's store–white starched shirt, black pin-striped suit, shoes shined till you could see your face in them, strong, handsome, well-trimmed mustache, wide smile, revealing even, white teeth. He might have been the President, from his appearance, but he had a more important job.

I do not remember how many weeks the evangelistic meeting lasted, but it was in December of 1951. Oregon was experiencing a cold snap with temperatures near zero and snowing. The building was heated with a makeshift stove made of two fifty-gallon drums hooked together with two smaller pipes. The building was too warm in the front and cold in the back. In spite of the conditions and inclement weather, the building was packed to capacity every night.

When Archie Word began to preach in his clear and powerful voice one could not help but listen. Many wished they could disregard or ignore what he said, but inattention was not an option. One person said, "I sat there the whole hour with my mouth open, and realized later that I had not even swallowed. My mouth and throat were parched. I was spellbound."

The sermons were biblical, fully illustrated, powerful, (sometimes when he spoke of hell it was almost as if one could smell the smoke. Maybe it was the old wood stove!) but filled with pathos, live and genuine tears of concern.

On Thursday evening of the last week of the meeting I was the first to step out, followed by my brother, David, and everyone in the congregation (over 100 people) with the exception of the elders, preacher and a few others. The whole congregation came to renewal and repentance. It was December 13, 1951.

Some people were offended by his personality and style. He was always completely forthright, sometimes on the verge of being crude. (This was almost certainly due to his early years living a life of sin. This left him fully convinced of the awfulness of sin and its consequences. He had no tolerance for those who wanted to keep one foot in the church and the other in the world.)

He always called sin by its first name and was quick to warn of the error of those who were given to compromise of the gospel or godliness. On some occasions his attacks on sin and compromise were taken as personal affronts.

If one only saw the side of him that was apparent in the pulpit they could get the idea that he was heartless. The fact of the matter was that he had a heart of love for people and especially for those who were sold out to Jesus.

If he discovered that a person wasn't honest he had no tolerance for them until they repented. He was then the first to welcome them back. To him right was always right and wrong was always wrong. No one could doubt where he stood. As he grew older he never faltered in his stand.

He had a distinctive style of making sermon notes. They were in bold print and color coordinated. One time I preached a sermon in his presence. He asked if he could borrow it. I loaned it to him and he preached it at Montavilla. Notes were written on my outline in his bold handwriting, color coordinated! Although this was over thirty years ago, I still have that sermon outline.

There were many other sides to this great man. he had a very strong body. Many know that he boxed in the Navy and seldom or ever lost. I visited the fitness gym with him while in college. At that time I worked as a truck tire repair man and was in near perfect physical condition. He was in his 60s. We were lifting weights. I managed to press 155 pounds over my head. He then pressed 165 pounds over his. He was always a man's man.

The opportunity came for me to live with the Words for several months. Their home was like a hotel with people always coming and going. My sleeping quarters were in the basement near the furnace. Several things impressed me about their family. The prayer times at the meals were always special for me. The family joined hands and after reading the Scripture, earnest prayers were brought before God. This was a truly godly home, like the one in which I was raised.

Upon graduation from The Churches of Christ School of Evangelistsin 1962, Brother Word and I continued to correspond about once a month. The writing continued until his death. I received the next-to-the-last letter he ever wrote.

For the first half of his correspondence I did not realize what a great man he was–he was just my friend and mentor. One day his true merit dawned on me, and I kept the rest of his letters.

The letters were really sermons filled with advice and exhortation. These proved of great value in my life and ministry. I feel sure that his great intellect, character, and love of people will shine through in this book of his sermons and essays.

Yes, Archie Word was probably the greatest gospel preacher of his day. Your time will be well spent in reading his messages.

Dr. Charles A. Crane, President

Boise Bible College

Boise, Idaho

# Introduction

When Archie Word was 87 years old a reporter for the *Eugene Register–Guard* described Word as a man who preached with "a voice full of thunder and a fist full of punch." I liked that description so well I used part of it for the sub-title of my biography of Archie Word, *Voice of Thunder, Heart of Tears* (College Press, 1992).

Archie Word did preach in thunder tones, no doubt about it. He was not afraid to climb into the ring (ex-prize fighter that he was) with sin and put it down for the count. In the first round if he could! Brother Word believed in calling sin by name. Roy Shaw once described Word's preaching: "straight-forward, clear-cut blows rang throughout the building, staggering blows to sin." Word absolutely refused to preach repentance "in the abstract."

When Word preached "REPENT!" he emphatically meant "REPENT!" Genuine repentance, to Archie Word, meant a radical change that was "actual," "entire," and "immediate." He firmly believed that without genuine repentance from sin there could be no authentic conversion to Christ. In five years of full-time work as a revivalist on the West Coast (during the Great Depression), Word saw 3,000 people converted to Christ–fully half of them church members who had never been converted in the first place. His famous slogan, "Hear A. Word Preach The Word," earned him a spot in Ripley's *Believe It Or Not!*

But "Brother Word," as many loved to call him (some used less endearing terms), balanced the thunder with tenderness. When he preached "OR PERISH!" he truly had a "heart of tears." Those who heard him can never forget the tearful tremble in his voice when he told true-life stories of sinful men and women he had known who either gave their lives to Christ or went to their grave without Him.

Word was a master of the illustration–rarely told to amuse. He was at his best when it came time to giving the invitation. His pleading was anointed with tears. Russell Boatman was an uncommitted 18-year-old boy when Word came to San Bernardino, California, in 1933. Boatman testifies, "Late, late in the extended invitation; long, long after most evangelists would have given up; I not only reconsecrated my life but I dedicated my life to the work of the gospel . . . I am grateful for the one who led me to that decision."

"The effectiveness in his preaching was in his pleading," says Boatman. "Some say he skinned us alive and poured salt on the wounds. If so, it was the salt of his tears. Towards the end his voice would mellow, his eyes moisten and he would plead with sinners. In that show of 'weakness' was his strength. He was a man of compassion, and remained ever mindful of what he had once been. I shall ever love him for shedding tears on my behalf."

Archie Word was born April 21, 1901, near Glasgow, Kentucky. Not long thereafter the Word family moved to Lindsay, California. Archie was baptized in the Lindsay Christian Church when he was about 12, but he ran away from home at 17, joining the Navy during World War I. In the providence of God he survived the sinking of the *U.S.S. South Dakota.*

Word returned from the war wordly-wise. He became a notorious bootlegger, prize fighter, and dance hall operator in California's San Joaquin Valley. After nearly being killed in a grisly automobile accident in 1925, he went to Eugene Bible University in Eugene, Oregon, (now Northwest Christian College) where he was finally converted in an upper room prayer meeting, Nov. 11, 1925.

In 1926 Word married his childhood sweetheart, Florence Procter. After graduation from EBU and ministries in Crabtree and Toledo, Oregon, The Word Revival Team took to the road in 1930. The Words began a 33-year ministry with the Montavilla church (now Crossroads church) in 1935. By 1943 the church was recognized by Standard Publishing as having sent more young men and women into full-time Christian service than any other church in the country. Under Archie's leadership the church helped start 9 new churches in Oregon and Washington. In 1952 Word helped found a new Bible College, Churches of Christ School of Evangelists (now Northwest College of the Bible).

The Words spent the last 20 years of their lives criss-crossing America, Archie continuing to preach with a voice full of thunder and a fist full of punch. He died Nov. 17, 1988, in Scottsbluff, Nebraska, a new half-finished sermon outline left on his desk. Florence joined him in death Jan. 29, 1992. They are buried in Willamette National Cemetery, Portland, Oregon.

In editing this book, I had to select from nearly 1,000 sermon titles and hundreds of articles and essays. I regret that I did not have access to most of his sermons from the 30s. A good number of his sermon outlines were mostly ruined late in his life when a car wreck sent a box of his sermon notes tumbling into the Snake River. (One wag said, "I'll bet the river boiled!") Some of those notes are smeared so badly you can barely recognize the multi-colored writing in that bold, familar hand. Others may be blotched with his tears.

-Victor Knowles

# 1

## MERRILY GOING TO HELL!

*Preached at the First Baptist Church, Paso Robles, Calif., March 12, 1934, on the "rest night" of his revival at San Luis Obispo, Calif.*

"For men shall be lovers of self, lovers of money. . .lovers of pleasure rather than lovers of God. . . ." (II Timothy 3:2,4).

The movies will take in 50 times more than the collection tonight! How do we merrily go to hell? Through worldly amusements!

**CARDS**

Playing tag with the devil is like playing tag with the undertaker—he'll get you in the end!

Cards were invented for the amusement of an idiotic king![1] The deck of cards is the infidel's dictionary, the blasphemer's lexicon, the harlot's handbook, and the backslider's Bible! And for some church members the card table takes the place of the Communion table!

Cards are a game of chance, not of skill (like checkers, baseball, or tennis). Someone says, "I believe in teaching my children to play cards at HOME, so they won't go out and learn it in some hell-hole." Sounds good, doesn't it? Yes. Then how about a beer barrel in your home? a prostitute in your home? a supply of dope in your home? Home life is ruined by cards. Ladies afternoon card parties cause cold suppers for Dad. Cards ruin church attendance and the Christian life. Only God knows how many people have rejected Christ and chose cards in preference to Jesus Christ.

The real meaning of cards is found in the "Gambler's code." The "ten spot" is in opposition to the Ten Commandments. "Clubs" represents a weapon of murder. "Spades," a tool to dig graves, suggests death. "Hearts" holds up the broken heart of Christ in derision instead of devotion. "Jack" represents a libertine who lives off the gains of fallen women. "King" represents the devil. . .Satan, the king of darkness (who) leads and entices men away from God and heaven, downward to hell. "Queen" represents Mary, but in a slanderous way. . .a slander on the name of the virgin mother of our Lord. "Joker" represents Jesus, and this is the most horrid blasphemy of all; for the joker is supposed to be a product of an illicit union between the "Jack" and the "Queen."

Maybe you did not know this but you do not have to KNOW a rattlesnake is poisonous for it to kill you!

Last year the FBI record said cards caused $3 million to be embezzled, 32 bank cashiers to misuse bank money, 1,443 people to commit forgery, 127 people to go insane, 1,116 attempted suicides, 124 committed suicides, 128 people to be shot or stabbed, and 500 divorces. The state of Texas now has a law against playing cards on a train—too many innocent people were jeopardized by flying lead! Shall we let state laws preceed Christ's principles? Anything that puts that much hell in the hearts of men ought to be expelled!

## THE THEATER

How do we merrily go to hell? By the theater route. The theater does not promote love for Christ or godliness. It is detrimental to spiritual growth. The average play today is indecent. Immorality is promoted there. Look at the titles of films today. "My

Office Wife." "Is My Face Red?" "What Price, Hollywood?" "Sunny Side Up." "Dancers in the Dark." "Wife Traders." "They Call It Sin." "Back to Nature." "Room Service." "Rage of Paris." "Shop-worn Angel." "Soiled Past." "Night Club Scandal." "Three Heat Waves." "Her Jungle Love." "Blondes at Work." "Sinners in Paradise." "Nudist Colony." The public wants this immoral and brazen wickedness.

Hear these testimonies. McReady, a great actor: "None of my children shall ever, with my consent, enter a theater. . .Not under any pretense, if I can help it." Edwin Booth: "I'll never permit my wife or daughter to go to the theater until I know its character." Mr. Durgs: "Both the place and the work of the place are immoral." Dr. J. M. Bulkey condemned 50 out of 60 plays in the best New York playhouses and rated the other ten as of "low merit."

The average play is full of drunkenness, conspiracy, fighting, adultery, robbery, forgery, murder, lust, envy, hatred, malice, passion and lewd morals. Harry Carr, editor of *The Los Angeles Times*, says, "The modern movie is a school and graduate school of crime."[2] Evil companionships corrupt good morals" (I Cor. 15:33).[3] Rabbi Stephen S. Wise says of Broadway plays, "They must be the product of moral scavengers." Former actress Anna Held, after her conversion, said, "The conditions of the stage are such that I cannot advise any girl to go on it."

The movies laugh at sin! Decency is made to blush! Take away the female anatomy display today and the sheriff's sign will hang on the door tomorrow!

Paul says, "Set your mind on the things that are above, not on the thing that are upon the earth" (Col. 3:2). Does the stage or screen elevate? Does it develop piety or devotion to Christ? Does it make you want to attend prayer meeting? A little Sunday School boy, after his first movie, said, "Gee, man. If you ever went to the movies once, you'll never want to go to prayer meeting again!" That's exactly what it does, too!

I hate anything that robs Christ and destroys the natural love of a child for Christ and God! I cannot be a friend of Christ's unless

I fight His enemies! Are you following Jesus? If you follow Jesus you'll never enter a dirty theater, or movie, or any other place that is responsible for the wholesale wrecking of character!

**THE MODERN DANCE**

The third way we "Merrily go to hell" is via the modern dance. Today the United States is dance crazy, living for this sensuous amusement. The dance has been fought by all great churches and preachers. Billy Sunday. Bulgeon.[4] Sabetti. Charles Reign Scoville.[5] D. L. Moody. DeWitt Talmage. Sam P. Jones.[6] Von Bruck. Charles G. Finney. George Truett. Charles Spurgeon. Rueben Torrey. Hyman Appleman. John R. Rice. (And you think I'm a radical?) Once God had MEN in the pulpit instead of politicians and pussyfooters. THEY ALL FOUGHT SIN!

You say, "Our church does not condemn dancing!" Have mercy! It must be a "pneumonia" church. Spiritually dead! No prayer meetings! No revivals! No missions! God pity a church whose conviction of Christ rises no higher than the Bunny Hug, Turkey Trot, Fox Trot, Tango, Camel Walk, Hesitation, Charleston, Texas Tommy, Hug-Me-Tight, Shimmey, Sea Gull Swoop, SKUNK WALTZ, Black Bottom, Farmer's Upscuddle and Cow Slip, Jive, Swing, Jitterbug, Boogey Woogey, and Rumbah![7]

Do you know Christians who dance? How do you know they are Christians? By their FRUIT! The nearer one gets to God, the less he cares for the world. Does the dance honor Calvary? the Cross? Christ? NO! Why is the dancer "merrily going to hell?" Because the dance kills spiritual life! In Pomona[8] Miss Goetsch was lost by the dance. But now she is studying to become a missionary! Old Cappy was a dance hound and card fiend–trying to teach a Sunday School class. A failure until he was converted.

"Merrily we go to hell" through the dance because it kills health! I speak as a physical instructor in university for four years.[9] The dance is a health destroyer. You say you dance for exercise? What do you do all that hugging business for? The dance violates all health laws. LATE HOURS (from 10 p.m. to 2 a.m.). Sit up at prayer meeting or church as long as you stand up at the dance and it will kill you! IMPURE AIR. Smoke. Close air. A hot stuffy room. OVER EXERTION. The average dancer covers 10 to 12 miles each full evening. First you get hot, then cooled off. I know a coffee salesman's daughter who died from a cold contracted at a forbidden dance.

Then there is the matter of the LACK OF CLOTHING. Say cloth is $5 a yard. It takes about forty-five cents to make a whole dance dress! From low neck to no neck! And the neck line is your waist line! From full dress to undress! Shame on any woman who dresses to cause men to stare and make remarks about her ANATOMY! "Whosoever causes his brother to stumble. . ." Nudity, licentiousness, and license does not build strong bodies.[10] More sickly, weak-kneed, watery-eyed, cigarette fiends and booze blokes walk our streets because of the dance than from any other one thing!

The dance kills spiritual life. It kills physical health. "Merrily we go to hell" because it kills MORALITY. Fully 207,000 out of 230,000 "fallen women" attribute their fall to the dance.[11] A New York Catholic priest's confessional records reveal that three-fourths blame the dance and the theater. The dance takes 50,000 young people out of high school each year. Visit any Salvation Army home! Many soldiers wives went to hell through the U.S.O. dances. F. A. Faulkner, a dance master who has been behind the scenes, author of *From the Ball Room to Hell* and *The Lure of The Dance,* says it is LUST and LUST!

"Merrily we go to hell" through the dance because it kills MODESTY! The greatest shield to virtue is modesty. No place in society outside of a brothel is such familiarity allowed as it is at the modern dance! Just try a dance for men only! For women only—even worse![12] For men dancing with their own wives only! That would terminate the dance! "I've got corns, a headache, gas, rheumatism!" Men don't dance to hug their own wives. They'd just as soon hug a barrel of skinned onions! One girl was overheard talking in an elevator. "I like the low-necked dresses best. You get more dances then!" You are right, girl! But you'll get more yet with no blouse at all! But the law won't stand for that.[13] Many a girl who has tried the dance all the way sits tonight with not only a broken heart but with an illegitimate child.

"Merrily we go to hell" through the dance because it means DEATH TO VIRTUE. Aldous Huxley, who certainly holds no brief for hidebound morality, laments: "American college boys and coeds copulate with the causal promiscuousness of dogs." And the dance is the breeding place for such rot! The lower the scale of morality in the town, the more dancing. Look at Reno! Chicago has 5,000 "Potter's Field" funerals for girls every year. How did they get there? Ninety percent came via the dance! And they are there to stay!

"Merrily we go to hell" through the dance because it means death to your Christian influence. Suppose you dance and are strong. (Not all dancers fall.) But suppose your dancing causes a weaker one to fall? Who will answer for that? Suppose your pastor danced around in the arms of other men's wives? He'd lose your respect! If it robs a preacher, it robs you too! You say society endorses it? What right has society to endorse that which is wrong?

A woman was trying to win her friend to Christ. "I do so want you to be saved and come to Christ."

"For what?"

"For salvation. Don't you want to be saved? You know we are all sinners."

"Yes, I know. But I do not cheat, steal, lie, swear, nor use tobacco. What do I need?"

"Do you pray?"

"No. Do you?"

"Yes. I pray for you."

"Why? When? Monday we danced. Tuesday we were at the Fireman's Ball. Wednesday we went to a party. Thursday I don't know where you were. Friday we played cards until 2 a.m."

"I was at prayer meeting Thursday night."

"What's that? Your church has prayer meeting on Thursday night?"

"Yes!"

"Did you pray for me there?"

"I tried to!"

"Well, all I have to say is that you need to pray for yourself and get something I don't have before trying to talk to me about salvation!"

A letter was written to Paul E. Brown, head of Christian Endeavor in California.

Dear Sir:

I am going to write you a long, long letter and tell you something that no one knows yet, and when I am through I am going to start down the last slide that stops in the center of hell. . .I am going to warn mothers about their daughters, I'm going to put into your hands something that will speak in letters of blood from the very gates of hell itself. . .I charge you to tell this story wherever possible, warn all young people you meet not to wander from their Savior. . . .

When you get this I will be non-existent, Mr. Brown, and there will be no one to mourn, no one to care, no one to weep or miss me, but if I can save one soul by exposing my life, perhaps I may not have lived in vain. . . .

I am here because of a dance given in a church parlor. I did not know it was wrong to let a young man take me. . .I was only 14. . .It was only a matter of six days from that day before I had taken the first step down. . .Then a scandal, and I was sent from home disgraced. . . .

My case now is hopeless but there are many young girls who have not yet taken the first step. . .O, when will the church get close enough to their Savior so they can feel His heart of love beating and find in Him their pleasures?. . . .

Here are two cases where the dance sends people to hell with no Christian influence!

Dr. Frank Richardson, speaking before the Homeopathic Medical Association of New Jersey, said, "Dance halls are the modern nurseries of the divorce courts, training ships of prostitution and graduating schools of infamy of vice. The modern dance was conceived in lust, born of heathen parentage, nurtured and reared in brothels. It has been introduced into and fostered by society because it gives lustful pleasure, but it is destructive to spirit, soul and body and is a menace to the integrity of our civilization."

Puck says, "The dance is the highway to the bawdy house, disease, insanity, suicide, the Potter's Field and Hell."

The modern dance sends people "merrily to hell."

Christ died to keep people out of hell!

---

1. This charge was made in the little tract written by one Rev. Grant Colfax Tullar, *Facts About Cards and Card-Playing* (Pilgrim Tract Society, Randleman, NC). It was paper-clipped to Word's sermon notes.
2. Word then listed 29 criminal techniques that boys and girls in reformatories and young men and women in jail said they had learned from the movies.
3. A news clipping in Word's notes, date lined Jan. 27, 1932, told of a 17-year-old Chicago youth who was found "mentally unresponsible" for the killing of a Chicago policeman. The jury determined that "the boy's mind had been excited by movie thrillers and lurid stories to such a degree that he was unable to discern right from wrong."
4. A great "union" revivalist. In 1927 Word sang for him at a union service in Oregon City.
5. A contemporary Restoration revivalist.
6. After a wild and liquorous youth, Jones was converted and became a preacher of the Methodist Church. Concerning dance masters Jones said, "I would not wipe my feet on the rotten rascal!"
7. In his "wild years" (1922-1925) Word operated three dance halls in Fresno, Calif.
8. Pomona, Calif., where Word held a 13-week revival in 1932.
9. Word, older than most students because of his "wasted years" of sin, was named Physical Instructor at Eugene Bible University his freshman year.
10. Here Word told two illustrations about "Leaney Henry" and "Cross-eyed Blalock" of Porterville, Calif. Like many of the illustrations in his notes, Word told them from memory.
11. Here Word quoted from a news clipping about a "white slave" ring in Los

Angeles. Four people were sentenced to San Quenton for "luring young girls from Los Angeles dance halls to houses of ill repute in Bakersfield and Pismo Beach."

12. This was 60 years before the "gay" bars of America!
13. Today's "law" permits both topless and bottomless dancing in bars.

Elsinore. 6/10/32

Marching Orders Of The King!

Intro:-
1. Hitler's Command Meant Misery To the World!

Vs.

King Jesus Command Means Happiness To The World.

2. Everything Worth While has Cost us Something.

A. Freedom — Revolutionary War
B. Hi-Seas Clear — War Against Pirates.
C. Schools — Free Educational War.
D. Prohibition — Campaign. (still on!)
E. Home = Sweat.
F. Children = Pain.

The G.C. Cost X His Life & Us Our Time But it Brings Us Joy & Lasting Happiness!

*One of Word's oldest "surviving" outlines, preached June 10, 1932, in Elsinore, CA. Note name of "Hitler" replacing "Kaiser."*

# 2

# REPENTANCE AND FAITH

*Christian Standard,* October 25, 1941

We who have been affiliated with the Restoration plea, commonly known as churches of Christ, have been taught "faith, repentance, confession, baptism, remission of sins and the Holy Spirit's gift," which is the true approach to a pagan unbeliever, with the gospel of Christ. But to one who knows God's will as revealed in His law, there must be REPENTANCE from sin as revealed in God's laws before there can be a real saving faith in His Son.

When Jesus preached (Mark 1:15), He was preaching in a country that had been under God's laws–faithful prophets and faithful preachers–for 1500 years. By divine revelation He had a right to demand REPENTANCE from their known sins, sins which they knew to be sins by their law, but when Paul preached to the Philippian jailer, he said to him, "Believe on the Lord Jesus Christ and thou shalt be saved." This was spoken to a man who was frightened, submissive and ready to be taught, but ignorant of Jehovah's[1] laws and standards. Soon after that we see him washing the backs of the men whom, a few hours before, his government had beaten—the fruit of repentance that grew out of faith based on Paul's true message.

When we know a thing is wrong, we must be willing to quit it because it is wrong before we can wholeheartedly and with a saving faith turn to Jesus Christ for salvation. God demands REPENTANCE just as surely as He demands faith. Some things MAY BE, but other things MUST BE! Repentance and faith are INDISPENSABLES; positive requirements for salvation. We may not like it, but there is no salvation without it. A little girl is found to have a "strep" infection in the blood stream. The doctor prescribes sulphanilamide; it tastes awful; the child doesn't want to take it. But it is a case of take it and live (bad taste and all), or refuse it and die. That is what the Saviour meant in Luke 13:3-5.

Repentance and faith complete each other like a boat and oars. Neither is of much value alone. God has joined them together; let no man put them asunder!

## REPENTANCE

Repentance means a change of mind that works a complete change of conduct, and it is caused by godly sorrow for sin. Change of conduct is not enough. Quitting sin because you have been caught at it is not repentance. Quitting gambling because you have lost in a gambling game is not repentance. Quitting loose morals because you are afraid of disease is not repentance.[2] Quitting cards just because you have been having hard luck and losing is not repentance. Quitting liquor just because you can't stand the sickness that accompanies a "hangover" is not repentance. Quitting swearing just because you fear hell is not repentance. REPENTANCE IS CAUSED BY BEING SORRY FOR SIN BECAUSE IT IS SIN AND GRIEVES THE VERY HEART OF GOD—ALL SIN—THEN FORSAKING IT FOREVER!

Suppose my boy[3] deliberately disobeys me. I talk to him about his infraction of my rules, but he determinedly keeps on. I refuse to let him have my car, force him to remain at home and turn down his appeal for a new suit. One day he comes to me and says, "Dad, I'm sorry I've been so bad, because it has caused me to miss a lot of good times." That is not repentance! Until that stubborn, unhumbled and rebellious boy is willing to confess his wrong and quit it because it is wrong, he has not repented. Godly sorrow and the goodness of God lead us to REPENTANCE–turning from all sin because it is sin!

Repentance from what we know to be wrong is literally based on faith, and it makes room for more faith and faithfulness. Faith gives birth to repentance and repentance makes a life fit for faith to command and bless.

The unregenerated man, whether he is in the church or not, is just the same natured-man as he has always been, except that all of us are more responsible now because we have had more opportunities to know better. Recently I purchased some cold meat, and the butcher guessed at the weight, threw it on the scales and, when he saw that it was off, cursed. Then he turned to me and said, "I beg your pardon, Reverend." He respected me, a man, while he despised the holy and righteous God who made him and equipped him to gloify his Creator. He begged my pardon, but did not repent and beg God's pardon. That man claims to be a church member, but his heart is filthy from sin of which he has not repented.

In order to put milk into a bottle that is filled with dirt, the dirt must be first removed. The two make only an unpalatable mud, and so it is with sinfulness and church membership. Only a complete dumping out of the old contents because they are vile (which act we call "repentance"), can make way for Christ's salvation and the abiding presence of the Holy Spirit. Deliberate and malicious sin that is not repented of cannot live in the same soul with the Holy Spirit. We need to repent in order to obtain salvation (Acts 2:38). We need to CONTINUE repenting of anything wrong that comes into our lives as long as we live.

Old Mr. Dodd, one of the earliest Puritan preachers, was nicknamed "Old Faith and Repentance" because he never failed to appeal for these two indispensables. I admire him for his orthodox stand and, as far as I am concerned, I intend to practice these two as long as I live, and I feel it would be a pleasure to go from this body to His presence preaching repentance and faith!

Any preacher can preach repentance in the abstract and no one will object, but let him begin to name sins to be repented of and there will be a furor among those who hear him but who are determined to remain in their sins. John the Baptist taught that certain things of which he knew his hearers were guilty were to be repented of. He told the publicans to quit overcharging in their tax deals. Surely it was a sore spot; some did not like it (and they knew better), but it was wrong and John named it. Probably all of them were guilty of this sin, but that did not excuse them in God's sight. To the soldier, John hit a solar plexus blow by demanding that he cease extortion by violence, false accusations and discontent with his wages. John knew the soldiers of that day, but he was true to their souls. (Sounds as if he had been reading some of our daily papers on labor difficulties,[4] doesn't it?)

Let us be just as definite, right now, with the sinner who desires to be saved. He has lived in the United States and knows much of God's standards; therefore his knowledge makes it imperative that he repent before he can be saved. Repent of what? I answer, "He must repent of everything he knows to be wrong and sinful!" To illustrate, any sinner who has lived in America from his youth knows that self-destruction is wrong,[5] and he also knows, in spite of the hundreds of millions of dollars spent by the tobacco companies in advertising, that tobacco is destructive to the human body. If a tobacco-using sinner, either man or woman, comes to a true preacher asking about repentance, he will be told (as definitely as John told the common people, publicans and soldiers about their sins) that HE MUST QUIT the use of this body-ruining and spirit-wrecking weed that has been capitalized by men who are willing to live off other men's weakness and misery. The sinner who has already gained admission to the congregation but insists on the use of the filthy drug that literally rots all flesh and strikes at our four most vital organs–lungs, heart, liver and kidneys–needs to be told (Acts 8:21-22). Wouldn't John the Baptist tell him? If you really love him, wouldn't you tell him, too?[6]

The liquor man seeks admission to the church of our Lord. He has money and is liberal with it. He is a "hail fellow" and well thought of by the city council because he is a heavy investor. His name is as good as gold at the city newspaper offices because he is a heavy advertiser. If he joins our church it will mean increased collections. What should the preacher do? Tell him read Mark 1:15 and connect it with I Corinthians 6:9-10, but don't overlook Luke 17:1-2 and Romans 14:21.

The same message of repentance goes for the worldly-minded jazz hound,[7] the thrill-seeking movie addict, the card-playing hypocrite and all the others who run after follies BEFORE THEY KNOW THE LORD AS A REAL SAVIOUR FROM SIN! It is not a message that will bring popularity to the minister among the unregenerated church members or preachers, but it is one that will bring honor to the faithful soul throughout eternity. One soul REPENTING makes the angels rejoice, and the soul that PREACHED repentance and LIVED repentance will be singing with the penitent and the angels forever!

The church needs to do some repenting right now![8] We who have been taught know better, and God will hold us accountable. We know how God expected His church to be supported financially,[9] and when we borrow from denominationalism the Ladies' Aid societies, circles, squares, councils and gossip clubs in order to raise a few dollars, we sin aginst God and make lazy men. Someone needs to tell us to REPENT!

We know God's method of church government, and when we allow a free convention of brethren to be dominated by a "pastor at large," "superintendent," "bishop" or "state secretary,"[10] to the place where a free man in Christ hasn't a chance, ordination is deprived the local church, and the preacher is told there is no place for free speech, then we need to hear some fearless prophet of God, who is fearless as far as men and women are concerned, sounding forth the message of REPENTANCE AND FAITH IN GOD.

When the Sunday School and the Christian Endeavor become independent and separate organizations distinct from the church, carrying on a program that stifles the church's power and divides loyalty, they need to be told it is time to repent and make restitution.[11]

God sought repentance of Cain in the beginning of our race. Repentance was the heart cry of every true prophet of God throughout the Old Testament. Repentance was John the Baptist's first and strongest appeal. Jesus preached repentance and sent His 12 and the 70 to preach repentance. Peter, on that great day of Pentecost, began his answer to the inquirers with an appeal to repentance.

Let us never forget that every preacher from that day to this—that has ever amounted to a hill of beans in God's sight—has been a faithful preacher of repentance and faith toward God. Big churches are not what God wants. TRUE churches that believe and practice repentance become His pride and joy. Let us all REPENT AND FEARLESSLY PREACH MORE REPENTANCE!

**FAITH**

Faith and repentance, and repentance and faith are inseparable—born together and die together like Siamese twins. Repentance is the result of an "unperceived faith" or "inward faith" or "latent faith." Repentance alone yields no conscious comfort, but it will work truthfulness of heart, purity of soul and will cause one to abhor all sin and impurity. No true repentance ever came apart from faith. Repentance is a dark cloud to most folks, but it always has a silver lining.

I'm afraid, however, that among the churches of Christ some have the idea that since they confessed Christ once, it is never necessary again, and others believe that a repentance at the time of their accepting Christ is sufficient to carry them safely through to heaven. Peter didn't think so (according to Acts 8:22-23). We all need to know that when we have outgrown repentance, we have become too proud to believe God. The Lord has put faith here to cheer repentance, and repentance is so placed as to make faith a sober thing.

We are being taught today to believe in the United States of America, because if we believe in our country we'll soldier for her, buy her bonds to support war and uphold our laws. God knew this and prescribed this 1,700 years before the United States was ever dreamed of. Faith makes loyalty. Faith causes us to serve God. Faith produces faithfulness. God knew this when He demanded that we believe. Faith in God was demanded when idolatry ruled the world, and because Christians BELIEVED, they were willing to go to the stake, be put on the rack, suffer crucifixion or be torn limb-from-limb by hunger-maddened wild beasts. Faith meets the test victoriously.

Faith was demanded when almost all of our leading psuedo-religions were in the embryonic state and Christianity met them in open combat. And while the noise of falling blows was heard, the anvil remains; the hammers are gone.

Faith was demanded in a day when the whole pagan world was seeking fleshly amusement, but Christianity developed self-controlled characters who "kept the faith" while Rome decayed.

We need that same repentance and faith tody that was essential to both Jew and Gentile in the beginning. We need faith when infidelity works through professors who belabor our children with skepticism in our public schools. We need faith out on the job while the air is full of dirty talk and cursing. We need faith at the community club when the devil's crowd seeks to turn into a dance-and-card club. We need faith in the Parent-Teacher Association to witness for the Lord when He has been forgotten under the superficial load of scholasticism. We need faith in some of our Bible colleges where Satan has set up his mightiest stronghold–faith to stand up for the God of the Bible, the Christ of that God and His sacrifical atoning death, even though all hell laugh and deride us.

We need faith in the pulpit when the church is infested with faithless, lukewarm and indifferent church members–faithfulness to preach about consecration and genuine repentance, not fearing to name sins; faithfulness to urge men and women to pray when sports activities call and social obligations are pressing, preaching the Word, urgent all the time; reproving, rebuking, exhorting while we teach and continue to suffer for it. For we are NOW in the times when men will not endure sound doctrine; but, having itching ears, they are looking for someone to preach to please them.

It is a hard task, but it is a God-given one–one that God will reward.

"The kingdom of God is at hand; REPENT ye, and BELIEVE the gospel."

(Editor's Note: Of Archie Word the *Christian Standard* wrote, "Our preacher of this week is a Kentuckian by birth and Scotch-Irish by race. Perhaps that account for his sterling firmness of conviction, unflinching courage and unflagging zeal. There appears to be some appropriateness about his name, for the Word of God is the dominating factor in his life.")

1. Word's use of "Jehovah" reflects his love for the American Standard Version (1901).
2. What would A. Word think of today's "safe sex" approach to AIDS?
3. Archie Word, Jr., was born Oct. 10, 1940, a little more than one year before this essay was published.
4. On Oct. 10, 1941 (Archie Junior's first birthday), 15 days before this article was published, tank output for the war effort was crippled in Michigan by inter-union struggles. The C.I.O. refused to handle parts made by the A.F.L. Word was an avid newspaper reader.
5. But today we are beset with "suicide doctors!"
6. Brother Word was sounding the alarm against smoking long before the United States government came out with their reports warning against it as a health hazard.
7. "Jazz hound" was one of Word's favorite terms.
8. If repentance was needed in the church of the 40s, then what of the church in the "Gay 90s"?
9. Word was a firm believer in "tithes and offerings."
10. All part of the U.C.M.S. of Word's day.
11. Brother Word believed all such organizations, and their treasuries, should be under the oversight of the local church elders.

*Caricature of Archie Word used in advertising revival in Lexington, NE in the 40s.*

3

# THE COST OF DRINKING

*Christian Standard,* July 10, 1943

Just for fear someone might be constrained to say, "Well, Preacher, that text you have taken is in the Old Testament[1] and is not applicable to us today," I want to use a New Testament text for my introduction.

"For I would not have you ignorant, brethren, that our fathers were all under the cloud, and all passed through the sea; and were all baptized unto Moses in the cloud and in the sea; and did all eat the same spiritual food; and did all drink the same spiritual drink; for they drank of a spiritual rock that followed them; and the rock was Christ. Howbeit with most of them God was not well pleased; for they were overthrown in the wilderness. Now these things were our examples, to the intent we should not lust after evil things, as they also lusted. Neither be ye idolaters, as were some of them; as it is written, The people sat down to eat and drink, and rose up to play....Neither murmur ye, as some of them murmured, and perished by the destroyer. Now THESE THINGS HAPPENED UNTO THEM BY WAY OF EXAMPLE: and they were written for our admonition, upon whom the ends of the ages are come" (I Cor. 10:1-7).

**A COSTLY PRICE TAG**

The "price tag" is always of interest to people. Most of us have millionaire tastes and pauper pocketbooks, and most of us have been "overcharged" in the business world at some time or another. Some of us have unwittingly signed papers that cost us dearly before the threatening letters ceased to come from our smooth-talking tormentor's attorney. We were talked into signing for a friend or we were "sold" on a policy and were told that the papers that we signed would not be binding, not realizing the cost until the awful realization came: WE MUST PAY!

That, I am sure, is the predicament of thousands here in my home city[2] right now, and they are just like millions of others in this liquor-soaked, blind and stupefied nation. Smooth advertising, misleading and creating appetities that are abnormal, aided and abetted, incited and misled by tools of hell through the movies, public press and radio[3] are, as they continue their sowing, also reaping from the poor "suckers" who do not realize the awful price they must pay in the end! The devil covers and blurs his price tags. God marks His price plainly and legibly to all who would examine them. God's Word has spoken! The price tag is plainly in view to those who will look where God displays it – in His Word.

"God changes not" (Mal. 3:6). And the price God demanded on the nation in Moses' day and throughout Israel's history He still demands...and in time will collect! God does not always take an annual inventory and balance His books, but He will in the end, and the guilty ones shall not escape.

What should be the preacher's part in meeting this age-old (Isa. 58:1) curse of mankind? He should remember he is no policeman to force people to obey; nevertheless, he is God's agent to warn. He is to cry aloud and spare no one, and declare to the people their transgressions. He is not to try to seek favors (Gal. 1:10) of men, either by free advertising in the dailies, by compromise or by silence, when "Old Moneybags" is present in the "three great annual feast days" of denominational tradition – Christmas, Easter and Mother's Day!

We honor the prophets of old who were faithful to their charge, but remember it is not going to be long until our children and their children will be reading about us and they will either honor us or despise us because of our stand today.[4] Let us be true to our God and to those to whom He has sent us to preach.

Many times we could learn profitable lessons from our grandparents, if we would.[5] Most of us have some folk on our family tree who could teach us to abstain from the very appearance of evil.[6] It was so in the nation of Israel. Away back on their family tree was an illustrious personage by the name of Noah. He did some fine things. He was righteous most of the time, believed God's promise and even did some preaching to warn others (II Pet. 2:5). From a human-prowess standpoint he built the most famous cargo ship of the centuries, because God used it to save the human race. That was quite a famous great-great-great grandfather for any person to look back upon. Then Noah branched out into the vineyard business and became a husbandman (Gen. 9:20). Like many other vineyardists (I used to live in the California vineyard belt),[7] Noah began to make wine and to sample his own product.

The awful shame of Israel's noble and distinguished forefather is recorded in Genesis 9. God has given the account for all ages, that we might profit by it. The great man became a senseless, helpless and naked drunk – exposed to his own children! How could Israel ever forget this awful account? In reality Ham's curse was the result of Noah's drunkenness. Noah caused the curse upon his own son.

How can we be led to imbibe of this "hell's brew," even though millions of dollars are being spent to entice the unsuspecting, when we have not only Israel's account of Noah, but to supplement this Biblical record we have the police records of the world for at least six thousand years back? God gave His sacred account not only to help Israel, but to help any nation where the Word of God is preached. The drinking of liquor, whether it be natural wine, fortified wine or distilled beverages, leads to indecent exposure and shame to both parents and children. If you think I am overstating the case, go down to your city jail next Sunday morning and take a look into the "tank" and see men and women with swollen faces, eyes cut and blackened, wives and husbands standing outside crying or in quiet preconference with the judge.[8] Then you will know that "these things in the Old Testament were written for our admonition."

"Righteousness exalteth a nation, but sin is a reproach to any people" (Prov. 14:34). Israel could have looked with profit at another one of her national heroes – at least he was a companion for many years of their "Father Abraham". This man Lot had money, position, honor, family, friends, personality and respect. Apparently everything that men hold dear he possessed, yet his sin – which culminated in the vilest, most disgusting sin recording in all the annals of God's inspired record (incest) – was preceded by drunkenness.

Many times men excuse themselves for acts committed on the ground that they were under the influence of alcohol, but remember, men knew what they were doing when they began to drink – and they knew that liquor makes men go out of their heads. They knew that almost always the sex desires are overstimulated. Even Lot's daughters, thousands of years ago, knew that much from their conversation in Gen. 19:31-32.

Man may excuse acts of sin and foolishness, but the Scriptures teach that the price tag has to be paid in full. There's no "shoplifting" with God and getting by with it. The drunken act was completed. The plan of Lot's daughters worked, but from this disgraceful act came two of the worst enemies Israel ever had – the Moabites and the Ammonites (Gen. 19:37-38). Liquor always brings dirt, and every time the Ammonites leagued with Israel's enemies it served to remind Israel of their unholy origin. They were children of incest caused by wine, one of the costs of drinking as recorded in the Bible.

Nations are made up of individuals, and as individuals go, so goes the nation. We as a nation have been slipping into the drunkard's grave ever since 1933.[9] For 10 years we've been spending millions to lead our citizens to become "sots". We have succeeded in this much! We have increased our fermented malt liquor from 6,000,000 barrels up to 55,000,000 barrels. (This comes from three-year-old figures.) We have increased our capacity for "still wines" from one million gallons to 62 million gallons in a year, while we have jumped from 6,000,000 gallons of distilled liquors in 1933 to 136,000,000 gallons in 1938. God only knows how much we "slopped up" this last year, with both men and women making big money in the war plants and high-school youngsters making more in four days than their parents used to make in a month.

The Bible says, "As you sow so shall you reap." Now let us see if we are running true to form or to the style that was set by Lot and his illegitimate and drunken brood. The FBI, by their records of our activities, prove that the Bible warning is true. "Ye have cast lots for my people, and have given a boy for a harlot, and sold a girl for wine, that they may drink" (Joel 3:3). Let us see if we haven't done about the same thing. J. Edgar Hoover said recently, "Fingerprint records of persons under 21 years of age showed that arrests of minors among girls increased 55.7% in 1942 over 1941. Commercialized vice among minor girls increased 64.8%, while those arrested for other sex offenses increased 104.7%. Increases of 39.9% and 69.9%, respectively, were registered for drunkenness and disorderly conduct."

We are reaping as a nation just what we have sown, and, brethren, the crop is not half in yet! As long as we have liquor billboards on the streets and highways, liquor advertising in our newspapers, neon signs emblazoning some alcoholic stupifier, large plate-glass windows with attractive displays of beer, wine and whiskey, and the movie industry portraying it glamorously as often as it dares, we can depend on it, we will pay the bill! And what a bill!

The Bible shows by example that no nation can be blessed that follows after Lot, and past history, as well as the present news, verifies that warning. I wonder whether, were we as strict with our children as the prophet of God said for Israel to be, if we would not be better off in the long run (Deut. 21:18-21). I believe less lives would be forfeited than we are losing now. Our "feather pillow" methods of handling drunkenness have developed crime rather than curbed it. If God thought it was bad enough to deserve stoning to death in the Old Testament, surely we are not so wise when we say we are going to pay the pensions of the aged and infirm through the taxes leveled on these debauchers of society that would have been killed in the Old Testament to keep purity. God does not change! He demands His price! The drinker must pay not only in person, but he passes his curse on to his children for their heritage.

Surely Amos drew a picture very applicable to our conditions in Amos 6:3-7. We have our houses, the best furnished in all the world. We have lamb and veal, the choicest cuts. No nation on record ever had as many "jackassified ditties" as we have over the air, on records and in sheet music. Then, to accompany this nest of ill-smelling vipers, we have the most in quantity and variety of alcoholic stimulants. Do you think that will make a nation that is ready to receive the blessings of God, about which Americans sing?

One of Israel's own kings would not heed God's warning, and he paid with his life (I Kings 16:8-10). Truly, God is no respector of persons. If any people on earth ought to be total abstainers, it is our government officials, but from all reports, liquor flows free from the White House[10] to the unpainted shanty on "Skidrow." God does not change! We will pay and we are paying now! The Bible repeatedly posts the cost of drinking.

So far we have used only the Old Testament for our reference work in this sermon, and you will notice that I have dealt with things of time, material and earthly possessions. The natural man can be appealed to in no other manner. He cannot understand spiritual things, but in the New Testament we have the standards being raised. God's new covenant is directed chiefly to those who are spiritually begotten and heaven-bound children of God. Naturally, the appeal to Christians is on a higher plane. The stakes are more valuable. It is not now loss of clothes, wife, children, home, nation or physical life. It is something more to be desired. Jesus said in Matt. 10:39 that He has something of more value than physical life to offer. What is it? Eternal life with God!

Some of our "stinkingest unsocial actions" are not named in so many words in the Bible. Jesus does not say to abstain from chewing tobacco nor from smoking "Lucid Streaks,"[11] but the new covenant does say, "Abstain from the very appearance of evil." However fine a dodger a sinner may be in defending his own sins, he has no loophole through which to dodge when it comes to the drinking of intoxicants. The Holy Spirit uttered and recorded the fact that the drunkard and drunkenness are excluded from heaven (I Cor. 6:9- 11).

It is bad for the drunkard to lose his wife. It is worse to grow old and lose the respect of one's own children. It is awful to lose good health over liquor. It is worse to be maimed or crippled for life because of booze, and to realize that every one knows why you limp or are deformed. Far above all those losses is the loss of heaven – the loss of the soul! With liquor it is: "What shall it profit a man if he loses everything worthwhile on earth, damns his family, community and nation, and then loses his own soul!" God does not change! God does not lie! He has no "sales". The cost of drinking in its finality is everlasting destruction from the face of God and His holy angels forever!

**CHRIST OFFERS HOPE!**

This would be an awful picture if I had to stop here. Surely there would be no hope. We as a nation are in the awful throes of a drunken spree right now, but the "hangover" is just around the corner and it will take more than Egypt's ancient antidote of boiled cabbage to relieve us of our headaches. There is hope, but, let us never forget it, there is ONLY hope in Jesus Christ and His salvation. When Jesus Christ is accepted as our LORD, He causes us to repent of all our sins. Repentance is a change of mind that works a complete change of our conduct. Old desires pass away and new desires take their place. Then in baptism the "old man" is buried and a "new creature" is raised up. Old habits are lost under the cleansing blood and through the Holy Spirit the life is kept in God' way.

Yes, there is hope IN the Christ of God for every drunkard. History is replete with living examples of drunken "stews" and "bums" who have found rest in Christ and complete freedom from the cravings of an alcoholic appetite.

In my own home town[12] we had a fine Christian woman who had a son who was a heartache from his early childhood. He would not go to church or Sunday School. He chose his friends from the element in society that kept the small-town police busy. He went "wild" at about 17[13] and in a drunken stupor had one arm severed from his body while bumming a ride on a freight train. That taught him nothing. Years went by and he became so bad he could not follow his painting any longer. One drunken spree followed another so closely that he was considered a fit subject for the insane asylum. He was a living illustration of Prov. 23:29-35 as well as of Isa. 28:1,7. He tried to kill his own mother with an ax and just missed killing his own twin brother.

The law came and put him in jail. He yelled and screamed and roared all night (and in a small town everybody knew about it). The next day a minister, who was not allowed to go inside the jail, came and stood outside and preached Christ to that poor suffering soul. He listened instead of cursing the preacher, as he had always done before, and through the bars he took the minister's hand and confessed his faith in the only One who could save a drunkard. Then, instead of demanding to be freed, he asked to be confined to his cell for 30 days where he might read his Bible and fight this battle with the Lord's help.

At the end of the 30-day period he was let out of jail. He made his way to the church and was baptized. He plied his trade for two years and faithfully attended all the church services. He became an ardent personal worker, leading many to know Christ right there where he had been a living example of the cost of drinking. He married a fine Christian girl, went to Southern California to the seminary to study to become a missionary to the Mexicans. His successful work there for years before his untimely death shows God is able to save even the worst of drunkards. He died 20 years prematurely, which also shows while God can and does forgive our sins, the old body has to pay the cost of drinking.

God changes not! The price tag has been made plainly visible in God's Word for those who drink. It is ruin here in this life, and eternal ruin hereafter to the unrepentant drunkard.

(Editor's note: Of Archie Word the *Christian Standard* wrote, "When he writes about the cost of liquor he knows whereof he speaks. He has seen the ravages firsthand. He has been around....No one who hears him can wonder at his power in evangelism. He speaks as one who knows he has divine authority behind the message. He speaks with brilliance, passion, zeal for souls, one of the real evangelists of our time.")

1. Word's article in the *Christian Standard* was based on two texts from the Old Testament, Deut. 21:18-21 and Prov. 23:20-21, selected by the preparers of the International Uniform Lesson Outline.
2. The Words settled in Portland, Oregon, in October, 1935, after nearly five years on the revival circuit.
3. In the early 1950's Word began assailing television as another "tool of hell."
4. On June 17, 1943, "the Last Word" was born at Adventist Hospital in Portland, Esther Elaine Word, the sixth of the Word children.
5. Unfortunately, Archie's grandfather (as well as his father) was a Kentucky moonshiner, "chasing his whiskey with a string of oaths."
6. In Archie's case it was his mother, Maggie Kenny Word, who warned him about the evils of drinking.
7. The Word family moved from Kentucky to California's San Joaquin Valley (which still abounds with wineries) in 1906. Archie eventually followed in his grandfather's and father's footsteps, becoming a bootlegger during the Prohibition years. By the time he was 24 he was running three saloons in Fresno.
8. A. Word practiced what he preached. For many years he worked under Judge Olson in the court handling domestic relationships. In 1941 he began taking Montavilla's young people with him in his regular visits to the city and county jail.
9. On Dec. 5, 1933, Prohibition came to an end. To his dying day Archie Word remained adament in his belief that Prohibition had not failed.
10. FDR was still occupying the White House in 1943. Word, and other preachers of his day, sometimes referred to Roosevelt as "Boozevelt."
11. "Lucid Streaks." A play on "Lucky Strikes."
12. Lindsay, California.
13. The same age as Archie when he ran away from Lindsay to join the Navy.

## CHURCH OF CHRIST

**ORIGIN**

1. Time—Pentecost, A.D. 34. Acts 2:1-15.
2. Place—Jerusalem. Acts 2:5; Luke 24:46, 47.
3. Founder—Christ. Matt. 16:18.
4. Foundation. I Cor. 3:11; Eph. 2:20; I Pet. 2:4-6.

**THE ORGANIZATION CONSISTS OF**

1. Immersed penitent believers. Act. 2:38-41 and Mark 16:15-16.
2. Pastors and Evangelists. Eph. 4:11; II Tim. 4:5.
3. Elders (or Bishops). Acts 20:28; I Tim. 5:17.
4. Deacons. Acts 6:16; I Tim. 3:8-13, and Romans 16:1.

**THE NAME**

1. Of Individuals—
   - Saints, Holy in Character. Rom. 1:17; Acts 9:13.
   - Disciples, Learners. Acts 6-1; John 15:8.
   - Brethren, relation to one another in Christ. I Cor. 15:6: II Pet. 1:10.
   - Children, relation to God. Gal. 2:26.
   - Christians, followers of Christ. Acts 11:26; Acts 26: 28, 29; I Pet. 4:16.
2. Of the Church—
   - Church of God. I Cor. 1-2. (Planner).
   - Body of Christ. Eph. 1:22, 23; I Cor. 12:27. (Activity).
   - Church of Christ. Rom. 16:16; Matt. 16-18. (Ownership).
   - THE CHURCH. Acts 8:1; 9-31. (Only ONE CHURCH).

**THE CREED**

1. Faith in Jesus Christ. Matt. 16:16.
2. Never changes. Heb. 13:8.

**DISCIPLINE**

The Word of God, only. II Tim. 3:16, 17.

**THE SIN OF DIVISION**

1. Christ prayed for unity. John 17:20, 21.
2. Paul pleaded for unity. I Cor. 1:10, 13; Rom. 16:17, 18.
3. The Scriptures condemn division. Gal. 5:19-21.
4. Division is carnal (sinful). I Cor. 3:1-3.
5. Divine basis for unity. Eph. 4:1-6; Heb. 8-5.

**ORDINANCES**

1. Lord's Supper. Matt. 26:26-28; I Cor. 10:16; 11:23-29; Acts 20:7; Acts 2:42.
2. Baptism. Matt. 28:18, 19; Mk. 16:15, 16; Acts 2:38; Eph. 4:5.
   - Purpose. John 3:3-5; Acts 2:38; 22:16; Gal. 3:27.
     - Only penitent believers were baptized. Mk. 16:16; Acts 2:38; 8:12; 18:8. (No babies were baptized).
   - What Scriptural baptism requires.
     - Much water. John 3:23.
     - Going down into water. Acts 8:38.
     - Form of burial and resurrection. Mk. 1:10; Rom. 6:2-5.

**PURPOSE**

Conversion of the world.

**"THE WORD" REVIVAL TEAM**

EUGENE, OREGON
CARE OF E. B. U.

## "The Word" Reminder! *Read It Again!*

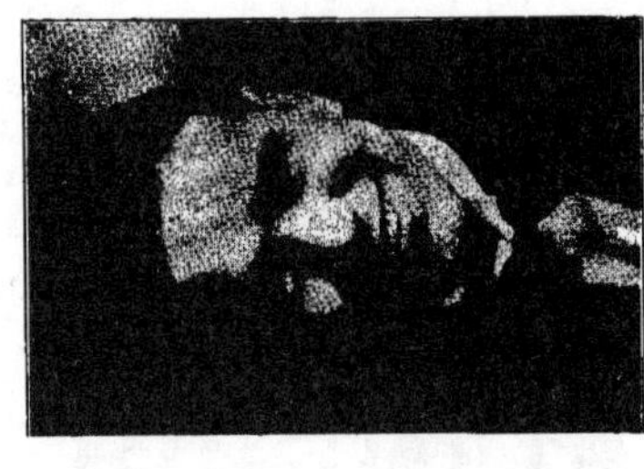

A. Word, *Evangelist*
"A Sinner Saved by Grace"

Dear Christian Friend:

It is with joy I leave this little token in your hands, for since becoming a servant of the King, joy is mine. It can be yours if you will live whole-heartedly for Him, and endure unto the end.

This pamphlet pasted in your Bible will help you to live for Christ, if you will obey its teaching.

With best wishes to you in Christ,

I am Evangelist

A. Word

*Front page of 4-page pamphlet Word gave to new converts. This one given to K. O. Backstrand in 1939.*
*Back page of pamphlet was revision of a chart by V. E. "Daddy" Hoven, Word's teacher at Eugene Bible University.*

## 10 Rules for the Christian

A Christian's growth depends on himself or herself. I Peter 4:16.
Physical growth depends on exercise and so does Spirituality!

1. *Systematic Bible Study.* I Peter 2:2; I Cor. 4:6; II Tim. 2:15.
   a. Regularly each day.
   b. Listen to God talk thru His Word.
   c. "The Word" is Soul Food.

2. *Pray.* Phil. 4:6.
   a. Prayer is a Christian's breath. Don't Suffocate!
   b. Pray about everything—Joys and Sorrows, Victories and Mistakes, Friends and Enemies! Col. 4:2-6.

3. *Be a Soul Winner.* James 5:19-20.
   a. Acts 1:8. Witness for Christ.
   b. Mk. 16:15-16. Souls out of Christ are Lost.
   c. "Christianity is like measles, if it goes in on you it will kill you."

4. *Stay Away from Bad People.* I Peter 2:9.
   a. Heb. 12:1-2. Throw off Sin.
   b. "Be not deceived. Evil companionships will corrupt good morals."
   c. Rom. 6:16-17 and Rom. 12:1-2 and II Cor. 6:14-17.

   Look out Christians! When company prevents prayer!

5. *Glorify God Always.* Eph. 5:20 and Col. 3:17.
   a. Col. 3:5-10.
   b. Gal. 5:22-24.
   c. I Tim. 6:11-16.

   } A Real Christian is a Christian Seven Days a Week!

   *Ask Yourself, "What Would Jesus Do?"*

6. *Do Not Miss Bible School, Church or Prayer Meeting!*
   a. Heb. 10:25.
   b. Sinners watch you; you're their Bible!
   c. Practice what you preach! Acts 20:7; 2:42.
   d. Eph. 5:25. Be like Jesus.

7. *Give Regularly.* I Cor. 16:1.
   a. Give Systematically. Mal. 3:7-11; I Cor. 9:13-14.
   b. Give because you appreciate! Gal. 6:6-7.
   c. Give cheerfully! II Cor. 9:6-7.

   "Until you have given one-tenth of your income you have not given Him anything."

8. *Co-operate With Your Pastor.*
   a. Don't criticize him; pray for him!
   b. Come to him for help, he is a minister. Mk. 10:45.
   c. Let him in on your joys. Eph. 5:19.
   d. You may need him some day; so be a friend!
   e. In unity there is power. Jn. 17.

9. *Do Not Become Discouraged.*
   a. Be cheerful.
   b. Expect temptations. Matt. 5. Jesus had them!
   c. Persecutions will come. II Tim. 3:12; Lk. 6:22; I Cor. 11:19.
   d. I Cor. 10:13. Trust in Christ.
   e. Jas. 1:12. Endure temptation.
   f. Mat. 10:22; 2 Peter 2:9.

10. *Remember! Heaven Is Our Home!*
    a. "It is better to go to heaven alone than to go to hell in a crowd."
    b. "It is better to go to heaven from a shanty than to go to hell from a palace!"
    c. "Eye hath not seen, nor ear heard, neither hath it entered into the heart of man the things which God hath prepared for them that love Him." I Cor. 2:9.

*Word's "10 Rules" were nearly identical to those in a pamphlet used by Billy Sunday.*

4

# GOD'S BLOCKADES ON THE ROAD TO HELL!

*A sermon preached at the historic Workman Street Church of Christ, Los Angeles, California, in 1945*

Even blockades cannot stop some people!

A driver of a Bearcat Stutz, probably drunk, ran through three road blocks and red lanterns, crashed, and then dived into the Columbia River!

The road to hell is filled by God with obstacles. Here are some blockades on the road to hell!

## A GODLY MOTHER'S PRAYERS

Before you were born they were praying for your protection and perfection. Mary found favor in the eyes of God because she was a devout woman. But some murderers may owe some of their desires to prenatal influence–their mothers tried to kill them before they were born!

During your babyhood they set a godly example by teaching you such prayers as, "Now I lay me down to sleep," or "Lord Jesus, we thank Thee for this food."

In later life they continued to pray for you. A man came to "after meetings" in Chicago, only to disturb. He stood outside the church offering free beer to new converts. But even in Chicago he was caught up with his mother's prayers. One night he could not sleep. He finally got out of bed and sought an evangelist to get right with God!

A godly mother sets up another barricade on hell's road—teaching. I well remember my mother's reading to us boys[1] about the hardships of the missionaries in India and the deaths of thousands of Hindu people during their great famines. While Dad made hay, Mother sat with us boys under a large haycock that Dad had set up with a fork. She read to us about Joseph, Moses, Elijah, Isaiah and Daniel. Who knows how much of an influence that she has had on my ministry? Only God will ever know all about it.[2]

My mother taught me honesty! When I was about six years old, I crossed over the tracks (we lived on the "wrong side of the tracks") to the hardware store where I picked up a cap pistol and brought it home. My mother said, 'Son, where did you get that gun? And how much did you pay for it?' I told her I got it over at Matheson's Hardware store, and that I had just picked it up. I was perfectly honest about the whole deal. I guess my mother decided it was time to teach me to be honest because after she had put on her bonnet, she took me by the ear and started across the tracks again. We took the gun back, and Mother paid the man 15 cents for it. Then she took me by the other ear, and we started home. When we got home, she took me out to the cow barn and from the noise that came out of there, the neighbors thought we had a whole herd of cattle! Then she took me into the house and put me to bed, and while I lay there she drove a nail up over the door (in my plain sight) and hung that pistol on the wall. I had to look at it all day and stay in bed all day and remember that when anything is taken out of the store, it must be paid for first.[3]

Peter P. Bilhorn's[4] mother's prayers won him. She was praying at midnight when he came home!

A boy who had a godly mother went to Alaska where he worked in a mining district. He worked days, but gambled nights! One day he took some of his employer's money...and lost it at the gambling table! He went out into the mountains and raised a gun to his temple, ready to pull the trigger. But then he thought of his old mother and her parting message: "If you are ever in trouble, remember the Lord! Turn to Him!" There on that mountain he found peace with God. The next day he made it right with his employer.

My own mother's prayers kept me from knocking a man in the head in San Diego. I saw my mother's face![5]

A poor drunkard at Newberg, Oregon, had a good Christian mother. But he married a non-Christian! Now one of his boys is a thief, one is in the pen, a daughter is a cigaret fiend and married to a confessed bootlegger, and his wife is a street-walking Communist! But this sermon and his godly mother's prayers brought him back to salvation!

Why aren't some of you men and women in hell? A mother's prayers and teaching have kept you out!

**THE BIBLE**

The Bible is one of the greatest hindrances—to sin! There it stands with its warnings (Gal. 5:14-21) and invitations (Matt. 11:28); its description of sin (Rom. 3:10-18) and consequences (Rom. 1:28ff); its beauty and rewards of righteousness; its wonderful pictures of God's love; its protection of faithful Israel (Israel lived while Egypt fell, Assyria fell, Syria fell, Babylon fell, Persia fell, Greece fell); its wonderful heaven-inspired church. A great blockade!

The Bible makes a man uneasy in sin! Men give excuses for not reading it, from Old Man Smith at Crabtree[6] to the writings of Bob Ingersol. They say the Bible is filled with filthy stories, bad morals and endorses the death penalty. But the real reason they don't want to read it is because their lives are filthy, and the Bible condemns it; their morals are bad, and the Bible shows it up; they are guilty and the Bible brings it too close to home for comfort!

The Bible turns men from sin. "The wages of sin is death, but the free gift of God is eternal life" (Rom. 6:23). Only God knows how many have been turned to Him by verses like Amos 4:12, "Prepare to meet Thy God," John 6:37, "Him that cometh to me, I will in no wise cast out," and John 3:16.

Over 400 years ago a pious German monk came to Rome. He thought it was a holy city! Instead he found it full of corruption and immorality. As he ascended the Saneta Scala (the sacred stairs) a verse of scripture burst upon his mind: "The just shall live by faith." Martin Luther was converted through a Bible text. One verse of scripture changed the whole religious world, brought the Bible's translation into common languages, ended the Dark Ages, broke the Pope's universal rule and, in time, brought religious freedom to America!

A wife attended a revival meeting. At home she began to read the Bible aloud. Her husband didn't like it. "Cut it out or I'll give you your fill of that d____ book!" She said, "I'll show you how to enjoy this book." Night after night she read from the Bible. One night he broke down. "I'm a sinner, a poor, undone sinner!" And God saved him when he yielded!

A boy who had grown up in a Christian home got mixed up in trouble and decided to steal from his boss. There was only a small chance of detection, but the next morning he found a slip of paper on his desk. "Lay up for yourselves treasures in heaven." That verse (Mark 6:19) changed his life and now he is a great worker for God!

O sinner firend, won't you let this wonderful Word of God (and the prayers and teaching of a godly mother) turn you with a whole soul to God and His salvation?

**GOD!**

May the Lord have mercy on the father or mother who is not leading their children toward God! An artist who lived in a regular art gallery had many beautiful masterpieces. But there was one picture he valued above all others. It had only the slight resemblance of a rose. Why did he value it? His mother made it! Who makes things has much to do with the value we place on it. Oh, what a world this would be if we only realized God made it!

A policeman rudely shoved an old lady out of the way–to save her from a speeding car! Sometimes we see God's kindness in His severity! God cares.

Bernard Shaw was a missionary to Cape Town, Africa. He was dismissed and forbidden to preach there. He loaded up his family and goods and started for the interior of Africa, not really knowing where he was going. He traveled 300 miles in 29 days. He encamped at night and found close by a camp of Hotentots. Shaw asked them where they were going. They answered, "To Cape Town or a missionary!" One day's difference in starting would have caused them to miss each other! God protects.

I once looked through a friend's telescope and saw a so-called Christian chewing and spitting tobacco. He did not know I was watching. God's all-seeing eye never sleeps. He sees all deeds and knows all thoughts.

God can be seen all around us in nature. Dr. Lampland, federal astonomer, said, "The undevout astronomer is mad." "I am thinking of God's thoughts after him," said the great Agasiz. A famous botanist, scrutinizing a flower, was asked, "What do you see?" "I see God!" was the reverent reply. A Christian microscopist, turning from his microscope, said, "I have found a universe worthy of God!"

God is revealed to us in His names. Elohim, Creator! El Shaddai, Almighty! Elyon, Most High! Adonai, Lord! Yaweh,

Eternal I Am! Father, Projenitor of life. Saviour, Rescuer of the wanderer!

Remember sinner friend–on hell's road stands the God who made you and loves you! We ought to turn to him wholeheartedly! An advisor to Abraham Lincoln said, "The fight is likely to be very bitter. Don't you think we ought to get God on our side?" "No," replied Lincoln, "Let us get on God's side!"

A sweetheart's love may fail. A dad's love may fail. A mother's love may fail. But God's love never fails! God stands in the way, hurling His warnings at every person on the road to hell!

**SERMONS!**

Philip's sermon saved the eunuch (Acts 8). Paul's sermon saved the Philippian jailor (Acts 16).

A girl in Marshfield, Oregon,[7] came after the meeting was over to give her heart to the Lord. She said, "There was one sermon God wouldn't let me shake off!"

Old Mrs. Tucker was saved at Marshfield by the sermon "7 Steps to Hell!" Another was saved by one sentence! "A woman that is immoral may listen to the world call her a 'Hot Mama,' 'Some Chicken,' 'Sweet Baby,' or 'Everybody's Doll,' but the truth of the matter is, 'You are a whore, and God says all whores are going to the lake of fire!'"[8]

Sermons were worth $5000.00 to C. A. Smith's loggers. He paid the revivalist "Haywire" Davis that much for the good he could do his men!

A hardboiled seaman was saved and saved from the "pen" after hearing a sermon at Lakeport, California.[9]

Sermons are a part of God's blockade on the road to hell! Lord, give me power to make them real obstacles!

**A BIBLE SCHOOL TEACHER'S INFLUENCE**

How many are there here tonight who were saved by a faithful Sunday School teacher? (Asks for show of hands.) Mrs.

Matthis had a great influence on my own life! I met her years after when I was in the Navy in San Diego.[10]

A fine young man took an unruly girl's Bible School class. But he came down with tuberculosis and was given up to die! But he asked the pastor to take him to talk to the girls about Christ until he was worn out. He returned the next day to continue his pleading until all but one of the girls was truly converted. On the last Sunday of his life all the girls came to confess Christ–and the only girl who had held out came to Christ! Just recently her daughter graduated from Bible College in Los Angeles!

I would to God parents could realize what an opportunity they have in some of their teachers. Miss Farley, a Marshfield junior high school teacher, gave up a Campfire Girls opportunity, a chance for promotion in teaching, incurring the Superintendent's wrath, lost a new contract and many friends–all to keep her Bible School class!

Bible School teachers are a powerful blockade on the road to hell! But for God's sake, parents, don't leave it all up to the Bible School teacher!

**THE HOLY SPIRIT!**

Right in the midst of a so-called "good time" have you ever had a feeling come over your heart? Unrest, dissatisfaction with the life you'e living, longing for something better, memories of home, church, the Bible, mother and God? The Holy Spirit was dealing with you (John 16:8)!

The Holy Spirit has mysterious power. How He moves in our lives! (Editor's note: Here Archie jotted down in his notes, "Lost Key" escapade at Lindsey. Years later daughter Barbara remembered the incident.)[11] "We were all ready to leave for another preaching point after the last service, and Dad could not find his car keys. We all looked everywhere, and Dad turned everything inside out...The preacher helped us look, and after an hour of fruitless searching, one of the people that had been deeply convicted by the sermon appeared at the church and was baptized on the spot. As soon as they were through with the baptism, Dad put his hand into his coat pocket and there were the keys in the little coin pocket inside the outer pocket. He just knew that he had looked there, but the Lord knew what was coming and kept us right there, just long enough for the lost one to get right with the Lord."

The Holy Spirit is the power needed inside our lives. A man working alongside a half-wit dropped dead. The half-wit was found trying to stand the dead man up, crying, "He needs something inside!"

What is that which stirs your heart RIGHT NOW? "I wonder if I should become a Christian tonight?" It is the Spirit of God! Obedience means eternal life! To say "No!" means eternal hell!

Friend, you can go right through these barricades: a mother's love, the Bible, God, sermons, a Bible School teacher's influence, and the Holy Spirit...but there is a final blockade on the road to hell!

**THE CROSS OF CHRIST!**

In the pathway of every unsaved man stands the cross of Christ! Where Christ was falsely accused! beaten! thorn-crowned! hands and feet pierced! in anguish of heart! side riven! rejected of men! bearing our griefs! carrying our sorrows! wounded for our transgressions! bruised for our iniquities! He went through–for us–unspeakable suffering on that hellish bloody gibbot! He carried all the sins of ALL the world on His person! Every man or woman who goes on toward hell has to step OVER, or ON the cross of Christ!

A godly old man had a worthless son. The father loved the son and wanted to save him from remorse. But the son determined to go into that infamous, soul-damning business of selling booze, coining money out of mother's tears, wive's broken hearts, the groans and sighs of children, and the blood of men. The father went to plead with his son. "You'll never sell

**another drop while I live. Only over my unconscious body can they enter!" He planted himself outside the door of the saloon. His own son came out, hit him, and over his dying body, sold booze!**

**IF YOU GO ON IN YOUR SINS YOU MUST DO IT OVER THE DEAD BODY OF CHRIST AND HIS CROSS!**

---

1. Archie had a brother, Walter, who was born exactly two years after Archie, April 21, 1903.
2. This story is related in *Voice of Thunder, Heart of Tears* (p. 37).
3. *Ibid.,* (pp. 38-39)
4. A famous 19th century revivalist.
5. This incident took place during Archie's wild years in the Navy. The man was Chinese and Archie intended to kill him, but when he raised his fist (or perhaps a blunt instrument) the face of the Chinese was transformed into the face of Maggie Word! Archie later testified that he had committed every sin except murder.
6. Word's first ministry was at Crabtree, Oregon.
7. Marshfield is now known as Coos Bay. Archie Word help many successful revivals in this fishing town on the Oregon coast.
8. The prostitute who attended that night came down the aisle a few nights later and surrendered her life to Christ. She won her husband and son to Christ and when Archie returned to Marshfield a year later, she was singing in the church choir and playing the piano for Sunday School!
9. It was at Lakeport that Archie Word preached his famous "dance" sermon–right in a dance hall! It led to over 100 conversions in the church. See *Voice of Thunder, Heart of Tears* (pp. 207-210).
10. Where Archie was prevented from killing the Chinese man by seeing his mother's face.
11. This incident took place the final night of Archie's third revival in Lindsay in 1935. It is recounted on pp. 262-263 of *Voice of Thunder, Heart of Tears.*

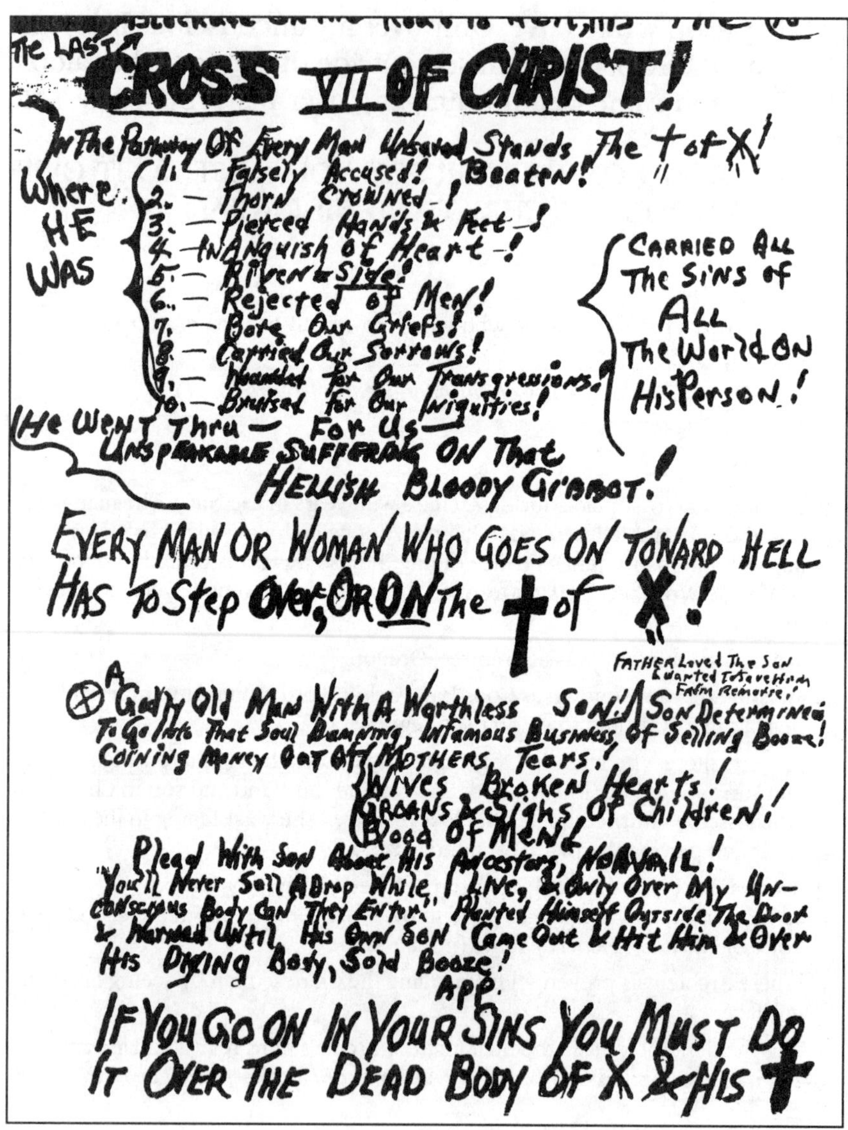
The Last CROSS VII OF CHRIST!

In The Pathway Of Every Man Unsaved Stands The † of X!

Where HE WAS
1. — Falsely Accused! Beaten!
2. — Thorn Crowned—!
3. — Pierced Hands & Feet—!
4. — In Anguish of Heart—!
5. — Riven Side!
6. — Rejected of Men!
7. — Bore Our Griefs!
8. — Carried Our Sorrows!
9. — Wounded for Our Transgressions!
10. — Bruised for Our Iniquities!

Carried All The Sins of All The World On His Person!

He Went Thru— For Us Unspeakable Suffering On That Hellish Bloody Gibbet!

EVERY MAN OR WOMAN WHO GOES ON TOWARD HELL HAS TO STEP OVER, OR ON THE † of X!

Father Loved The Son & Wanted To Save Him From Remorse!

A Godly Old Man With A Worthless Son! Son Determined To Go Into That Soul Damning, Infamous Business of Selling Booze! Coining Money Out Of Mothers' Tears! Wives' Broken Hearts! Groans & Sighs of Children! Blood of Men!

Plead With Son About His Ancestors, No Avail! "You'll Never Sell A Drop While I Live, & Only Over My Unconscious Body Can They Enter." Planted Himself Outside The Door & Warned Until His Own Son Came Out & Hit Him & Over His Dying Body, Sold Booze! App.

IF YOU GO ON IN YOUR SINS YOU MUST DO IT OVER THE DEAD BODY OF X & HIS †

*Last page of notes from sermon "God's Blockades on the Road to Hell." Note use of cross illustration and "X" for Christ.*

5

# BAPTIZED, BUT NOT RIGHT WITH GOD!

*The Church Speaks,* September 10, 1945

This is going to be a specifically Biblical sermon and if you want to understand the message it will be imperative that you read Acts 8:9-24.

The old proverb writer truthfully spoke when he said, "The scoffer loveth not to be reproved; he will not go unto the wise." But remember right along with that piece of news, there is another one that says, "He that turneth away his ear from hearing the law, even his prayer is an abomination." So we know that the person who expects, in any sensible way, to get along with God must listen to HIS WORD and heed it. The same proverb writer says, "He that rebuketh a man shall afterward find more favor than he that flattereth with the tongue" (Prov. 28:23).

Personally, I would rather have the favor of God upon my ministry, and in the END have the respect of the sinner that has come to his right senses, than to know in my heart I was wrong with God and only running on public sentiment that could at any moment turn upon me when the proper stress should be put upon it. Every man in the ministry has to make his choice to either serve God and buck public sentiment or to "chisel" on God and court the sentiment of the general public at that particular time. Public sentiment changes so rapidly. Once we hated Communism[1] and many pulpits were open and abusive in their attack on it, but today the pendulum has swung to the opposite extreme. If Communism ever was wrong it still is, and public sentiment does not change a thing that is organically and structurally wrong. And public sentiment does not change a thing that is RIGHT, either. IF GOD'S WORD SAYS IT, IT WILL STAND THROUGH ALL ETERNITY! I am dealing with a Biblical doctrine in this sermon. Follow carefully and read well for your life may depend upon your right decision in this matter.

**BAPTISM OVEREMPHASIZED**

In many instances baptism has been overemphasized. For centuries the Roman Catholic church and various denominations taught that the application of a few drops of water on an infant (which they called "baptism") was essential to the babe's salvation. They even went so far as to design instruments to apply water to the baby before its birth (in cases where they thought the mother could not give birth to the child). The Bible teaches no such damnable foolishness, neither by precept, command or example. That is the outgrowth of man's so-called "wisdom," and it represents some of his foolishness in drawing conclusions from a false syllogism.

Baptism has been overemphasized when men were taught to wait until they were on their deathbeds before having the rite of baptism performed. If it was for "remission of sins," they would be sure to commit no sins after they were baptized. You may say, "That sounds silly." Well, it is silly! But it is some of man's "wisdom" that we can now look back on and see how silly it really was.

There is another form of overemphasis on baptism, and it is practiced in many so-called Christian churches today–teaching people that they can depend upon water baptism (and I mean IMMERSION, which is the only meaning of "baptism") for their salvation, WITHOUT HAVING BEEN BEGOTTEN OF GOD AND CONVERTED BEFORE THEY WERE BAPTIZED. Remember this: if baptism ALONE can save you or any other sinner, then we might just as well get a garden hose and start sprinkling the city in the name of the Father, Son and Holy Ghost; or start hiring some big brutes to go out and bring in the citizens and force them to be immersed. Baptism, WITHOUT REGENERATION, is depending upon water alone for salvation, and it is a devil's substitute with too much emphasis laid upon baptism. If baptism ALONE can save people, we will be held accountable for not using force, if necessary, in getting people under the water. (Notice, I said IF baptism ALONE can save sinners!)

## BAPTISM SLIGHTED

On the other hand, baptism has been slighted by some groups of people in various denominations. How is this done? Some preachers have not preached on baptism and its connection with the God-given plan of salvation in 10 years, even though it is the ONLY command in the entire Bible that is ever given in the name of the Father, Son and Holy Ghost.[2] Why do they not speak on this subject? The answer is easy. It is because there are many "nice" people who want to come to church and assume a certain air of respectability, but they will not become obedient from the heart to the Lord, and they do not want to be told about their sins, nor their rejection of the Christ of God,[3] nor their own condemnation under which they lay until they are released by the blood of Christ! It is a thorny path to travel and sometimes lonesome (to preach what Jesus told us should be preached).

Others slight Christian baptism by teaching people that we are saved by faith ALONE. We are saved by faith, but we are NOT saved by faith ALONE, or "faith only". The worst form of deception is that in which there is a half-truth mixed with an utter falsehood. Scripture says, "Yea, a man will say, Thou hast faith and I have works: show me thy faith apart from thy works, and I by my works will show thee my faith" (James 2:18). Baptism is a work demanded of God–to show the world we have faith. Read Mark 16:15-16. Baptism is an act demanded of God and no man can say that he truthfully knows God who refuses to obey Jesus' command. "And hereby we know that we know him, if we keep his commandments. He that saith, I know him, and keepeth not his commandments, is a liar, and the truth is not in him; but whoso keepeth his word, in him verily hath the love of God been perfected. Hereby we know that we are in him" (I John 2:3-5).

James says, "Ye see that by works a man is justified, and not only by faith" (James 2:24). This had reference to Abraham having been obedient to the command of God. By his obedience he showed his faith. Abraham is known as the father of the faithful and we become sons of Abraham, according to Gal. 3:9, when we have faith enough to do what God has told us to do, believing that He will keep His promise to us upon our completion of our obedience. Just as Abraham was commanded to offer up his son, we are commanded to be baptized. We show our FIDELITY or our INFIDELITY by our obedience or our disobedience to this divine command.

Baptism is slighted again by telling people to put off their obedience to Christ in baptism until Easter, or at some other convenient time. Notice the difference in the book of Acts! The Pentecostians were baptized the same day (Acts 2:38-42). The eunuch from Ethiopia was baptized immediately (Acts 8:37-39). The Philippian jailer was baptized the same hour of the night (Acts 16:33-34). Apparently these men of God believed that God's test of faith was to be applied (and that it was not to be done next Christmas). They believed that God had given His oath as to WHEN He would apply the blood to the sinner's past records.

Another way baptism has been slighted is in telling the candidate that they may have their choice of the "mode" in baptism. The Bible says there is ONE baptism, not three or four.[4] Men have invented substitutes they have deceived people into believing God will accept, but there is not one word from the throne of God corroborating their claim. The Bible knows nothing about sprinkling, nor does the Bible sanction pouring. Baptism pictures the DEATH, BURIAL AND RESURRECTION of Jesus, as set forth in Romans 6:2-6. Baptism is also a form of BIRTH (birth means "to come out of"). For 1300 years the church practiced immersion. Not until A.D. 1311[5] did a Pope even assume the prerogative of changing this divine command of God's only begotten Son!

Baptism is immersion, but Christian baptism MUST be preceded by faith and repentance which works conversion before it is effective. See Acts 2:38 and notice that repentance is placed BEFORE immersion and the promise of remission of sins is AFTERWARD!

But it is possible to be baptized in water and still not be right with God! Read Acts 8:13-21 (the account of Simon the sorcerer). You will find that it is possible to be baptized in water–immersed–and have a desire to be a teacher, even wanting to be on a par with the apostles, and still not be right with God!

In some congregations it is quite common to find folks who want places of leadership–and many times they will do anything under God's heaven to get it. I've seen gossip campaigns started with just one objective in mind: to gain some coveted place in the church, possibly a teacher's place, or the pianist's position, or the choir director. Prominent positions gained by gossip and slander do not glorify God, and the person guilty of any such conduct ought to be in politics instead of the church of the living God! People doing those kinds of things may be baptized, but they are not right with God. Simon the sorcerer was baptized...but he was not right with God!

How may we know we are not right with God, even though we have been immersed?

## BAPTIZED, BUT NOT RIGHT WITH GOD!

If COVETOUSNESS is in your heart, you may be baptized, but you are not right with God. Simon reverted to his old desire to be a "Somebody" and to make money (Acts 8:18-19). He coveted the power that belonged to an apostle only. Covetousness is foreign to the child of God. If you are coveting the things that belong to another person, you may be baptized but you are not right with God!

A legend tells of Gabriel sweeping a street, and as he swept he sang. Someone asked him how he could sing while he worked[6] at such debased labor when he had been used to being in the presence of God in heaven. Gabriel answered, "I am doing my Father's will." He was equally happy doing his Father's will on the streets of earth as he was on the streets of heaven. He filled his own position. He did not covet someone else's position. He was right with God!

Covetousness is a strong desire for something that belongs to someone else. If you desire money, the tithe that belongs to God, you are coveting, and you are sinning. If you take that money, the tithe, you steal. Coveting leads to stealing.

The Bible says that covetousness is idolatry. It compares covetousness to wolves in its savage and rapacious nature. It says that covetousness is like a greedy dog, a horse leech, a blood sucker with a double-forked tongue. With one tongue it gorges itself and with the other it empties itself. There are four insatiable things, according to Proverbs 30:15-16. The grave, the barren womb, the parched land, and fire. They never are satisfied! They never have enough, and covetousness is the epitome of them all!

The Greek word for covetousness means, "A desire to have more than belongs to one." The great Hippocrates called a consultation of all physicians in the world to find a cure for covetousness, but found they could not cure it. Two thousand years still finds the medical profession up against insurmountable barriers in dealing with this disease of the heart. Philosophers, too, have failed. Only Jesus Christ can cure this malady of the heart, and He makes it right again by TRUE REPENTANCE and GENUINE PRAYER (Acts 8:22-24).

How may we know if we are not right with God, even though we have been baptized?

If a person is still WORLDLY he may be baptized, but he is not right with God. "Ye adultresses (those who break your marriage vows to God), know ye not that the friendship of the world is enmity with God. Whosoever therefore would be a friend of the world maketh himself an enemy of God" (James 4:4).

God knows that worldliness distracts the thoughts of men. Worldliness drives away their moral convictions and leads men and women into the quagmires of the sex morass. Worldliness binds their souls with chains of sensual pleasure that can only be broken with the fires of hell–and then it is too late for the poor unfortunates to get away. Worldy pleasure deadens our spiritual senses or right and wrong. Napolean put the Duke D'Enghien to death. All Paris felt such a horror that his throne was threatened. There were threats of a counter revolution. Napolean caused a great ballet to be brought out. It was produced with the utmost splendor at the grandest opera hall, with free admission. Paris soon forgot the murder of the innocent man.

Church members who have been baptized, but who are not right with God, go to the show to forget their cares instead of going to God with their burdens. They go to their tobacco for comfort instead of going to the loving heavenly Father. They sit at the card table and try to forget instead of coming to the Lord's Table to remember the blood of Christ that cleanses from all sin. They try to drown their sorrows in the liquor bottle instead of coming to Him who said, "I will give you rest." All too soon they forget about the God of heaven and His teaching. It is not long until they have drifted from His divine commands, becoming rebels who have not only lost their own souls, but have become the instrument through which the devil has damned their entire family.

A group of boys, while playing in a pond, discovered some frogs and at once began to throw rocks at the poor creatures. Many of the helpless things were killed, and many more were maimed. Finally one old frog poked his head out, and said, "Boys, stop your cruel sport. Consider that what is fun for you is DEATH to us!" Worldly church member, what is fun to you is death to Christ's influence on others. It is death to your own influence for Christ. It is death to your chance to ever teach a class or become a real deacon or elder. It is the most expensive fun, this being a wordly, backslidden church member, that is baptized, but not right with God!

You may be baptized, but if your heart is UNCHANGED, you are not right with God. "Jehovah is nigh unto them of a broken heart, and saveth such as are of a contrite spirit" (Psa. 34:18). God works from the OUTSIDE (the ears) to get to the INSIDE (the heart). It is the INSIDE that needs to be cleansed.

I watched a window washer working on a large showcase window downtown. He worked by the piece, and not by the hour. He was busy and he wanted the job done well because other work depended upon his doing every job well. He applied the soap and water; ran the sponge over the surface and brought the squegee down the smooth surface. Glancing at his work, he saw a spot. He stepped over to it and tried a razor blade on the spot, rubbed it with his finger nail, and then putting his head around the corner, he yelled, "Hey, Jack! It's on the inside!" So it is with the baptized-but-not-right church member. The problem is on the inside. The heart is not right and from the unconverted heart comes covetousness and worldliness.

Remember, washing the heart with the tears of sorrow is not enough. Scrubbing it with the soap of good resolutions is insufficient. Rubbing it with the chamois of morality will not work. Covering it up with self-justification will not take the dirt out. God has given us a method that will work every time, and nothing else on earth will work. It is found in Acts 8:22, "Repent of this thy wickedness and pray the Lord if perhaps the thought of thy heart shall be forgiven thee."

A heart right with God seeks forgiveness (Matt. 6:14-15). A proud Greek woman was a nurse in an American hospital in Turkey. She had been baptized, but she was not right with God. She carried a grudge in her heart and had carried it for years. She heard about "being baptized, but not right with God" and she decided she was going to be right. She walked three miles to ask forgiveness of an old enemy. Her kinfolk and friends thought she was crazy, but the next day they knew better for they heard her say, "We made peace and the stone in my heart is gone!"

God's Word says, "Create in me a clean heart, O God; and renew a right spirit within me." The changed heart loves his fellow men–and he loves them enough to preach the truth to them without fearing the consequences! He loves God FIRST and trusts God to keep him when all men turn against him. Love is the natural fruit of the changed heart. I love God because He first loved me, but I love my neighbor enough to show him that I am like Christ. Show me the man who loves God, and I'll show you a man who loves prayer meeting; he loves his fellow men; he loves sermons; he loves his enemies; he loves the Word; he is not afraid to publicly testify to the power of God in his own life.

In one of our meetings after the sermon had been preached, a dear old Christian sister came forward after the invitation and said, "I just wanted to tell you that there is nothing between my soul and the Savior; none of this world's delusive dreams." (We had sung that song that evening).[7] She went on to say how happy she was that nothing divided her love. She was free from the worldly vices of the theater, cards, bad literature, gossip, worldly friends and covetousness. It was a sweet testimony from a sincere heart. She did not know that she would be in the hospital and dead in four days, but she was. She called for her adopted daughter to come and kiss her goodbye...and then she went to be with Him who made her right with God!

Dear friend, don't be foolish and wait until you are crushed to the very earth before you listen to the voice of God. How many have done that and then tried to bargain with God for a blessing. I once baptized a man and his wife some years ago. She was really converted, but he was just baptized. He said he loved his wife, but he lived like the devil and made her life as miserable as he could. She became terribly ill. She was rushed from one state to another by plane and landed in Portland to be under a specialist's care. The husband drove through and arrived in our city exhausted. He sat in silent vigil near the door of the private ward while the angel of death hovered near. Loving relatives and Christian prayed, but the battle was a losing one.

One day this man came to my office and in the course of conversation said, "Oh Brother Word, if God will just save her, I'll do anything He wants me to do."

I waited for awhile, for my heart went out to him in his heart-broken distress, but I could not be faithful to him and not say, "Friend, do you not think you are acting foolishly by trying to drive a bargain with God? Would it not be better to say, 'Oh God, whatever happens, whether she lives or dies, or whether

I live here or there, if you will give me grace from heaven, I will do your will as long as I live."

He sat there for some time, debating, and finally, he said, "You are right. I'll do it." We had prayer together. His wife died. She was tenderly laid to rest by loving friends, but the man LIED TO GOD, for he did not keep his bargain. One of these days he may be on the deathbed himself. Or, worse yet, the next time the Lord may say, "Man, you lied to me before, but this time 'He that hardeneth his neck shall be suddenly cut off, and that without remedy.'"

Nothing can be used as a substitute for genuine repentance. You can not fool God! He knows the heart! Man may misjudge you, but God knows all about you!

If you have been baptized, but are not right with God, for Jesus' sake, repent of whatever is wicked in your life and pray to the Lord to forgive you and accept you back into His household, before it is too late. Then you may know that you are BAPTIZED AND RIGHT WITH GOD!

---

1. Archie Word was an ardent anti-Communist, especially in his writings in *The Church Speaks.*
2. See Matthew 28:19.
3. Brother Word loved to refer to Jesus as "the Christ of God."
4. See Eph. 4:4, "One Lord, one faith, one baptism."
5. When the Pope, a Frenchman named Clement V, was ruling from Avignon in Southern France, a virtual prisoner of the French king.
6. Archie Word was "singing while he worked" when he was discovered by W. S. Lemmon, a preacher from Porterville, California. Archie went to Eugene Bible University on a music scholarship.
7. *Nothing Between* by Charles A. Tindley.

# THE CHURCH SPEAKS

**Published with the sole purpose of causing people to think about Christ's Teaching especially relating to His church and the holiness of its members.**

ADDRESS ALL COMMUNICATIONS TO THE EDITOR,
A. WORD, 550 N. E. 76TH AVENUE, PORTLAND 13, OREGON

VOLUME 13 No. 3 "MAKE ALL THINGS ACCORDING TO THE PATTERN." MAY 1961

## *Hate-Monger*

A. Word, Editor

CATHOLICISM is like any other sin; always trying to cover up. It is all right for them to sin, but it is all wrong for anybody to expose them in it. They are the "LOVING PEOPLE" when they massacre Christians and destroy their houses of worship, but if anybody dares to say anything about it, they are labeled forthwith "Hate-Mongers".

It is O.K. for the Pope Pius IX to say, "You ask, if the Pope were lord of this land and you were in the minority, what would he do to you? That, we say, would entirely depend upon the circumstances. If it would benefit the cause of Catholicism he would tolerate you; if expedient, he would imprison or banish you, probably he might hang you: but, be assured of one thing, he would never tolerate you for the sake of your glorious principles of civil and religious liberty." BUT IF anybody digs that answer up and broadcasts it when there is a possibility of one of the Pope's boys getting into the Capitol, he is an awful "HATE-MONGER"!

It is loving and kind for "Ryan & Miller" "The State and the Church" page 38-39 to say: "But constitutions can be changed, and non-Catholic sects may decline to such a point that the political proscription of them may become feasible and expedient. What protection would they have against a Catholic State?" BUT it is the height of hatred for anybody to spread

Continued to page 35

## THE EDITOR

By Stewart Baker

I want to introduce the editor, Bro. Archie James Word, to you new readers of THE CHURCH SPEAKS. I have known him for over 20 years and have grown to love and admire him more

ARCHIE JAMES WORD, EDITOR

*The Church Speaks reached a circulation of 25,000 under Archie Word's editorship.*

## 6

# REPENT OR PERISH!

*The Voice of Evangelism,* October 26, 1946

"Except ye repent, ye shall all likewise perish" (Luke 13:3,5).

There is a great deal being said today against the receiving of "the pious unimmersed",[1] but there is very little being said about the "UNPIOUS IMMERSED" who are already in the membership. Let us remember this, brethren,[2] REPENTANCE is just as important in God's plan of salvation as is BAPTISM. Repentance changes a man's life! Baptism, when it is applied to the penitent believer, is where God applies the blood of Jesus Christ for the remission of past sins. But if the sinner will not repent of his sins, the blood is not applied, the Holy Spirit is not given, and the baptized UNREPENTANT sinner perishes just the same as the repentant sinner who REFUSES to be BAPTIZED. Both are rebels against the authority of God.

There is no acceptable substitute for repentance, and the one who refuses to repent of his sins still claiming to have a knowledge of Christ is just as big a liar as the man who refuses to be baptized while claiming to know Jesus. "He that saith I know him, and keepeth not his commandments, is a liar, and the truth is not in him" (I John 2:3-4). REPENTANCE is a commandment of the Lord Jesus Christ and is an immutable condition upon which rests the forgiveness of our sins.

It is still, as it has always been under Jesus Christ's regime; "Except ye repent, ye shall all in like manner perish" (Luke 13:3). John the Baptizer introduced Jesus with a message of repentance; the disciples were sent out by Jesus to preach repentance; Jesus taught the people repentance throughout His ministry; all the prophets had pled for repentance from personal and national sins; and when the Holy Spirit came to supervise the construction of the long- prophesied church which was to become the Kingdom of Christ on earth, His first demand of the sinners on that memorable day[3] was "Repent ye!"

My topic is my proposition, and this sermon will have but two divisions. First, **"REPENT YE!"**

Peter commanded repentance (Acts 2:38). Paul preached repentance (Acts 17:30). He declared to both Jew and Gentile that they should repent and bring forth work worthy of repentance (Acts 26:20).

A penitent life is exemplified in Col. 3:2, "Set your minds upon the things that are above, not upon the things that are upon the earth." Repentance is illustrated in I Thess. 1:9, "How you turned unto God from idols, to serve the living and the true God." Repentance was urged in Heb. 12:1-2, "Let us lay aside every weight and the sin that does so easily beset us."

First, repentance that is acceptable to God must be ACTUAL, not fictitous.

It is not just a promise or a vow, but it is a real change of one's life's actions. Perhaps you said, "I'm going to turn to God," but you did not do it. Or you said, "I'm going to cut out my sinning," but by tomorrow you forgot all about it. Maybe you said, "I'm going to live a life of holiness from now on," but on the morrow you forgot all about your vow. Possibly you said, "I'm giving up my vices and crimes against God," but you did not give them up; you kept right on deserting the church and wickedly loafing your life away as far as Christ's church is concerned.

A few tears yesterday, which are all dried up today, is not repentance. A promise made but broken, is not repentance. That weak and broken vow you made is not repentance. A transient emotion is not repentance. You may say, "I'm sorry, I repent, I'm going to quit my devilishness," yet go on tomorrow in that same sin! That is NOT repentance! YOU BROKE YOUR VOW TO GOD! That makes your curse all the more certain; you attempted to deceive God! You lied to God about a commandment of His Son. You did not repent, and my text still stands—abbreviated, pointed, pungent. ACTUALLY repent or perish!

Second, true repentance must not only be actual, but it must be ENTIRE.

How many foolish sinners say, "I will give up my old stinking tobacco sin." (And God knows that every person who names the name of Christ as Savior from sin ought to give up such a vile, smelly and vulgar habit as the use of the weed.)[4] Someone else says, "I'm going to give up my lying and gossiping;" another says, "I'm leaving off the card playing[5] and gambling;" or "I'm giving up the filthy companionship of Hollywood in the theaters and dance." Now, all these are worthy of genuine repentance, but if you quit one of them, that would not necessarily constitute repentance, for repentance means ALL KNOWN SIN MUST GO!

Hear me, O saint and sinner, it is not ONE sin nor 50; it is a solemn renunciation of ALL sin! One accursed snake of lust in your heart makes repentance a sham! One leak sinks the ship at the dock! It is ALL or NOTHING with God! True repentance makes one hate sin as a "race," not just one particular sin. True repentance makes a child of God hate sin en masse.

A true sinner's repentance makes him say, "Guild thee as thou wilt, O sin, I abhor thee! cover thyself with pleasure, make thyself gaudy, like the snake with azure scales–I hate thee still, for I know thy venom, and I will flee from thee."[6] Why? Because true repentance makes us hate sin. All sin must be given up or you have no Christ. All transgressions must be renounced or heaven's gates are barred to you. It is repent–sincerely and entirely–or perish!

Third, repentance that is effectual must be IMMEDIATE.

Many people say, "When I'm a little older I'll repent." "When I'm near death's door." "When I'm facing eternity." "In that quiet season before death." "After my heart and lungs are ruined and I can't smoke anymore." "After I'm too old to dance, I'll repent and turn to God." But listen, brother, it is terribly few who ever change after long lives of sin. Put no faith in repentance on your deathbed. If you don't repent in health, you probably won't in sickness. Life is always uncertain. Men drop dead on the job. Men drop dead on the street. Men die in their sleep. You may die on the dance hall floor! When death comes it is bad enough to have a tortured body without having the pangs of repentance eating into your remorseful soul! God says, "TODAY, if ye will hear my voice, harden not your heart."

An old Jewish rabbi said, "Let every man repent one day before he dies: and since he may die tomorrow, let him take heed and turn from his evil ways today." Repentance that saves must be ACTUAL, ENTIRE and IMMEDIATE.

The second part of this sermon is, **"PERISH!"**

A hundred years ago[7] pulpits rang out with messages describing the terrors of hell! Sermons filled with warnings about the wrath of God, certain judgment, a terrible hell. But, brother, that was a hundred years ago! Today's preachers say very little about God's punishment, but dwell almost exclusively on His mercy. They are afraid sinners won't like it, so they emphasize God's love. They don't want to frighten anybody, but hell is a frightful place! They don't want to be called "narrow-minded, hell-fire" preachers, but in their blindness they have run into the "broad way that leadeth to destruction."

Personally, I don't care what men or churches may say about me for preaching the revealed will of God. I'm going to tell sinners of God's awful and certain punishment whether they like it or not. I feel I MUST warn all men, everywhere! I don't preach on hell because it brings me joy, but because I MUST! Because God has spoken! People may laugh, ridicule and slander me, but some day they will be laughing out of the other side of their mouth. I expect that King Ahab laughed–maybe a little uneasily–when Micaiah told him he would not come back from battle. But when that fatal arrow struck the vitals of Ahab, and his life's blood began flowing down his legs and out of the chariot, he turned to his chariot driver and cried, "Take me from the battle for I must die!" At last he knew Micaiah had spoken the truth!

I would rather be true to God and to every man, and take the blaspheming tongues that call such preachers "liars" and "narrow," than I had to face you at the Judgment with you calling me unspeakable names. I would rather speak what I know–and what everyone else knows God has told a preacher to preach about the awfulness of hell–while scoundrels and Jehovah's Witnesses and other "No Hellers"[8] blend their voices in epithets, than to have you yell at me throughout eternity. "Preacher, you flattered us, but you didn't warn us; you didn't tell us of eternity's doom; you left the wrath of God out of your message to please us, AND HERE WE ARE IN HELL TOGETHER; you spoke feebly and faintly instead of lifting up your voice like a trumpet to warn us of this awful place; you took our money, but you were unfaithful to our souls!" Brother, you would curse me forever in eternity!

Sometimes the knife is necessary to save the patient's life. In such instances, the surgeon does not hesitate to use it. God has said we must "repent or perish." Why has He said this?

First, because God is a God of justice. Who can imagine the JUST Jehovah allowing sin to go unpunished? Some may dream of such a God, and others may intoxicate their brains to where they can imagine a God without justice, but no sound mind or healthy brain can imagine a God without justice. Could a king be a good king and not be just? Could a government be a good government and function without justice? Could a judge be a good judge and not be a just judge? Then answer me this, my friend. How can God, who is a king, governor and judge, be a good God and not be just? He, being just, MUST punish sin! He, being loving, must WARN us! Can you imagine a just God looking on good and evil with the same pleasure? Can you imagine a just God rewarding both the good and the evil with the same reward? God is just, and He says, "Repent or perish!"

Second, to reject punishment for sin is to fly in the face of all the sacred writings. Does not the record show that God has always punished men for sin? Has God changed? Malachi thunders, "I Jehovah God, changeth not!" (Mal. 3:6). Were not Adam and Eve punished? Driven from their beautiful garden home to wander upon the face of a world which would become unfriendly because of their sin and disobedience. Did not God drown those on the face of the earth because "the wickedness of man was great upon the earth" and their imaginations were continually evil? Did not God punish sin? See the hail of fire and brimstone as it rained down upon the perverts in Sodom and dare doubt that God punishes sin. Witness the gaping jaws of God's earth as it swallowed up Korah, Dathan and Abiram. God has never spared the rebellious. Wicked Pharaoh, with his generals, chariots, horses and horsemen, were overwhelmed and buried in the Red Sea. God punishes sin! Look upon 180,000 soldiers of war who were slain in one night by the angel of Jehovah's justice; Sennacharib's army annihilated! Then, call to mind, that God has warned He is just and that all inspired Scripture corroborates the statement that GOD PUNISHES SIN!

Third, your own conscience, unless it is utterly dead, says, "God punishes sin!" You may laugh and say you do not believe it. But you will find that your conscience can and will change your intellectual belief. You say, "I cannot believe God will punish me for my sins," but you KNOW that He will!

When you are at your extremity, you will cry to the God of love who sent His Son to die for you, but, you rejected His love while on earth. Now you must take His justice! Dying men believe in God's justice. Do you remember in *Pilgrim's Progress* where Mr. Conscience had a very loud voice, and though Mr. Understanding shut himself up in a very dark room where he could not see, yet he used to thunder out so mightily in the streets that Mr. Understanding would shake in his house because of what Mr. Conscience said.

A guilty conscience makes a coward out of the bravest talking infidel. A country minister came to the city to visit with some relatives. In the evening he decided to go for a quiet walk for a period of meditation. He walked in a great park of the city. Darkness was upon him before he knew it, and he started his return. As he walked along he saw a great crowd assembled around a loud-speaking soap-box orator. His first impression was, "Here is a man proclaiming the kingdom of God even in this city, and is it not wonderful to see such a crowd?" But, to his surprise, he heard a young man blaspheming God, daring God to do His worst to him while he spoke terrible things against God's justice.

The people listened intently to this young skeptic. They were pleased with his cutting sarcasm and his boasting logic. When he sat down, the whole audience thundered its approval. The old minister was horrified and felt that he must say something for the honor of his God to the souls of these men who had just been subjected to such poison, but before he was able to get his wits together, a middle-aged man, strong and hardy, stood up in the midst of the people and spoke.

"My friends, I have a word to speak to you tonight! I am not about to refute any of the arguments of the orator. I shall not criticize his style. I shall say nothing concerning what I believe to be blasphemies which he has uttered. But I shall simply relate to you a fact, and after I have done that, you can draw your own conclusions.

"Yesterday I walked by the side of the river. I saw on its flood a young man in a boat. The boat was unmanageable, and was going fast toward the rapids. He could not use the oars for fear, and I saw that he was incapable of bringing the boat to shore. I saw the young man wring his hands in agony. Soon he gave up any attempt to save his life, knelt down in the boat and cried, 'O God, save my soul! If my body cannot be saved, save my soul!'

"I heard him confess that he had been a blasphemer. I heard him vow that if his life were spared, he would never be such again. I heard him implore the mercy of heaven for Jesus Christ's sake. These arms saved that young man from the flood! I plunged into the river, brought the boat to shore and saved his life. That same young man has just now addressed you, cursed his maker, ridiculed his justice, and bragged of his unbelief and bravery. Now what do you say, sirs!"

What do YOU say, my friend?

I am saying to you, my text and proposition are true! It is, REPENT OR PERISH! It is God's unalterable ultimatum! Repent–ACTUALLY, ENTIRELY, IMMEDIATELY–or perish under the condemnation of a JUST God, foretold by the sacred Scriptures and the fact that He has given you a foretaste of His wrath in your conscience that is stirring and lashing you now!

O Brother, won't you repent tonight?

1. The Disciples of Christ practice of "open membership" was a hot issue in 1946.
2. This watershed message was the opening night sermon of a preaching rally held in Cincinnati, Iowa, in 1946.
3. Pentecost, A.D. 30.
4. One of Archie Word's most ramous sermons was "Ten Reasons Why My Mother Told Me To Leave Tobacco Alone," a sermon so strong it got him kicked off radio station KALE in Portland.
5. Brother Word, in his sermon "Merrily Going to Hell," called cards "the Backslider's Bible." He opposed card playing because of the real meaning of cards in the gambler's code. The jack represents a pimp; the king, the devil; the queen, Mary, the mother of Christ, but in a blasphemous way; the joker, Jesus Christ, the product of an illicit union between the jack (a pimp) and the queen (Mary).
6. Source for quote taken from Spurgeon's sermon "Turn or Burn!"
7. The mid-1800s saw many great revivalists, including D. L. Moody, Charles G. Finney and Charles Haddon Spurgeon.
8. In his sermon notes Word included SDA (Seventh Day Adventists) and Herbert W. Armstrong as other "No Hellers."

My Text & Proposition Are True—!
It Is "Repent Or Perish!"
It Is God's Unalterable Ultimatum!

Repent { Actually!, Entirely!, Immediately!

or PERISH—★

Under The Condemnation of
A JUST God!
Foretold By The—Sacred Scripture!
—And—
He Has Given You A Foretaste Of His
Wrath In Your Lashing, Guilty, Conscience!

Rev. 14:9 + 20:11-15

Oh Brother, Wont You
Repent Tonight?

Conclusion to Word's fiery message "Repent or Perish!"

# 7

## WHY I BELIEVE IN A PERSONAL GOD

*The Church Speaks,* January 5, 1947

"The heavens declare the glory of God; and the firmament showeth his handiwork" (Psa. 19:1).

I am convinced we do not talk enough about our God. The unbeliever in your community talks more about his unbelief in God than most Christians do about their belief in God. Atheistic anarchists will get up on their soapbox in the park and denounce God and Christianity,[1] but very few Christians are willing to get right up on the same box and testify to to their faith in the God who has been ridiculed. Why should we not talk about God? Is it not a fair question?

God is the foundation upon which Christianity rests. If there is no God then there is no Christ. If there is no Christ then there is no atonement for our sins—and no real hope after this life. Without Christ, the grave is the end and all is darkness!

God is the foundation upon which all real government is built. Moses, under God's leadership, gave the people the first known republican form of government where the people had a say in their government. In this land of America we believed in God and were so bold as to put it on our money ("In God we trust"). Germany tried to do away with the God of the Bible,[2] and the natural results were seen and are being seen there now.[3] Russia has denounced God and the Christian religion, and has developed what is known as the dictatorship of the proletariat.[4] Communism, today, is the worst form of dictatorship in the world, and the most uncooperative civilization in all nations.[5]

God is the foundation of all MORAL law. The 10 Commandments are the basis upon which all civilized laws were built. Where the laws of God are not recognized, morality, as we know it, does not exist.[6]

History has definitely proven that no nation ever rises above its concept of God. The United States today proves that statement. When we believed in God, we were a moral people, but since the evolutionary theory has come in, with its kindred evil doctrines, we have become a nation unheard of in criminality. Our crime bill will run well over the $15 billion figure. Those are really "New Deal" figures in crime.[7]

"The fool has said in his heart, 'There is no God'" (Psa. 14:1; 53:1). Notice where the fool said it: in his heart! Why? Because he had no REASON for saying it, but it was his DESIRE.

Here are some reasons why I believe in a personal God.

## NATURE PROVES THE EXISTENCE OF GOD

Paul appealed to this argument. "For the invisible things of HIM since the creation of the world are clearly seen, being perceived through the things that are made, even His everlasting power and divinity; that they may be without excuse" (Rom. 1:20).

Nature in the vast shows the work of God through the telescope, and nature in the minute shows God through the microscope. The handiwork of a designing engineer is seen everywhere. Suppose I should show you my watch. Would you think it had an intelligent designer and maker? You would be bound to answer, "Yes." Why? Did you ever see a watch made? Maybe you haven't, but you would still have to say the watch had an intelligent designer. Why would you think so? Because everything about it says so! It has a barrel, a stem to set and wind, springs to make it run, wheels that mesh, a crystal to protect it, screw to hold it together. It all fits. And it works perfectly! But suppose I would say, "No, my friend, the watch had no maker at all. It is merely the result of fortuitous concurrence of atomic matter!" You would say, "Word, you are a fool!" Why? Because your reasoning mind would not allow you to accept such reasoning. With all the vast universe to look upon–billions of times more complicted than any watch (and far more accurate)–no wonder God said, "The fool hath said in his heart, 'There is no God.'"

An appeal to the created universe, demanding a great Jehovah God, was made by the apostle Paul in the first century as he wrote to the Romans (who had turned from the Creator to worship creatures (Rom. 1:18-23).

The very eye with which we see; the ear with which we hear; speaks to us, and says, "Who made us?" Surely no personage of less power and intricate skill than God could have made us as we are! "The fool hath said in his heart, 'There is no God.'" The great universe demands God as its answer in the beginning, and it demands God to keep in in order.

Someone says, "Well, what about the doctine of modern evolution?" Evolution? In the first place, it is not modern at all. The modern popularizer of evolution was born more than 150 years ago. He wrote his first evolutionary hypothesis in 1844. That is over a hundred years ago. He produced his *Origin of the Species* in 1859. But remember that Charles Darwin did not originate it! He merely mouthed what the devil had been saying through men for centuries before his time. Darwin found a ready market in the minds of infantile scientists (so called).

Evolution is not true. It is not based on one single solitary scientific fact. There has never been one single instance of scientifically observed and recorded transmutation of species, nor has it ever been scientifically proven that any animal ever inherited any "acquired characteristics." There are developments of varieties, but there is always a tendency to revert to the original type the minute the superintending hand of man is removed from the experiment.

Burbank took potatoes and by careful studies and selection was able to produce Burbank Irish potatoes. But he started with potatoes and finished with potatoes! If you would leave those potatoes unguarded by man for 10 years they will, by themselves, revert to the little pills that nature produced in the first place.

It is the same with horses. A scientist can breed certain horses to produce fast racing stock or heavy draft horses. He has not made a species at all. And all he has to do to lose all he has made is to leave it up to natural selection. In 50 years he will lose all he has worked for. Take a look at the wild horses on the plains of Eastern Oregon and you will see the irrefutable facts that knock the daylights out of the theory of natural selection causing anything to evolve! Nature, unaided by man's genius to improve, does not Evolve–it DEvolves!

But suppose, for the sake of argument, that evolution is true. Let me ask you this question: "Do you think you have gotten away from God Almighty?" If you think you have, then ask yourself this question: "Who put into that primordial piece of protoplasm (in that slime pit that evolution cannot account for!) the inherent power to develop into the intricate and complicated world that we see all about us? Life cannot make itself–that has been demonstrated for certain! Then who supervised it, to bring it into its form we see today? Was it just blind chance? You couldn't take a meat grinder's parts, put them into a pan, shake them for a million years, and make them, purely by chance, turn out to be a meat grinder! It wouldn't work...and you know it! Back of every working machine is a machinist; back of every piece of architecture there must be an architect; and back of this greatest of all machines (the universe) is the all-powerful and wise machinist–GOD!

Evolution hangs itself in the very beginning, because it has to have a self-starter! It denies itself in facts, for it must have more power to keep it going.

I believe in a personal God because this universe in the minute, or in the vast, microscopically or telescopically, says, "GOD!"

## THE ACCOUNT OF JESUS OF NAZARETH PROVES THE EXISTENCE OF GOD

It is a well-known axiom that every effect must have an adequate cause–and there is only one cause that is adequate to account for the character of Christ. He was without sin, and only God is good! Jesus was unassuming, although He had the unlimited power of Deity at His disposal. He was kind, just, irreproachable, perfect, without guile, fearless. The only cause adequate to account for the matchless teaching of Christ is God. He gave us the greatest law (and that on a moment's notice); taught us of a loving heavenly Father, holiness of life, cleanness of mind, sacrifice of self, and the highest ideals of character. These are attributes of Deity!

Only God is adequate cause to account for the supernatural power of Jesus. He had power over time, space, nature's laws, unmanageable sin's damages, and His power extended beyond the grave and into heaven. He had power to raise up, not only others, but Himself from the dead, and I say, the only cause adequate to account for Jesus Christ, is God!

You may ask, "Well, what about Modernism's view of miracles?" Again I answer–it is not very "modern!" The first notable attempt to delete the miracles in the Bible was given to us over 113 years ago. David Strauss gave us *Laben Jesu* in 1833. Strauss was as qualified as any man then living to do the work that he set out to do. He was in many ways a remarkable man. He had a profound scholarship, as men count scholarship. He had matchless powers of critical analysis, was untiring in his industry, driven by almost demon-possessed powers of endurance. His destructive criticism swept the great universities of Europe in a generation. Strauss worked just the opposite of Jesus. He began at the top in institutions of learning (that had their origin in Christianity), and let it sift down to the laity, while Jesus gave His teaching to the common people, and gradually it worked up to the so-called learned.

Friends, I doubt if one-half of one percent of the people reading this sermon will ever have heard of David Strauss, and I doubt seriously if one one-hundredth of one percent have ever read one page of the writings of David Strauss, although, at one time, Strauss was widely read in Germany, England, Scotland and France. Why? The answer is simple. His writings are rejected as unsound–and it was critical analysis that ruined them! The closer you examine the critics of Christ the sooner they fall, and the closer you examine the teachings of Christ the more dear and real they become to you, the more you will love them, and appreciate them.

Next, a very distinguished Frenchman by the name of Ernest Renan gave all his talent (which God had endowed him) to prove that Jesus was an illegitimate son, or, worse than that, a fictitious character. He gave the world *Vie De Jesus (The Life of Christ).* He had a smattering of Semitic scholarship, possessed an imagination superior to that of H. G. Wells, displayed matchless literary style, and had the public sentiment of that day with him. He became internationally famous almost overnight. His hellishly deceptive philosophy and half- truths cursed the scholastic world for nearly 30 years...then it faded. Not nearly as much noise was made about its falsity as was made in heralding it as the very truth! Textual criticism, his keenest implement, was used to ruin his house of cards.

There have been thousands of attempts to discredit the four gospel records, and every attempt has failed. The accounts have been proven to be ACTUAL HISTORY. If Jesus lived as the four gospels say He lived; if He worked as the four gospels say He worked; if He taught as the four gospels say He taught; if He died as the four gospels say He died; and if He arose as the four gospels say He arose; if He ascended to the heavens as the four gospels say He ascended, then back of His sinless life, and back of His miraculous demonstrations, and back of His matchless teachings, and back of His atoning death, and back of His resurrection, and back of His ascension to the heavens STANDS ALMIGHTY GOD, THE ONLY CAUSE THAT IS ADEQUATE TO ACCOUNT FOR JESUS CHRIST!

**I BELIEVE IN A PERSONAL GOD BECAUSE OF MY OWN EXPERIENCE**

Once upon a time I was skeptical, and I drifted in my skepticism until I was almost an atheist.[8] I was brought back to a faith in God through nature's design, cause and effect, plus the record of Jesus Christ and His teaching. Now God is the one great reality in my life that gives reality to all other realities! I shall never cease to give thanks for the many people who helped me to clearly see the hand of God.[9] But now I have futher corroboration–and to me it is still more unanswerable than the others–my own experience.

Suppose I should find you wandering out in the street; hungry, cold and naked. Suppose you were so hard pressed that you came to me and asked me for help. Suppose I should say, "I was once in just about as bad a condition as you are in, and here is what I did. See that hole in the wall? Well, you go over there and give your order for something to eat." That may sound silly to you, but a hungry man will try anything! So you go over and ask for a hamburger...and out comes a hamburger! It tastes so good that you try it again. Then you ask for an egg sandwich, and again out comes your order. Suppose you keep this up for a month, each time changing the order to something more elaborate. Would you not believe that some caring being was behind that wall, answering your requests?

Twenty-one years ago we found that hole in the wall that men call "prayer." For 21 years we have been living from hand-to-mouth, that is, from GOD'S hand to OUR mouth.[10] We have never missed a meal. I cannot get into my Navy uniform that I could wear quite comfortably in 1925.[11] We have been cared for better than we could have asked for. We have been allowed to come precariously near the bottom a few times, to show us we need God, and then we have had our cup to more than run over. From the hand of God we were given a new Plymouth car at a time when we needed it badly.[12] We were allowed to go on the air when it looked impossible, and by the grace of God we have been moved from one station to a better one through the years.[13] The finances came in and we never lacked. We have been given one of the finest churches in America,[14] and now in response to a heart desire, through prayer, we have been allowed to publish a newspaper that goes to most of the states in the union.[15]

My personal experience proves to me the reality of God!

I once had a very dear friend named Mitchell Finch.[16] You might come along with some idealistic philosophy and try to prove to me that he had no actual existence. And I might not be able to put my finger on the weak spot in your argument, but do you really think for a moment you could make me believe that there is no Mitch Finch? Not by any means! I would still believe that Mitchell Finch IS. Why? Because of my personal experience with him.

God is! God has spoken! The prophet of God has said, "Prepare to meet thy God." That is one thing that is absolutely certain–every one of us MUST meet God. It makes no difference what your place in life is, nor your profession. Every mother, father, son, daughter, school teacher, laborer, university professor, chemist, doctor, lawyer, butcher, baker, bartender, and brilliant orator–all must meet God!

The question of paramount importance is: ARE YOU READY TO MEET GOD? Christ is the only way! If we do not have Christ, we do not have God. Rebels in Communist Russia, we are told, have the words "Against God" tatooed on their chests. We may think that is terrible, but until we come to God through His Son Jesus Christ, we have it written in eternal letters in the records of heaven that we are "against God."

Up in Alaska,[17] where thousands of gamblers take chances in the Nenana Ice Pool, happy is the man who has the right ticket. He is a winner of about $100,000. Few people ever get in on that, or ever hear their names read as the winner...but at the judgment seat of God, every name will be called, and happy is the man who can say, "I am ready. I have believed on Christ. I have repented of all my sins and have been baptized into Christ. I have had my sins washed away by the blood of Christ. I have received the Holy Spirit into my life. I AM READY TO MEET MY GOD!"

---

1. See the closing illustration in Word's sermon "Repent or Perish!" (chapter 6).
2. Word may have had in mind "German rationalism" or even Hitler's national socialism.
3. This essay was published in 1947, a little more than two years after World War II ended. Germany was left in ruins.
4. The working class in a modern society.
5. A. Word did not live to see the collapse of Communism, but he would have rejoiced with the rest of the world. (Word died Nov. 21, 1988, just one year before the fall of the Berlin Wall in East Germany.)
6. Since the United States Supreme Court ruled against the 10 commandments in public schools in the mid-1960s, morality has steadily declined.
7. In 1993 the annual crime bill in America had risen to over $648 billion! (Those are really "Raw Deal" figures!)
8. Baptized at age 12 or 13, in 1913 or 1914, Archie Word backslid and was not truly converted until Nov. 11, 1925, in an upper room prayer meeting at Eugene Bible University.

9. Perhaps the most influential person was Dr. Harold E. Knott, Archie's favorite professor at Eugene Bible University.
10. Archie Word and Florence Procter were married July 7, 1926.
11. Archie was in the Navy for about a year-and-a half (1918-1919). In his early years of ministry he would don his old uniform, sing "Lost Ship" in the light of a spotlight, and preach a sermon about the night his ship, the *USS South Dakota,* was torpedoed and how he nearly drowned in the icy Atlantic.
12. After healing a 12-year split in the church at Ceres, California, Archie was presented with the keys to a brand new 1935 Plymouth. Seventy-six people reconsecrated their lives to Christ and made reconciliation with their brethren–right in the middle of Archie's sermon. Archie called it one of the most moving services he had ever been in.
13. On radio programs, some "live" broadcasts, for many years on Portland and Vancouver radio stations.
14. The Montavilla Church of Christ, where Archie preached for 33 years (from 1935-1968), recognized by Standard Publishing in 1949 as having sent more young people to Bible College and into the ministry than any other church in the brotherhood.
15. *The Church Speaks,* originally a full-size newspaper, was begun in 1944. Eventually the circulation grew to 25,000, and was even sent to the White House.
16. A boy who ran away from home to join the fighting forces in World War I along with Archie. They remained lifelong friends.
17. Archie had conducted a revival meeting in Anchorage, Alaska, the year before (1946). Alaska did not become a state until 1959.

# 8

# WHY I BELIEVE THE BIBLE TO BE THE INSPIRED WORD OF GOD

*The Church Speaks,* December 5, 1948

The Scripture I am about to read was first directed to a young evangelist. Some of it is prophetical in scope, and some of it is just plain godly instruction.

"Yea, and all that would live godly in Christ Jesus shall suffer persecution" (II Tim. 3:12). (That prepares the young man who thinks that living a preacher's life is going to be a bed of roses for what he MUST expect if he is true to God!)[1]

"But evil men and imposters shall wax worse and worse, deceiving and being deceived. But abide thou in the things which thou has learned and has been assured of, knowing of whom thou hast learned them; and that from a babe thou has known the sacred writings which are able to make thee wise unto salvation through faith which is in Christ Jesus. Every scripture is inspired of God and is also profitable for teaching, for reproof, for correction, for instruction in righteousness; that the man of God may be complete, furnished completely unto every good work" (II Tim. 3:13-17). This Scripture states definitely that the sacred writings are INSPIRED OF GOD (which literally means they are "God-breathed").

In this day of so much confusion, it is wonderful to know that God has spoken to us and that we have HIS MIND on certain things. In fact, it is the most important, fundamental truth concerning our lives on this earth! If the Bible is the Word of God, then we have a means of knowing the mind of God. Without it we are hopelessly in the dark.

Only in a land where the Bible has gone is there a knowledge of Jehovah God. The Bible tells us of God's nature, character, purpose, will, plans, method and work. Without it we would be in the same dark ignorance as is the Oriental stepping in front of a fast-moving car to scare away his evil spirits, or those who bury their dead sitting up (so they could fight their evil spirits better), and a thousand other devilish teachings that men have invented in their ignorance of the true and living God, made known to us through the Word of God.

With the Bible as a dependable guide book from God, we are warned concerning man's nature, his fall from God's glory, his ruin, his means of salvation from this awful condition, his duties, his labors, and the final destiny of this creature that is made in the image and likeness of God.

If the Bible is the Word of God, then we have a foundation, a starting point. If it is NOT the Word of God, then all is chaos and speculation. Every man is a law unto himself. Your guess is as good as mine. Within a short time we would be living just as other nations who do not have the divine revelation to guide them in their spiritual lives.[2]

There was a time when I did not believe[3] (and honest doubts are perfectly legitimate). Doubts, however, are like bed bugs. It is no disgrace to have them, but it is a disgrace to KEEP them! Any man who wants to know the truth can find the truth. The evidence has been given upon which he can build faith and destroy his doubts.

I made up my mind when I was forced into a corner to find out whether there was a Book from God—a real God, a living and loving Saviour and salvation in His name.[4] If there was, then I was going to make my life according to the pattern that God had directed. But if I was convinced that there was not God, that we are mere animals, that it is "dog-eat-dog," then I would pattern my life along the lines of Al Capone, and live a life motivated by greed.[5]

I'm thankful to God I found out—absolutely—that the Bible is the Word of God, and if it pleases the Lord, I would like to present some of these thoughts and best evidences to you. These reasons have convinced thousands and thousands of people, and I expect millions, through the past centuries. They are like the sun: old, but indispensable. They have convinced men in every walk of life, from ditch diggers to presidents and king. Read carefully and weigh the evidence!

**I BELIEVE THE BIBLE TO BE THE INSPIRED WORD OF GOD BECAUSE OF ITS UNITY AND COHERENCE**

I realize this is an old reason, but it is still a very good one. The Bible is made up of 66 books, 1,189 chapters, 31,102 verses. It is written in three different languages: Hebrew, Aramaic and Greek. It was written on three different continents: Asia, Africa and Europe. It took approximately 1600 years for it to be written, not including Job. (Only God knows when Job was written, for it preceeded the time of Moses.) The Bible's authors were separated by as much as 400 years in their writings (there was that much time between Malachi and Matthew). And there are 40 authors that wrote the 66 books, coming from at least 20 different vocations.

The Bible displays every known form of literary structure. It contains every form of poetry. There is the rhapsody, or excited composition; epic, or heroic; elegy, or funeral song; kyric, or songs; erotic, pertaining to love; and the didactic, which is plain teaching. Besides this, the Bible contains every form of prose. There is the oration, satire, allegory, historic, didactic, epistolary, argumentative, theological treatise, proverb, parable and apothegm.

From the foregoing, it would be natural to expect variances, discrepancies, contradictions, discords, with an utter lack of unity. But, what do we find? The Bible is not a book ONLY, it is a united library. Yet, it is intensely ONE book, in that it deals with just one theme from beginning to glorious end. It is more united than any one author's book. This is a fact that philosophers jump over, evolutionary theorists evade and skeptics fail to consider, but facts are facts, unchanged by man's neglect or unbelief.

This marvelous unity is two-fold. It is not a superficial unity, but profound and deep, taking much study and research. The more one studies the Bible the more convinced one becomes that it is TRUTH EMBODIED. The closer the study is made of skepticism, the sooner it falls. The Bible wears well!

This unity is like an organic unity; living, vital and developing constantly. First there is the seed, then the sprout, the plant, the mature plant, the sapling, the bud, the blossom, then the ripened fruit! Revelation is the ripe fruit of Genesis! Paradise lost in Genesis 3 is Paradise regained in Revelation 22. And from the time Paradise was lost until it was regained, every chapter in the Bible leads in God's developing plan to that end. Try to account for that without admitting it is a book from God Almighty! It takes more than some puny theory, born of some dreamer's imagination, to account for this superhuman fact. The only sensible answer is that back of the 40 authors, using three different languages, was one all-governing and controlling mind of God; back of the men who came from 20 different vocations in life, yet wrote harmoniously with each other, was one all-superintending and shaping mind of God; back of these men who wrote over a period of 1600 years, on three different continents, was one all-knowing and wise God who formed the eternal message in their minds and recorded it for the blessing of all future generations! He is revealed as Jehovah, the Eternal God, El Shaddai, the Almighty God, to a weak, short-lived race of people.

To illustrate it futher. Just suppose that here in Portland, Oregon, we decided to build a national monument. We notified every state in the union that they were expected to contribute something for its construction. Suppose that is all we knew about the arrangements, but at the end of a two-year period there arrives aboard trains, steamships and airplanes, stone from 27 state quarries, each stone cut to fit its exact place in the building. Suppose there were cubical, spherioidal, cylindrical, conical, trapezoidal, rectangular and square stones, all trimmed to fit before arriving on the job scene.

Suppose iron came from 14 states, and each piece had to be untouched on its arrival. There comes pipes, truss rods, reenforcements, furnace and tubes. Suppose tin fittings from three states arrived, and all pieces were cut before their shipment to the exact size. Suppose that four states contributed brass and bronzed hinges, lock facings, reenforcements and castings, even down to the drinking fountains. Suppose these different states[6] sent their own carpenters, tinsmiths and general mechanics, and they began to build. As they progressed they find that there is not one stone too many, not one out of shape, there is exactly enough and every stone fits! Suppose they find that not one plate needs to be rebored or shaped. Everything fits perfectly and not one ounce of bronze is wasted.

How would you account for that? Brother, there is only one answer! Back of each workman in each shop, mill or quarry, was one all-governing mind of a master architect and builder who planned that monument from beginning to end, from foundation to superstructure.

Behold with me, my friends, the Bible. It is the monument. Not national, but international. The books are the material from the mind of God. It is not six stories high, but 66. It did not take 16 years to construct, but 1600. It was wrought on three different continents. Each stone fits exactly. There is none lacking. How can you answer it? I challenge you that back of every movement made from Genesis to Revelation is the ONE MASTER MIND OF GOD who controlled every author and his message, making the Bible the INSPIRED WORD OF GOD to His lost creatures. The evidence is irrefutable and the conclusion is inescapable.

Any person who wants to know, and will study, can find for a surety that the doctrine is of God, and that salvation is found through Jesus Christ, as revealed within the sacred pages of the Holy Bible!

**I BELIEVE THE BIBLE TO BE THE INSPIRED WORD OF GOD BECAUSE OF ITS FULFILLED PROPHECIES**

In the Bible we have two varieties of prophecies. There is the explicitly verbal and the prophecies in types and symbols. The verbal prophecies are divided into three groups: the Messianic, Jewish national prophecies, and the prophecies pertaining to the Gentiles.

Someone once asked a preacher if he could prove the Bible to be a divinely inspired book. "Yes, I can prove it in just one word–'JEW!'" The divine inspiration of Moses and the prophets is proven by the destiny of the nation of Israel (Deut. 28; Jer. 9:13-16; 25:10-11).When Moses wrote this (Deut. 28), Egypt was a great nation. How was he to know that Egypt was going to go down to oblivion (and many other empires and great nations with them), yet the small nation of Israel would last until Jesus comes again? Read the above scriptures and then pick up your daily newspaper and read it. See how graphically he describes the Christ-rejecting nation of Israel. They have been killed, massacred,[7] expelled, exiled, cursed and publicly maligned; yet they exist in almost every land under the sun. They are men without a country,[8] priesthood or sacrifice.

That is a literal fulfillment of the prophecies of their own great prophets of God.

Let any man study the history of the Jews from the time of Moses to the present hour and see if he can add anything to what the prophets have said. Then, after giving their complete history a careful reading, see if they can subtract anything from what the prophets of God have said. Answer me one thing: How could Moses and these other men of God write the history of this nation of Israel, 2000 to 3000 years before it happened, without the aid of the Almighty God who knows from the beginning what the end will be?

From these prophecies and their historical fulfillment, even the feeblest logician can draw the conclusion that the message of these men was inspired of God! When the chaplain to Prussia's Frederick the Great was asked for proof of the divine inspiration of the scriptures, he replied, "THE JEW!" Now we can see more clearly why he answered thus. Moses stands vindicated as an inspired writer.

I want to deal especially with the prophecies concerning the Christ that was to come. Keep in mind that prophecy simply means history that is written BEFORE it comes to pass. One of the outstanding prophecies concerning the coming Christ is Isaiah 53. It is denied by the rationalists as being an impossibility, simply because they will NOT believe in predictive prophecy. It is denied by the Jew because to admit this prophecy was concerning their Messiah would force them to accept Christ as that one. But we know it was referring the the Messiah for the records of the rabbis' teaching, during the later prophets and under the Maccabees, prove conclusively that they taught it as such. If it is nor referring to Jesus Christ, then to whom could it refer? Someone says, "The nation of Israel," but if you will read Isaiah 53 again, you will find that to be an impossibility because the One suffering is suffering for others! How could Israel be suffering and still be the one for whom the suffering is being done? The Rabbi says, "It seems to be the

Messiah, but it isn't." He is wrong! It seems to be the Messiah, and it is!

Remember that Jesus Christ is the first and ONLY man who ever lived on this earth who had his biography written BEFORE he was born! It was done through the power of predictive prophecy, which is only possible with God. Prophecy is history written before it happens.

Micah foretold the place of Christ's birth, and that He was an eternal being. Daniel gives the exact time of His coming. Jeremiah foretells the exact family, and the condition of that family in the day He would make His appearance. Genesis says He was to be born of the seed of woman (in contrast to all other genealogies of the Old Testament). And He was! Isaiah tells us that he was to be born of a virgin, and that His ministry would be in Galilee. Genesis tells us He was to come from the family of Shem. Jeremiah warns of the Massacre of the Innocents. Deuteronomy says He was to be a prophet, and Acts 3 says he was. Isaiah branches out to tell us He was to suffer vicariously, and to die with malefactors. The Psalms add that He was to be a priest after the order of Melchizedek, purify the temple, be rejected by Jews and Gentiles alike, be betrayed by a friend, and would have His hands and feet pierced (this was written hundreds of years before crucifixion was practiced as a form of capital punishment), lots would be cast for his clothing, His burial was to be with the wealthy, and that He would be resurrected and ascend to God.

Any book that has the power to look centuries into the future, predicting the most minute details, with precision and accuracy of time, place, persons and circumstances of events that were to occur centuries later, MUST have for its author the ONLY Person in the universe who knows from the beginning just what the end is going to be...and that is GOD the ALMIGHTY!

There are two great lines of prophecy concerning the Messiah and, upon surface examination, they appear to be directly contradictory. They foretell a suffering Christ and a conquering Christ. We now know that one was telling of His coming into the world, the first time, to save the world through His death; but the other tells how He will appear a second time to be the Lion of Judah, ruling with a rod of iron from the throne of David!

The Old Testament is filled with predictive prophecy. The personages, institutions, ceremonies, offerings, sacrifices, feasts, tabernacle, brazen altar, Holy Place, laver, Holy of Holies, showbread, candlesticks, ark of the covenant, the mercy seat–ALL were clearly foreshadowing the coming church of the Lord Jesus Christ, of which He is head.

I cannot help but conclude that any book that has the power of putting into legislation (intended to meet the needs of the people THEN living) the clearest foreshadowings of happenings and truths not to be fully revealed for at least 15 centuries, MUST have for its author the ONLY Being in the universe who knows the end from the beginning...and that is the omnipotent, omniscient and omnipresent eternal God, Jehovah. All Scripture is "God-breathed."

Suppose a man should come into your community and publicly demonstrate that he could take a small bean shooter and hit targets, direct "bulls eyes," every time, at 400 yards, 500 yards, 3000 yards, even though he was heavily blindfolded. Would you not believe that someone was working with him who was beyond human power? Well, consider with me that the prophets of God took their pens in hand to look into the pitch black darkness of the future–from 400 to 3000 years–and every time they wrote a prophecy they hit a bulls eye! That would be a human impossibility. Without turning to the one all-wise God, who knows the end from the beginning, there is no human answer that can be given.

**Therefore, I conclude that back of every author of the entire Bible stands God...the only answer to this supernatural book that contains these miracles and thousands of others not mentioned in this treatise.**

---

1. Brother Word, when reading a text, would often interject with his own commentary.
2. Today's relativistic society shows how short a time it takes for this to happen in a nation!
3. A period of time from 1918 to 1925 (age 17 to 24), when he was "bootlegging, brawling and boozing."
4. Word's son-in-law, Donald G. Hunt, believes Archie was "forced into a corner" in the classes taught by Harold E. Knott during Archie's first semester at Eugene Bible University. "There were times in the professor's presentation that Archie held up his hand with the intention of challenging some statement only to have his hand seemingly go unnoticed. Invariably the teacher brought out something that caused him to be glad he had not had his say. In time he came to see that all the intelligent fellows were not atheists and agnostics, and gradually his faith returned" (*Voice of Thunder, Heart of Tears*, p. 105).
5. While running three saloons and dance halls in Fresno, Archie was nearly killed in a terrible automobile accident. Two men were killed and the driver was sentenced to San Quenton.
6. There were only 48 states in the union when this illustration was made in 1948.
7. This was written only a few years after the Holocaust.
8. Brother Word probably failed to edit this sermon before it was printed in the Dec. 5, 1948 issue of *The Church Speaks,* because Israel was declared a state in May of 1948.

# 9

# WHY I BELIEVE IN THE ACTUAL DEITY OF CHRIST

*The Church Speaks,* December 5, 1948

"Now while the Pharisees were gathered together, Jesus asked them a question, saying, 'What think ye of Christ? Whose son is He?'" (Matt. 22:41-42).

That question, asked by the Lord Himself nearly 2000 years ago, of those who were the religious leaders of His day, is still the most vital, fundamental and unique question that comes into the mind of anyone who studies the life of Christ.

The influence Christ has had upon history shouts aloud, "He is more than a mere man!" It was His claim of Deity for Himself that finally caused His enemies to crucify Him. They said He blasphemed when He said, "Thou has said" in answer to the challenge made by the high priest, "Tell us whether thou art the Christ, the Son of God." Christ was crucified for His claim to Deity. If one was to be the vicarious sufferer for all sinners, and then must pay the substitionary sacrifice for all their sins, He MUST be more than a mere man!

The most fundamental question concerning Jesus Christ that is ever asked concerns His status as Deity. Is He actual Deity, not merely divine? There was a time when a man said, "I believe that Jesus Christ is the Son of God," and everyone knew he meant that Jesus was God in the flesh, but the devil has been awfully busy digging away at this foundation in recent years. Now theologians and self-styled scholars are subtly taking the very same words, but giving them quite a different meaning. It is a subtle, shrewd move on their part, for when words do not mean what they say, utter confusion has come in among the brethren.[1] Beware of the Unitarian, modernist and subtle deceiver who mixes up the meaning of old and sacred words. By this method they seek to lead even the elect astray, if it were possible.

Just because a man says he believes in the divinity of Christ no longer means that he is a Christian at all. He may mean that Christ was a very good man and no more. Men speak of the atonement, but they do not mean what enlightened Christians mean when they speak of the atonement. When they use the word "Christ," they do not mean at all our Lord and Saviour Jesus Christ–the actual, historic Jesus of the four gospels–but rather, they mean an IDEAL Christ, or a PRINCIPLE that they choose to call "Christ". We need more than a divinity, we need DEITY if, by Christ, we are ever to be saved from our sins! We need one who is worthy of our absolute faith, supreme love, demanding our unhesitating obedience and our whole-hearted service.

Jesus is the One that all men should honor, even as they honor the Father (John 5:23). He is more than a fine example that we should follow. He is God whom we can rightly worship! His word is as authoritative as the word of His Father. If we have a faith that is deeply rooted and founded upon the eternal and unerring word of God,[2] then let the Christian Scientists come, let the Unitarians subtly deceive, let the Russellites[3] put "curves" on words and tell half-truths, let the

Theosophical societies slyly mix oriental philosophies with some truth...and they will be unable to uproot your well-founded faith! It is vitally important that every Christian be thoroughly informed concerning the central figure of the Christian faith. Every one of us should be students of the Word of God because "these things are written that ye may believe that Jesus is the Christ, THE SON OF GOD: and believing ye may have life in His name" (I John 5:13).

The purpose of this message is to instruct the ignorant and confirm the ones who know what they believe concerning the Deity of Christ. No subject in the entire Bible is as important as this one, for without His Deity, Jesus is nothing but an illegitimate bastard[4] who lived a good life and died a martyr's death. There have been thousands who have done as well, if that is all He is. If Christ is not Deity then His miracles are fakes, for they could not have been genuine except by the power of God. If Christ is not Deity then His death on the cross was a farce, and He is the greatest deceiver the world has ever seen. If Christ was not Deity then His resurrection was a hoax.

EVERYTHING depends upon His Deity, and that is why the infidel world has centered EVERY gun they have upon this central target and for 2000 years years they have been blasting away at the Deity of Christ! If the infidels can find enough IGNORANT people, they will be able to acclaim their infernal doctrine to be the one that is popular. The Federal Council of Churches, through their radio program, is sowing through the air waves their doctrine. Thousands of people who know nothing at all about what the Bible teaches take in all that the Federal Council radio speakers teach about Christ–doctrines born in the figments of their own delirious imagination.[5]

**I BELIEVE THAT JESUS CHRIST IS ACTUAL DEITY, GOD IN THE FLESH, BECAUSE OF THE DIVINE NAMES**

**APPLIED TO HIM IN THE SCRIPTURES**

The names applied to Jesus in the Word of God clearly imply His Deity. Some of these names are used over and over again, and I will be unable to give an exhaustive number of references in this brief treatise, but I believe, to any person who WANTS to know, these scriptures will be sufficient.

To begin, Paul speaks of our crucified Lord Jesus as "the Lord of Glory." His exact words, "Which none of the princes of this world knew: for had they known it, they would not have crucified THE LORD OF GLORY" (I Cor. 2:8). To any Bible student there is no doubt that Paul meant Jehovah God, "the Lord of Glory" referred to in Psalm 24:8-10, "Who is this KING OF GLORY? Jehovah strong and mighty, Jehovah mighty in battle. Lift up your heads, O ye gates, yea lift them up, ye everlasting doors, and THE KING OF GLORY will come in. Who is the King of Glory? JEHOVAH OF HOSTS, HE IS THE KING OF GLORY." The crucified Christ, Jesus, is Jehovah, eternal God.

Then Thomas, speaking to Jesus, said, "MY LORD AND MY GOD" (John 20:28). Unitarians and other Christ-deniers try to get around the plain statement here by saying that Thomas was swearing politely (as some people do when they are excited or astonished). This shows how hard-pressed they are to find something on which to defend their doctrine. Note carefully that Jesus commended Thomas for stating his conviction. "Because thou hast seen me, thou hast believed: blessed are they that have not seen, yet have believed" (John 20:30).

Again Paul describes Jesus as God: "Our GREAT GOD AND SAVIOUR JESUS CHRIST" (Titus 2:13). And he adds this statement: "Christ is OVER ALL, GOD BLESSED FOREVER" (Rom. 9:5).

Infidels and other philosophical rejectors of Christ have made almost superhuman efforts to overcome the force of these God-inspired words. There can be no doubt, to the one who goes to the Bible, to see that Jesus is spoken of by many titles that are applicable only to Deity; thus He is declared to be

God. "But unto THE SON He saith, Thy throne O GOD, is forever and ever: a sceptre of righteousness is the sceptre of Thy kingdom" (Heb. 1:8).

It should not be necessary to go farther than this to prove that in scripture Jesus is referred to as God, but for fear someone may need more evidence, I turn now to Revelation 1:17 where John says, "And when I saw Him, I fell at His feet as one dead. And He laid His right hand upon me saying, 'Fear not: I AM THE FIRST AND THE LAST." It was the Lord Jesus speaking, and He distinctly called Himself the FIRST and the LAST—attributes of Deity.

This is not a new saying, for Isaiah had said, by inspiration, many centuries before, "Thus saith Jehovah, the King of Israel, and his redeemer, JEHOVAH OF HOSTS: I AM THE FIRST, AND I AM THE LAST: and besides me there is NO GOD."[6] Compare this with Revelation 22:12-13 when Jesus said He was the first and the last (the "alpha" and "omega"). "Behold I come quickly; and my reward is with me, to render to each man according as his work is. I AM ALPHA AND OMEGA, THE FIRST AND THE LAST, THE BEGINNING AND THE END."

Is this not enough to convince the most skeptical that it is record in the Holy Writ that Jesus calls Himself by the same names that were recorded of Jehovah God? If Jesus is God, then He is not merely a good man, and it is blasphemy to call Him such in the presence of these witnesses we have heard.

## I BELIEVE IN THE ACTUAL DEITY OF CHRIST BECAUSE OF FIVE DISTINCTIVE ATTRIBUTES THAT ARE ASCRIBED TO CHRIST

All the "fulness of God" is said to dwell in Christ. Only God, distinct Deity, can possess these five attributes: omnipotence, omnipresence, omniscience, eternality and immutability. Each one of these are ascribed to Jesus Christ, making Him actual Deity—God in the flesh. In this world, and in the world to come, Jesus is said to have power over all principality, dominion and might. All are to bow before Him. Does that sound like Jesus is merely a good man who set a good example? God's Word says, "He put all things in subjection under his feet, and gave him to be head over all things to the church, which is his body, the fulness of him that filleth all in all" (Eph. 1:22-23). The writer of Hebrews adds, "Who being the effulgence of his glory, and the very image of his substance, and upholding all things by the word of his power..." (Heb. 1:3). That is OMNIPOTENCE, clearly stated, belonging to Jesus Christ, our risen Lord.

OMNISCIENCE is also ascribed to Jesus, who knew men's minds. Speaking to the woman at the well, Jesus told her, "Thou saidst well, I have no husband: for thou hast had five husbands; and he whom thou now hast is not thy husband: this hast thou said truly" (John 4:17-18).

Jesus told a man with palsy, "Son, thy sins are forgiven" (Mark 2:5). The Scribes did not like this or believe Him, so Jesus gave them some private proof of His Deity by reading their minds for them! They said, "Why doth this man thus speak? he blasphemeth: who can forgive sins but one, even God? And straightway Jesus, perceiving in his spirit that they so reasoned withing themselves, saith unto them, Why reason ye these things in your hearts?" (Mark 2:7-8). Then He demonstrates His omnipotence by performing a miracle of healing before their very eyes!

Christ's omniscience is clearly shown in John 2:24-25, "He knew all men, and because he needed not that any one should bear witness concerning man; for he himself knew what was in man." II Chronicles 6:30 says only God had this attribute. "Then hear thou from heaven thy dwelling-place, and forgive, and render unto every man according to all his ways, whose heart thou knowest (FOR THOU, EVEN THOU ONLY, KNOWEST THE HEARTS OF THE CHILDREN OF MEN)." The disciples of Jesus testified, "Now know we that thou knowest all things, and needst not that any man should ask thee: by this we believe that THOU CAMEST FORTH FROM GOD" (John 16:30).

The OMNIPRESENCE of Jesus Christ is taught in the Great Commission as recorded by Matthew. After the commission had been given, directing the apostles to "make disciples of all the nations," He promised to be with them ALWAYS, including all the nations in which the gospel would be preached. The doctrine of omnipresence is stated further in Matthew 18:20, where Jesus said, "For where two or three are gathered together in my name, there am I in the midst of them." And John 14:20, "In that day ye shall know that I am in my Father, and ye in me, and I IN YOU." Paul says, "Or know ye not as to your own selves, that JESUS CHRIST IS IN YOU?" (II Cor. 13:5). Jesus Christ was in each one of them, in every nation, and that is an attribute which only Deity possesses–omnipresence!

ETERNITY is attributed to Jesus. "In the beginning was the Word, and the Word was with God, and the Word WAS God" (John 1:1). Jesus declared His eternal existence. "Verily, verily, I say unto you, Before Abraham was born, I AM" (John 8:58). "I am" is the word used for the eternity of Jehovah God. He did not say, "Before Abraham was, I WAS," but "I AM," denoting eternal existence. Long before Jesus was born, while the Lord was laying in the prophetic cradle in which Jesus should appear, the prophet Micah said, "But thou, Bethlehem Ephrathah, which art little to be among the thousands of Judah, out of thee shall one come forth unto me that is to be ruler in Israel; WHOSE GOINGS FORTH ARE FROM OF OLD, FROM EVERLASTING" (Micah 5:2).

Isaiah adds this information concerning the eternal existence of the coming Christ: "For unto us a child is born, unto us a son is given; and the government shall be upon his shoulder: and his name shall be called Wonderful, Counsellor, MIGHTY GOD, EVERLASTING FATHER, Prince of Peace" (Isa. 9:6). "Jesus Christ is the same yesterday and today, yea and FOR EVER" (Heb. 13:8). His eternal existence is stated in these inspired words, and that should be final to the one who believes the Bible is the Word of God.

Christ's IMMUTABILITY is also taught in Scripture. Speaking of the heavens, the writer says, "They shall perish; BUT THOU CONTINUEST...THOU ART THE SAME, AND THY YEARS SHALL NOT FAIL" (Heb. 1:11-12).

Everything that man makes, changes. There is constant deterioration, but not so with the Lord Jesus Christ, for He is eternal and immutable. All five of the distinctly divine attributes are applied to the Lord Jesus Christ, implying that He is, as He claimed to be, DEITY GOD. No wonder Paul says, "In him dwelleth all the fulness of the Godhead bodily" (Col. 2:9). Jesus was God in bodily form.

The evidence given already should be sufficient, but we are not going to rest our case yet, for we believe Jesus Christ to be Deity for another great reason.

## I BELIEVE THE ACTUAL DEITY OF CHRIST BECAUSE ALL THE DISTINCTIVELY DIVINE OFFICES ARE PREDICATED OF JESUS

There are seven distinctly divine offices, or seven things that God alone can do; and each of these distinctive works are attributed to Jesus Christ, proving Him to be Deity. He is our creator, preserver, forgiver of sins; He raises us up from the dead, transforms our bodies, judges us at the last, and bestows eternal life, God's greatest gift, upon us. He could be none of these, nor do any of these, if He were not Deity.

Jesus is the creator of the universe. "And, Thou, Lord, in the beginning didst lay the foundation of the earth, and the heavens are the works of thy hands" (Heb. 1:10). The context (Heb. 1:1-10) clearly shows that when Paul spoke by inspiration, he agreed with John, who wrote, "All things were made through him; and without him was not anything made that hath been made" (John 1:3). Christ is our Creator, THE Creator of the entire universe, God!

Jesus is the preserver of us. The entire universe is held together by Him. "Who being the effulgence of his glory, and the very image of his substance, and UPHOLDING ALL THINGS by the word of his power, when he had made purification of sins, sat down on the right hand of the Majesty on high" (Heb. 1:3). Life is a sustained miracle and He is the SUSTAINER. Only Deity is able to create and sustain life, and both of these are attributed to Jesus Christ our Lord. He is Deity incarnate.

The forgiveness of sins is ascribed to Jesus in Mark 2:5-10. It came about this way. Jesus told the man sick of the palsy that his sins were forgiven. The opposing faction immediately said that was the work of ONLY Deity. Then Jesus said, "But that ye may know that the Son of man hath authority on earth to FORGIVE SINS..." (Mark 2:10). He healed the man and promised to him forgiveness of sins–both acts of DEITY!

The power to raise the dead in the future was distinctly ascribed to Jesus. "And this is the will of him that sent me, that of all that which he hath given me I should lose nothing, but should raise it up at the last day. For this is the will of my Father, that every one that beholdeth the Son, and believeth on him, should have eternal life; AND I WILL RAISE HIM UP AT THE LAST DAY" (John 6:39-40). Either that is truth or Jesus was an egotistical maniac, yea, a megalomaniac! Do you think He was a fool? Does not His life and influence speak and shout from the house tops–"HE IS THE LORD! DEITY!"

Judgement is the work of Jesus. Paul wrote to Timothy, "I charge thee in the sight of God, AND OF CHRIST JESUS, WHO SHALL JUDGE THE LIVING AND THE DEAD, and by his appearing and his kingdom: preach the word..." (II Tim. 4:1). Jesus was the one who declared with no equivocation that He was to be the judge. "For neither doth the Father judge any man, but he hath given all judgment unto the Son; that all may honor the Son, even as they honor the Father" (John 5:22-23).

He is to be recognized and honored as an equal with the Father. Does that sound as though Jesus is a mere man, just a good man? If He is not the Judge then He is a liar, and He cannot be a good man and be a liar at the same time. O my unthinking friend, forget about this nonsense of calling Jesus a good man, and then denying His Deity, for when you do, you make Him a liar, and no man is a GOOD man who is a deceitful liar!

The Word of God makes it perfectly clear that it is Jesus Christ who bestows eternal life upon His children–and no one but God has eternal life or the power to bestow it on others. "And I give unto them eternal life; and they shall never perish, and no one shall snatch them out of my hand" (John 10:28). His sheep hear His voice, and they follow Him. When an old goat refuses to follow the Lord, he proves that he is not a sheep at all! Jesus prayed, "Father, the hour is come; glorify they Son, that the Son may glorify thee: even as thou gavest HIM authority over all flesh, that to all whom thou hast given him, HE should give ETERNAL LIFE" (John 17:1-2).

This is a summary of the seven distinctively divine offices that are predicated to Jesus Christ Himself. If there was nothing else, this would be sufficient to prove that He is Deity, god, and I could, without fear of successful contradiction, rest my case right here; but I want to pile up even more incontrovertible facts to substantiate my affirmation that Christ is Deity.

Here are some statements that you may look up for yourself–statements made in the Old Testament, which are made distinctly of Jehovah, are used in the New Testament to refer to the Lord Jesus Christ, and never applied to any other living man. For example, Jeremiah 11:20 and 17:20, when correlated with Revelation 2:23, proves conclusively that Jesus occupies the same place as Jehovah.

Another evidence of the Deity of Christ is the way the name of God the Father and Jesus Christ the Son are coupled together. See John 14:1 and 14:23. If Jesus Christ was not Deity, then this is a shocking blasphemy! There can be no middle ground between admitting Christ's Deity, and charging Christ with the most daring and appalling blasphemy of which any man in all history was ever guilty. He is either Deity as He claimed or He is a scurrilous blasphemer! Judge for yourself the results of His life and teaching.

Jesus gives rest to the weary, which no man can do (Matt. 11:28). He demands that we put the same faith in Him that we do in God, which should never be done to any mere man (John 14:1). He demands our supreme and absolute love for Himself, which no man has the right to do (Matt. 10:37). He proclaims His absolute equality with the Father, which no one except Deity could honestly do (John 10:30). He proclaimed that those who had seen Him had seen the Father, which is either truth or blasphemy (John 14:9). He claims that a knowledge of Himself is as essential to eternal life as is the knowledge of God (John 17:3).

There is no room to doubt the absolute Deity of Jesus Christ when the evidence is examined. HE IS DEITY! O what a glorious truth! The Saviour whom we preach, and in whom we believe, is very God! Nothing is too hard for Him. He is able to save from the uttermost unto the uttermost. For Him, His ALL SUFFICIENT DEITY, we thank the Father, because it was the Father who loved us and sent His Son to save us!

If you have not accepted Jesus as your Saviour, do you not see, my friend, you are turning down God when you turn down Jesus? You may say, "I do not believe in Him." But that only adds insult to an already injured Deity. Doubting a fact or disbelieving a fact does not change the fact, not one bit.

Suppose a man has a wife who is noble, pure, true and good[7] and her husband doubts her integrity. Would that make her ignoble, impure, false or bad? NO! It would prove just one thing–that her husband was guilty of an awful slander against her! So it is with the man who rejects and refuses to believe in

**the Holy Lord Jesus Christ as actual Deity and Saviour of all men who will submit and come to Him for salvation. Rejecting Him and refusing Him slanders His substantiated claims!**

---

1. Brother Word probably had in mind the liberal views of Christ espoused by many in the Disciples of Christ. Five years earlier Archie was one of 49 signers of the *Christian Standard's* historic "Call for Enlistment" (which Stephen Corey called "a blueprint of separation for the brotherhood of Disciples of Christ").
2. Though the word "inerrancy" was seldom used in those days, Archie Word was a firm believer in the inerrancy of Scripture.
3. The Jehovah's Witnesses were sometimes called "Russellites" after Charles Taze Russell.
4. Word's use of words like this often brought him criticism, but he would tell his critics that if the Bible used such words (i.e., Heb. 12:8), he would use the same.
5. Throughout the early years of his 33-year ministry at Montavilla, Archie Word had his own radio program where he blasted things like the Federal Council of Churches!
6. Isaiah 44:6 ASV.
7. Four words that certainly described Archie's good wife, Florence!

# 10

*"AND JESUS SAID IT!"*

*A sermon preached at the historic Montavilla Church of Christ, Portland, Oregon, in 1948*

"He said therefore again unto them, I go away, and ye shall seek me, and shall die in your sin...I said therefore unto you, that ye shall die in your sins: for except ye believe that I am he, ye shall die in your sins" (John 8:21,24).

It was Jesus defending Himself. Even He had to! It was Jesus vindicating His Word. He had spoken! It was Jesus proclaiming His Deity. There was no other way!

There are three points in this text that stand out to me.

## "YE SHALL DIE!"

Jesus said it! This text teaches men shall die! WE shall die! Someone says, "Preacher, you're not going to waste time on that, are you?" Jesus did! Some say, "We already know that!" Do you know that all people must die? Every soul you meet? Has it really dawned on you that YOU must die? I do not think this had dawned on lots of people. Do you realize you are dying right while you sit there looking at me?[1] Do you know a baby begins to die the moment it is born? The seeds of death are sown in every physical body.

God has said, "The soul that sinneth, it shall die" (Ezek. 18:4). There are a lot of things I don't know. But there's one thing I know about you! I do know you are dying! I don't know whether you are saved or not, if you are a lazy sponger or not, if you lie or tell the truth, are a secret boozer or sober, are honest or dishonest, are a worker or a shirker, are above board or a sneak, are a Christian at home or not, mistreat your wife and children at home, pray or don't pray, pay your debts or even try to, read and study your Bible or not, let things keep you from the assembly, use tobacco or are clean, are faithful or a backslider, gossip or keep your tongue, are an immoral fornicator or an adulterer, rich or poor, write bum checks when you know you do not have money in the bank (a "paper-hanger"), try to win souls to Christ or not (I know you are not a TRUE Christian if you do not), have a tender conscience or are a hardened TV addict (would you want to be found dead in front of one? Nobody was ever helped spiritually by one of those things but many have been ruined)[2], but I DO know you are a DYING man or woman, boy or girl!

Funeral directors make a mighty good living, doing away with the bodies of those who die in bed alone.[3] I see death in hospitals, homes, on the street, in cars, by water, air and earth—daily! I cannot get away from it! People die! The sooner you realize you must die, the sooner you'll begin to live right! (If you are not fit to die, you are not fit to live with!) Do you think that "Sunday morning only," "Bible School only" church members who put their work or wife or business ahead of Christ realize they must die? Do you think that people who value real estate above heaven (fattening their Black Angus cattle), those who refuse to meet for prayer, people who have heard many sermons but have done nothing about it, preachers who play politics and try to ride two horses at once, church members who absent themselves and let others bear the load, cursing foul-mouthed backsliders, gossiping and slanderous women (or men), idolatrous "Hellywood" supporters, women who have quit praying for their husbands, church members who refuse to sacrifice for Christ and His church, God-robbing church member thieves, people who put friends and parties ahead of Christ, Christ deserters, church deserters, people who argue and fuss among themselves, belly-aching sob-sisters who always want somebody to do something for them, tobacco-using, booze-drinking, body-destroying church members (in name only) REALIZE THEY MUST DIE?

But they must, just the same! Jesus said, "Ye shall die!" Paul said, "It is appointed unto men once to die!" (Heb. 9:27). God said, "The soul that sinneth, it shall die!" (Ezek. 18:4). The wages of sin is death! When a preacher realizes people MUST die: he will preach the truth fearlessly (thank God for your faithful preacher!), he will not be content to just take it easy, he will be willing to be spent for Christ (calling on the lost), he will "go" and give up luxuries, he will try to win souls, he will keep on burning himself out to keep sinners out of a burning hell (I want to tell every man, at least once, how to keep out of a burning hell!), he won't be cowed by some old "bell-weather" sinner not liking it! I tell you, people must die! Jesus said it!

I heard an old judge preaching at the North American Christian Convention in Springfield, Illinois.[4] He told me, "If preachers realized, as I do, that this may be my last sermon, they would preach differently! I realize I may never raise my voice again for God!"

## SOME PEOPLE WILL DIE "IN THEIR SINS"

There's no legitimate excuse for anyone who has ever heard the gospel just once to die IN their sins! "That whosoever believeth on him should NOT perish, but have eternal life" (John 3:16). But Jesus said, "Ye shall die in your sins: for except ye believe that I am he, ye shall die in your sins" (John 8:24). If a person BELIEVES (adheres to, trusts in, relies upon) on Christ, He will do what Jesus tells us to do to have our sins removed! If he believes Christ, he won't argue about Mark 16:16, "He that believeth and is baptized shall be saved; but he that disbelieveth shall be condemned."

I have seen people dying in their sins–begging the preacher to keep them out of hell! When you are dying, no preacher can keep you out of hell! NO PRIEST CAN EITHER! No honest priest will lie to a dying man! No honest preacher will either! I've seen people dying–screaming for help to keep snakes out of their bed! I've seen them die, trying to hold back as they peered into eternity's firey pit! Old Mrs. Hammer screamed, "My feet are in hell already!" I've seen so much of it that it's burned into my soul! We'll never live perfect lives here, but by God's grace every sinner can be equipped to die right by accepting Christ's sacrifice. I want to teach them, tell them of Christ, warn them of hell, invite them to Christ and heaven!

It is true, brethren. Without Christ people die–IN THEIR SINS! When people are dying in their sins it does not matter how gruff they've been in life, how many times they've insulted those who have tried to help them, how onery and stubborn they've been with their Christian wives, how tenaciously they've clung to their sinfulness; when they are dying they want someone around in whom they have confidence! People are afraid to die...IN their sins! Maybe you've tried hard to win that loved one to Christ. You don't seem to be able to get anywhere. Don't give up! He'll be afraid to die, when death comes. He won't want to die in that condition. For the Lord's sake, do your best to teach them, to tell them of Christ, to warn them of hell, to invite them to Christ and heaven! Don't give up! Keep pressing the battle! Knowing HOW men die (in their sin) gives me heart to try. Knowing there is a hell awaiting them, how can we give them up?

People seem so hard. They seem to have deadened brains and hearts. Even young people, when they are deadened by worldliness and sin, seem to have a blank stare. They are untouchable! Even church people have very few tears in their eyes, no weeping over the lost. They seemed to be seared! HARD! But they will not be so hard when THEY are facing death! Dying in sin makes whimpering babies out of what appeared to be strong men! They will not want to die without God. That should encourage us! Let's do our best to help them! Remember that, tomorrow, when you meet lost people!

Not only did Jesus say, "Ye shall die...in your sins," but–

### WHEN PEOPLE DIE, THEY GO SOMEWHERE!

Jesus said, "I go away, and ye shall seek me, and shall die in your sin: whither I go, ye cannot come" (John 8:21). Jesus tells them, "I must die...BUT I'm not going to STAY dead, I'm not going to stay in the grave, I'm going somewhere. But if you die in your sins, you cannot come to the place where I am going!" We know where Jesus is! He is seated at the right hand of God. Stephen and Paul saw Him!

Yonder on Golgotha's hill stood three crosses. One man is dying IN his sins! One man is dying TO his sin. One man is dying FOR our sins. One turns to Christ, "Jesus, remember me when thou comest into they kingdom" (Luke 23:42). He was dying, but he knew he was going some place, so he turned to Him who was not going to stay dead, going to have a kingdom, going to rule and reign forever! The dying thief believed–on the small amount of evidence he had upon which to base his faith (Christ was not raised yet!). His faith ought to shame us forever! Jesus' promise is a billion times more believeable today! We can die "in our sins" or we can die, with Christ TO our sins, and live and reign with Him! No one can make this choice for you!

Sometimes it takes a tragedy to make us realize "Ye shall die...in your sins." Unless Jesus is our LORD, we go to hell! Mr. and Mrs. Nellie Maynard were nice people. She was quite faithful to the church. He came some. Usually he stayed home and cooked the Sunday dinner...and smoked. She was not certain she could trust God. But one day their little girl was hit by a car. She died in the hospital. Mrs. Maynard now knows death is real. She was saved! She trusts Christ–now! Mr. Maynard was converted. Now he trusts Christ and the church comes first. Prayer is a part of their lives–now! Christ has become vital to them–NOW! But it didn't come until they realized, "Ye shall die!"

Only Christ can keep us from dying IN our sins. He wants to prepare you HERE for that eternal home THERE!

I was called, as many times a minister is, to go to the undertaker's parlor with a family to help them decide which casket they should buy. The undertaker wanted to show me around the place, so he took me down to the embalming room and showed me how the incisions were made, how the fluid was injected, and so forth. I listened from "long distance"–with one foot in the door!

Then he insisted I see ALL the caskets in the large show room. They had large ones, small ones, metal ones, wooden ones, all kinds of colors and prices. He pointed out the good features of the caskets with all the enthusiasm I would show in demonstrating a fine car.[5]

There was one casket, in particular, the undertaker was proud of. It was made of beautiful, high-polished wood. It was air-tight. He showed me how to make it airtight by turning a small aparatus on the side of the casket. He assured me this was the "last thing" in caskets.

Then he opened the casket and showed me the fine lining on the inside. He pointed out the comfortable mattress and springs, which he pressed down with his hand, and enthusiastically exclaimed, "Just feel those cushions! Why, man, a person could rest as comfortably here as on the finest 'Beautyrest' mattress! Just feel how nice and soft this is!"

I was not very anxious to do so, but I did put one hand down and cautiously pressed the lining with one finger! Then the undertaker urged me, "Just GET IN AND LIE DOWN a minute, and you can REALLY see what it is like!" He was only joking, but that was the last straw for me! I had seen everything I needed to see, and was ready to go, when he stopped me by saying, "Preacher, let me give you a good illustration; one you can use in preaching as long as you live. It is this. This casket is made NOT for a dead man, but for a living man. Dead men are already buried, and have no need of this casket. But this casket is made for some man who is now alive. Soon he will be dead, and buried in this casket."

It is true! Caskets ARE made for "living men"–those who will soon be dead. The undertaker added, "Furthermore, the person who will use this casket may have heard you preach. He may have no idea in the world of ever being in this casket. But he will be!"

It was altogether too true! For the man who showed me the casket–the one he thought was so beautiful–was the very man who was buried it in! He was killed on his way home from a funeral!

"Ye shall die...in your sins...for except ye believe that I am he, ye shall die in your sins!"

---

1. According to a list Brother Word kept on his notes, this message was preached 37 times between the years 1948 and 1983.
2. The last three things on this long "run" were added at a later date on a fresh sheet of paper.
3. Instead of writing the word "bed" in his notes, Archie drew a picture of a bed. He would also draw a cross and use a large X for Jesus.
4. Willis H. Meredith of Poplar Bluff, Missouri, founder of the Missouri Committee of One Thousand, an organization of concerned Independents who charged the Disciples of Christ with "abandoning the Word of God." The 1948 NACC was the only one Archie ever attended.

*5. Archie Word knew cars like nobody's business. He was a master in making car deals for himself and others.*

7.
HE WONT BE
COWED BY
SOME
—old "Bell-Wether"—
SINNER NOT
LIKING IT!

*Sometimes Word used a whole page for one potent sentence. This one from the sermon "And Jesus Said It!"*

# 11

# TWO INDISPENSABLES

*The Voice of Evangelism,* August 21, 1948

How easy it is to become side-tracked in the Christian race. And how many people do we see who have failed to heed Paul's admonition, "Let no man rob you" (Col. 2:18). Many have been robbed by some little thing of the world being thrown in their way to turn them aside and, thus, causing them to lose the race.

An old fable says that swift-footed Atlanta challenged her suitors to race her, with herself as prize or death as penalty for losing. Many competed and lost their lives; but a certain Hippomenes secreted on his person three golden apples and entered the contest. Atlanta swiftly passed him...and he threw an apple. Amazed, she stopped to pick it up. The race was on again and Hippomenes, again feeling himself failing, threw an apple. A second time she was caught by the glitter, and she stopped to seize the beautiful apple. Soon she passed him again, and as they neared the goal, Hippomenes threw the last golden apple. Atlanta succumbed to the bait, swerved, picked up the apple, but lost the race.

The devil has been using three golden apples on poor, sinful humanity throughout the centuries: "The lust of the eyes, the lust of the flesh, and the pride of life" (I John 2:16). These three temptations have side-tracked many from following the Lord, caused them to miss the prize, and to stumble into the devil's hell.

"Let no man rob you of your prize" (Col. 2:18). We constantly need to watch the race that we are running. When we turn aside, take our eyes off the Lord and His Word, then we sink even as Peter did in the Sea of Galilee when the wind and waves caught his eyes instead of the Lord.

**WE MUST CONTINUE IN THE PATHWAY OF HOLINESS**

We do not need to kid ourselves; we simply are not saints of God unless we are living lives of holiness. Brethren, HOLINESS OF LIFE will stop the mouth of every HONEST opponent that you may have. "But sanctify in your hearts Christ as Lord: being always ready to give answer to every man that asketh you a reason concerning the hope that is in you, yet with meekness and fear: having a good conscience: that, wherein ye are spoken against, they may be put to shame who revile your good manner of life in Christ" (I Pet. 3:15-16). Of course, the DISHONEST will show themselves to be just what they are by their continuing to gouge you, even though your life shows that you have been begotten of God and your ministry is God-blest.

Later, Peter says, "Seeing that these things are thus all to be dissolved, what manner of persons ought ye to be in ALL HOLY LIVING AND GODLINESS..." (II Pet. 3:11). Christians MUST continue in lives of HOLINESS if we are ever to make the goal, heaven. God help us, all of us, who claim to be New Testament Christians, to repent of our own sins. God help us, all of us, to confess humbly our sins. God help us, all of us, to plead the blood of Christ and not try to cover any one of our sins from the eyes of man or God. God help us to come again and again under the blood with our sins, according to I John 1:7-10. (So many times, after baptism, we forget the blood of Christ.)

Loving John, guided by the Holy Spirit, said, "If we SAY we have fellowship with him and walk in the DARKNESS, we lie, and do not tell the truth. But if we walk in the light, as he is in the light, we have fellowship one with another, and the BLOOD OF JESUS HIS SON CLEANSETH US FROM ALL SIN. If we say that we have no sin, we deceive ourselves, and the truth is not in us. If we CONFESS OUR SINS, he is faithful and righteous to forgive us our sins, and to cleanse us from all unrighteousness. If we SAY that we have not sinned, we make him a liar, and his word is not in us."

After we have become Christians, it is our heaven-bound duty to see that sin is continually erased from our lives by humbly confessing our sins to the Lord, asking for the cleansing that He alone is able to give. He wants us clean, HOLY, and the only thing that keeps us from holiness is our own wilful stubbornness.

*Jesus stands ready to pardon,*
*Jesus stands ready to save.*
*Down in Gethsemane's garden,*
*All that He had, He gave.*

And it was for the purpose of giving primary cleansing and a CONTINUOUS cleansing as long as we are on this sin-infested earth.

God has promised to give us VICTORY over our sinfulness as well as forgiveness when we fall (I John 5:4-5). If we believe that Jesus is our Saviour then we live in HIS strength, and we seek forgiveness immediately when we are unexpectedly caught in anything that is wrong. Thank God that we do not have to wait to get to a priest in some confessional! We can go immediately to our GREAT HIGH PRIEST "who ever liveth to make intercession for us." We do not have to wait for the "Mass" on Sunday morning, for "If we confess our sins, he is righteous to forgive us our sins, and to cleanse us from all unrighteousness.

God have mercy on us, and God help us to come to Him with all manner of our sins! God help us to seek forgiveness for church desertion, yes, even the sin of desertion on Sunday evening when the church is seeking the lost![1] When every member of the church is needed to give an impression of the strength of Jesus in the lives of those He has cleansed, and you deserted to do something of far less importance, seek God's forgiveness for Jesus' sake! God help us to seek forgiveness for our cowardice! O, what cowards I've seen in the ranks of the church membership–wives afraid to speak to their husbands about salvation in Christ![2] Husbands afraid to speak to their wives about the forgiveness of their sins! Parents afraid to speak to their children about the soul-saving Jesus! Employers afraid to speak to their employees about what God wants to do for them through Jesus Christ!

Do you know the greatest contributing factor to the sin of cowardice? I'll tell you so you can "examine yourselves." It is the sin of INCONSISTENCY in the life of the professed believer. If you are doing things that you know are not right; if you are saying things (in the presence of those you know you ought to try to save) that you know you should not be saying, THAT is what it is that takes the fearlessness of God out of you and leaves you a cringing coward! Live right, and you'll feel right. And you'll do right too, because you will not be afraid.

God help us to repent of the sin of "cooling off" and becoming LUKEWARM church members. Jesus has said that the lukewarm church will be "spewed out of His mouth." It is a sin to cool off. It is a dangerous sin to be lukewarm in our service to the Lord Jesus who died for us! O, God, help every church member to repent–and repent immediately–of half-heartedly serving Jesus! No one can stand before the world and speak of "holiness" who is a cooled-off, half-hearted, lukewarm servant of a crucified Christ! Seek the blood of Christ for your forgiveness before it is too late! Ask God for more strength so you can be of more service to Him who demands our ALL–body, soul and spirit. Don't cheat Christ any longer! Get forgiveness and get to work! Give God the glory, and then, by His grace, give Him every ounce of your strength to press the battle!

In our plea for holiness let us not forget the sin of pride. O, let us always rejoice in the victories that Jesus gives! Let us always praise HIM for every victory, and let us seek to be used of HIM as we go on seeking to conquer even greater obstacles. But, for Jesus's sake, let us never become vainglorious and proud! Of what do we have to be proud? We were sin-wrecked sinners! We were dead in our sins and trespasses! We were unclean! far from God! aliens! without citizenship! BANKRUPT! Everything that we have, we have from the Saviour God sent to rescue us. Why should we be proud? If we follow His word and do His will and He gives us the victory, then should HE not be the one to be glorified? God help us to be humble enough to thank Him for every victory we have! Christ is so wonderful, and we are so near nothing. What do we have that He did not give us? From the time you were conceived in the womb, it was Christ who watched over you. What defect do you have that SIN did not bring into your life? We were created perfect from the beginning, and into our veins has come SIN from our SINFUL PARENTS. Every defect came from men (that we honor), but often times God, who has blest us with every blessing, we forget.

Let us ask God for forgiveness for our trying to justify ourselves in our sinfulness. The man who tries to justify his sins is never going to repent of them. Just listen to people trying to justify themselves for their quick tempers, white lying, theater attendance, lodge on prayer meeting night,[3] attendance at the basketball tournament instead of loyalty to Christ's church,[4] Ladies Aid method of gaining a few extra pennies (while they cheat God our of $10,000.00 in tithes and offerings).[5] O, the sins that men and women try to justify! It is enough to disgust the Lord! Sometimes even the God of heaven gets enough of our sinfulness and gives up on people (Rom. 1). We need to REPENT and quit justifying ourselves in our sinfulness!

God demands lives of holiness. "For without holiness no man shall see the Lord" (Heb. 12:14). In order to live lives of holiness we need to repent and turn to God, seeking the cleansing of the blood of Christ. Let us repent of the sin of evil companionships. People are a lot like water. They seek their own level. What you are shows up in the companionships that you seek. If you are a compromiser at heart, you will find a group of fence-straddlers. If you are a denominationalist at heart, you will soon align yourself with a denomination. If you are a coward, fearing to launch out into the deep for God, you will soon find yourself surrounded by your own kind. If you are a bartender at heart (no matter how well you keep it covered up, no matter how nice you appear on the surface), you will be running around with a bartender before long. If you are a pussyfooter, seeking only to build a large congregation in order to build an impressive edifice of worship, you will somehow find men of that stripe for your companions.[6] "Birds of a feather flock together," but you will never find canaries flying around with a flock of buzzards! Choose very carefully your companions if you would be well pleasing to God.

God, help us to flee from the very appearance of evil and to trust our souls to Thy care! O, GOD, help us to live lives of holiness before an unbelieving and skeptical world, that they may behold our good works, and seeing the source of them, be forced to glorify Thee![7]God, help us when we are tempted to turn from the "straight and narrow" way to recall the lives of the early followers of Christ. Help us to remember how the pleasure-mad Romans hated them. Help us to remember that the same class of people in every land will do the same thing if we are true to Thee. Help us to remember that the religious Jews despised the followers of Christ when they stood uncompromisingly for their Lord, and that they will do the same thing if we are true, refusing to become infidels to please them.[8] Help us to realize that the higher-education crowd, the Greeks, laughed at the true followers of Christ, and that many faltered and became agnostics instead of true Christians. Help us to remember in this day when church folks are seeking the path of least resistance that our forefathers in the faith were persecuted, imprisoned, stripped of their property, their women were outraged, their children were sold into slavery...and the bodies of the saints who would not yield were crucified! O, the fearful terrors they suffered in the days when Christians were indeed CHRISTIANS!

God, help us to remember that the early Christians were sawn asunder! thrown to the lions! ripped to shreds by starving wild dogs! burned at the stake! torn on the rack! drowned a little at a time to make their deaths a bit more hideous to anyone who might be thinking about accepting this religion of Jesus Christ! Their blood was shed like a river–but they OVERCAME! Where is pagan Rome today? They were forced by the conduct of the Christians to say, "See how these Christians live...and see how these Christians can DIE!" Death is the "fire test" of life. If you are not ready to die, you are not living right!

Recently a lawyer and I visited in the home of an old saint of God who had suffered a stroke. He had been a real Christian for many years and had labored in the church for over 30 years. He had been stricken in the basement and at first was unable to speak.. His wife found him and through super-human strength managed to get him on an old cot in the basement before running to call the doctor. By the time the doctor arrived, his speech began to come back. After a consultation, the doctor retired to the next room to tell his wife what he had found. But before they could get the door shut, this old man of God called out in his deep bass voice, "Doctor, come here! I know what you are about to do. You are going to tell my wife of my condition privately. You do not need to do that. God has saved my soul and made me His own child many years ago. He has given me power to overcome. If I am going to drag one side of my body around the rest of my days, talking out of one side of my mouth as I am now, His grace is sufficient for me. And if, in your professional opinion I am about to cease this life and go to meet my Lord, I wish that you might stay here and witness with my beloved wife how God cares for His own in the hour of death." He was ready to go!

He who puts Christ FIRST in his life will find the Lord with him at the LAST! God wants to help us live right, and God wants to help us die right! What is the strongest argument against the church today? Is it not the charge of a lack of real love? the lack of genuine faith? the lack of undying loyalty to Christ? O, Christians, professed followers of Christ, let us return to the precepts of our Saviour! May God help us to out-live, out-love, out-give, out-shine, out-pray, and out-work all the false religions on the face of the earth, showing them lives of holiness!

**ANOTHER INDISPENSABLE IS HOPEFULNESS**

We have hope in Christ. It is "the hope" of which Paul speaks in Acts 26:6-7, "And now I stand here to be judged for the hope of the promise made of God unto our fathers...And concerning this hope I am accused by the Jews, O King!" The hope of our resurrection is THE HOPE that makes Christians hopeful when all else seems to fail.

We must continue in hopefulness. Sometimes in the past I have doubted God, become discouraged, felt God-forsaken and blue, but that was a long time ago. I've had good old Christians come to my side and say, "Brother Word, don't become discouraged. We know there have not been many responses, but if you will keep on pouring on the Word of God, we'll keep on praying, and in the end God will give victory."[9] I've seen some wonderful victories come out of the almost impossible. I'm ashamed that I ever doubted God. I've made up my mind that never again will I mistrust the Lord. I'll fight the devil and trust the Lord to make the blows count for the most!

Centuries ago a great evangelist named Oncken came to Europe to preach the gospel. He was arrested, fined and imprisoned (just as any true preacher will be in any Catholic-dominated country). Every time he was let free, he preached again. The magistrate before whom he was brought time after time finally lost patience. Standing up, leaning over the bench with the crucifix above his head, he shook his finger in the face of the preacher, and said, "Mr. Oncken, you are not going to preach!" The preacher straightened up, smiled, looked the magistrate right in the eye, and softly said, "Your honor, as long as I can see GOD above your finger, I will keep on preaching."

Brethren, that is a combination of holiness of life and hopefulness in one's life's work that is hard to beat! We need more of just that variety of preaching today.

Recently, while trying to console a little girl whose brother had been hurt in a terrible automobile accident, a grandmother, who had never given God or church much thought, said, "Don't you worry, little dear. God will take care of him." In terrible trials we turn to God. Why not let the world know of our hope in God? God is not dead! He is not even sick![10] Underneath we have faith in God. Why not let it out? Why not let the world know about it? Is it something about which we should be ashamed? Let us exercise our hope! Let us practice our hope.

As a minister, I need your prayers. You show your hope in the Lord by praying for His faithful minister. You pray for me that I'll keep right on pouring the Water of Life into the old "snake holes," and if we are faithful, in time the snakes will be drowned. Pray God that I'll be faithful, and that "new creatures" will be raised up where the old snakes of Satan died because I was faithful in preaching the Word of God.[11]

Remember that the cause of Christ is being opposed today by a bare, black, hopeless world. It is getting "no better fast." As man goes farther in sin, he becomes worse and worse. But there is still a God in heaven! His Son is still able to save! His gospel is still the power of God unto salvation–even to the most hopeless person on earth. His promises are true though all men be liars. We are His children by new birth. He ever loves and cares for His own. All hell cannot prevail against us, for we are backed by God's omnipotent power! It is up to us to sow the good seed, and in due time we shall reap a glorious crop. "Fear not, little flock, for it is the Father's good pleasure to give you the kingdom" (Luke 12:32). "Fear thou not, for I am with thee; be not dismayed for I am thy God; I will strengthen thee; yea, I will help thee; yea, I will uphold thee, with the right hand of my righteousness" (Isa. 41:10). "Jehovah is on my side, I will not fear. What can man do unto me?" (Psa. 118:6). "I will fear no evil, for thou art with me...Yea, though I walk through the valley of the shadow of death, I will fear no evil" (Psa. 23).

Christians, professed followers of our Lord, Let us live in HOPE!

*Be thou the rainbow to the storms of life!*
*The evening beam that smiles the cloud away.*
*And tints tomorrow with prophetic ray.*

If we could go together down the narrow passageways of the catacombs under the ancient city of Rome, we could find the symbol of the early Christian's hope. There carved in the "ageless stone" that is showing signs of age, we would find the "Cock"–symbol of Peter's denial, and, thank God, his restoration! We would see carved with unskilled hands the Phoenix, symbolizing the resurrection of the body. We would see the vine, symbolizing the union we have with our ever-living Lord. On another grave we would see the palm branch, symbolizing the Christian's victory over all his enemies. Then the fish, symbolizing, in acrostic form, Jesus Christ, God's Son and our Saviour. And the crude symbol of the anchor, that through the ages has told of the HOPE Christians have–secure and eternal!

God, help us be like Jesus–Holy and Hopeful!

1. Sunday evening services at the Montavilla church were highly evangelistic in nature.
2. A Christian wife once told Archie she never talked to her lost husband about Christ. Archie responded, "Sister, you could be married to the devil and get along very nicely with him too–if you never mentioned Christ to him!"
3. Word, a former Mason, in time became opposed to lodge membership, period.
4. Archie, a former athlete of renown, was not opposed to basketball unless it interfered with church services.
5. Word was a firm believer in supporting the church only by means of tithes and offerings.
6. Word's method of church growth was to "swarm" when the congregation reached 200 in number and start a new church. Nine new churches were started by this method during his 33- year ministry at Montavilla.
7. Here begins a long and passionate prayer, right in the middle of this sermon.
8. Not to be construed as an anti-Semitic statement. Word here is classifying three groups who opposed the early Christians (Romans, Jews and Greeks). Felix Freedman, a Jew of renown, was converted to Christ during one of Word's revivals in San Jose, California.
9. Word testified that in many of his revivals nothing happened for two or three weeks. But then the gates would open and as many as 100 or more would be converted.
10. This statement was made long before the catch phrase to the "God is dead" movement in the 1960s.
11. One of Archie Word's most popular revival sermons was "Shaking Out Snakes."

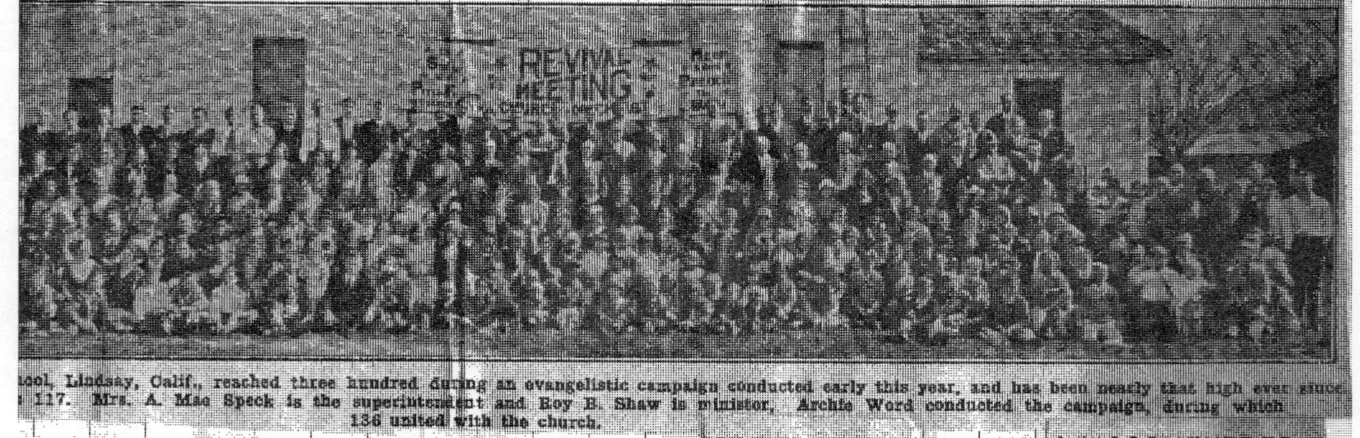


...ool, Lindsay, Calif., reached three hundred during an evangelistic campaign conducted early this year, and has been nearly that high ever since ... 117. Mrs. A. Mae Speck is the superintendent and Roy B. Shaw is minister. Archie Word conducted the campaign, during which 136 united with the church.

*This picture of the great Lindsay revival of 1931 still hangs in "Memory Hall." Taken from* The Lindsay Gazette.

# 12

## SALVATION AND DAMNATION, ALL IN THE SAME TEXT!

*Preached in 1948 at First Christian Church, Inglewood, California*

"And he said unto them, Go ye into all the world, and preach the gospel to the whole creation. He that believeth and is baptized shall be saved; but he that disbelieveth shall be condemned" (Mark 16:15-16).

The marching orders of Genghis Khan, Alexander the Great, Sennacherib, Ashurbanipal, Napoleon and Hitler sent soldiers on killing missions that wiped out millions of people. But the marching orders of the King of Kings–Jesus–has brought life, happiness and hope to millions!

The crucifixion was past. The resurrection had been demonstrated. The 40-day period was drawing to a close. Jesus' ascension was at hand. Christ's coronation was in the immediate future. Pentecost was eminent. Jesus gives one compact statement involving His chosen one's business. It is a command with a promise (salvation), and a warning with a promise (damnation).

Rejecting salvation means soul suicide! self-condemnation! shuts the door of heaven! seals God's sentence!

**SALVATION IS PRECEDED BY THREE SEPARATE STEPS**

(Yet, these steps are so placed as to be inseparable!)

First, the gospel must be preached. "Go ye into all the world, and preach the gospel to the whole creation." This is addressed to every child of God! If any professed Christian is not anxious and interested in the salvation of others, I doubt seriously whether he has ever experienced salvation!

And it must be Jesus Christ's gospel! It must be the gospel of the virgin-born Jesus, the prophesied Redeemer, the sinless miracle worker, the only begotten Son of God: the One who suffered vicariously, died on the cross, made atonement for sin, was victoriously resurrected, our only hope–the Jesus who commanded, "Go ye into all the world, and preach the GOSPEL (not some denominational creed or lodge obligation) to every creature!"

This is our responsibility! If there was only ONE person on earth who had not heard the gospel and he lived in Tibet's highest plateau, it would be worth all the money, sweat and tears of all Christians on earth to win that soul to Christ! God says EVERY creature is to have that gospel preached to him! That is why I am here preaching![1] O, my heart yearns that ALL people might have at least ONE chance to hear the gospel before they must die and meet their God! We MUST preach it! Not A gospel, but THE gospel! Whatever else is preached, THE GOSPEL must be preached (Rom. 1:16; I Cor. 9:21), or there is NO salvation!

Prophecy has it's place, but salvation is by the GOSPEL! I know prophecy is more spectacular–but there is no repentance in it! I know prophecy has more room for speculation–but there is no conversion in it! I know prophecy tickles folks' ears–but it doesn't change them! I know prophecy feeds some folks' ego–but Jesus said, "Preach the GOSPEL!"

The gospel has two parts. Man's sinful and lost condition. "There is none righteous, no not one" (Rom. 3:10). God must and WILL punish sin (Rom. 6:23a). Every sacrificial offering in the Old Testament pointed to sin's punishment. That is one part. But the gospel also tells of God's means of atonement whereby sin is punished and the sinner is given redemption! "Christ died for our sins according to the Scriptures" (I Cor. 15:3). The gospel must be PREACHED!

Second, the gospel must be HEARD. Why must the gospel be heard? Because of Romans 10:17, "So belief cometh of hearing, and hearing by the word of Christ." Preaching to empty seats is useless! The gospel must be heard by people. But preaching to an empty head is useless, too! Many people are preoccupied with thoughts of jobs, dinner, boy friends, girl friends, babies, games, the world. Lost sinners must hear the gospel OR THERE IS NO HOPE FOR THEM!

Listen to me now! God will hold responsible every lost sinner who has come to this revival as much as one time. He will hold responsible every lost sinner who could have come but did not. God will not only hold sinners responsible for the gospel they have heard but for the gospel they could have heard and did not. The gospel is to be heard![2]

If you are here LOST, you'd better LISTEN! You had better pay attention to this humble old God-sent preacher. The gospel of Christ DEMANDS your hearing it! It is not something I fixed up. It is not something some church cooked up. It is the gospel of CHRIST, your ONLY Saviour! The gospel offers God's only way of salvation. There's no other gospel and there's no other method!

Third, the gospel must be OBEYED. Jesus demands it! Jesus commands it! The lost sinner is to be saved by hearing, believing and obeying the gospel (II Thess. 1:7-8). I've read the Bible. I've studied the Bible. I've prayed over the Bible. I've wept over the Bible! There's no text that makes salvation plainer than Mark 16:15-16. It contradicts the whole structure of denominationalism! It is what JESUS said about salvation! He was God manifest, omniscient, all-knowing! He was not deceived and He would not deceive you! He died to save you! It is the truth from God! We are not to earn it, pay for it, buy it, or "just believe" it! Others may add "altar calls," "tarry meetings," or experiences. Some may subtract repentance and baptism (Acts 2:38), but they will have to answer to God. To be sure, DO WHAT JESUS SAID! "He that believeth and is baptized shall be saved."

**WHY WILL THE CHRIST REJECTOR BE DAMNED?**

"But he that disbelieveth shall be condemned." Belief ONLY will not save you, but unbelief ONLY will damn you! Here is how souls are damned. Any man who WANTS to, CAN believe. He who hears and WILL NOT believe, shall be damned. WHY is the Christ rejector damned?

First, because by NOT believing Christ, he has become a party to His death. You may think you are a pretty good guy. You may think, "I've never done anything very bad." But if you've ever heard the gospel one time–and you've rejected it–you are partners with those who crucified Christ! Jesus died because of "man's" sin. Not His own. But YOUR'S! And MINE! Our sins nailed Him to the cross! Our sins thrust the spear through Him! And the sin of unbelief is one of the worst! When you hear the gospel you either receive Him with a heart of gratitude and loving devotion, or you help crucify Christ–your substitute, your Saviour! You either accept His sacrifice or become guilty of His blood.

Many people misunderstand the gospel. They think only GOOD people can be saved, but they are the only ones who CAN'T be saved! There's not a verse of Scripture offering salvation to a good person. Christ died for sinners! for the unjust! for the ungodly! for His enemies! If you are a sinner, Christ died for YOU! But if you are one of those "good" folk, who never sinned (in your own sight), self-righteous, then I guess you'll just have to go to hell! Jesus did not die for the SINLESS, but for SINNERS! A lot of people are going to hell, lost forever, because they THINK they are good.

Second, by not believing he makes God a liar (Acts 4:12). It takes faith and obedience to save. God has no other method to save. You cannot get by by merely being good, joining a denomination, turning over a new leaf, reforming, feeling good, crying, begging, just being baptized or by a plan of salvation all your own. You must accept Christ in HIS OWN WAY—upon HIS OWN TERMS—believing God's Word concerning His Son, or you call God a liar because you did not believe His testimony!

Third, by not believing he chose darkness rather than light (John 3:18-19). Every man makes his choice—between heaven and hell, between salvation and damnation. God will not send you to heaven against your choice, your will, your desire! Every man who has an opportunity to hear God's good news has an opportunity to choose heaven. If you choose to be blind, you must suffer the consequences.

Take this illustration.[3] A man is born blind; he cannot see. You cannot hold him responsible for the fact he cannot see: he is not responsible for the fact that he cannot see because he was born blind. But suppose a great physician comes and says, "I'll give you sight. Just turn yourself over to me and I'll make you to see." But the man will not believe him; he will not turn himself over to him. That physician heals the blind all around. But he does not heal this man because the man, born blind and unable to see, refuses the gift of sight when he is offered it. The doctor says, "I'll give you sight." But the man goes away, having chosen to stay blind.

O, the awful judgment of God upon that one who heard the gospel—but chose his own destruction!

Fourth, by not believing he refuses God's pardon. God has offered His pardon—salvation—on simple terms. No one can be neutral. You've got to decide. For Christ or against Christ! Do you dare turn down God's pardon? O, how people work for a new trial, seeking pardon, here! Reprieve! Life! A little longer!

Years ago I was in a revival campaign in one of your Northern cities.[4] While I was there a poor woman was electrocuted in the state penitentiary. She had been arrested for certain crimes and tried in the courts of that state. She was found to be guilty. One day she was brought before the judge. He had her stand up before him as he sentenced her to be electrocuted on a certain date. She spent every dime she had in appealing high and low, in getting petitions signed. Being a woman, it was in all the newspapers of that state. People thought that a woman ought not to be electrocuted.[5] It aroused a good deal of talk, but the governor of the state would not do a thing. He examined the evidence over and over again. He said, "This woman has been tried in the courts of the land. She received a fair trial. The evidence points to the fact that she is guilty of the awful crime. She has been sentenced to die, and I will not interfere with the just carrying out of the law." He was right, because a good judge will see that the law and its penalty is carried out. You could not have civilization five minutes unless that were so.

One of the guards on death row in that penitentiary was a friend of mine and a member of the church with which I was engaged in a campaign. I will never forget the night he told me of that awful crime. He told me that the woman had one of the most vulgar mouths he had ever heard, that her cursing was even offensive to the hardened criminals on death row. He told me that she fought and raved and ranted. But, he said, about an hour before she was to be killed, when she had lost all hope that she would be pardoned, she broke down and became a little, whimpering, sobbing mass of flesh and bones. When the two guards went into the jail cell she got away from those two men. He said they called him. And one guard took her left hand and one her left foot; another guard took her right arm and another guard her right leg, and it was all the four of them could do to hold her. By the strength of four men they carried that screaming, pleading, begging woman down that little corridor, put her in the room and held her for dear life, sat her in the chair until the straps could be fastened. As they blindfolded her she begged and sobbed. He said, "Preacher, I have seen a good deal. The other men in the room were not Christians. But they sobbed like babies. There was that poor woman, a human being led like a dumb animal, held in the strength of four massive men, sat down forcible in a chair and strapped in it, blindfolded. Then the warden went over and pressed a button and electricity burned the life our of the body and sent her soul out into eternity to meet God."

O, my soul! What a scene the Judgment will be! Hardened sinners who would not accept God's pardon. Careless sinners who passed by God's pardon. Thoughtless souls who paid no attention to God's pardon. Cheating souls who presumed on God's mercy, gambled with time, and lost God's pardon. A prisoner in Canada foolishly rejected a pardon. He said, "Here I am dying alone, friendless, forsaken in prison, when I might have been home, forgiven and free!" Why choose the devil's hell when you can have God's pardon? God waits to fill your heart with power, hope and joy! You must choose! While this preacher preaches his heart out, while I'm begging and pleading, while the people sing and pray, do you dare turn down God's pardon?

---

1. This message was eventually preached 27 times in Word's travels from California to Maine and Washington to Florida.
2. This paragraph was taken from a clipping pasted in Word's notes. No source was found.
3. This illustration, source unknown, was also pasted in Word's sermon notes.
4. This author of this story is not identified in the clipping found in Word's notes.
5. Word, himself, was a strong supporter of capital punishment.

FINALE:—

OH My Soul!

WHAT A Scene The Judgment Will Be!

1. "Hardend Sinners" Who Wd Not Accept God's Pardon.
2. "Careless Sinners" Who Passed By God's Pardon!
3. "Thoughtless Souls" Who Paid No Attention To God's Pardon!
4. Cheating Souls, Who Presumed On God's Mercy, Gambled With Time, Lost God's Pardon!

You Chose The Devil's Hell! Instead Of God's Pardon!!!

⊗ "Here I Am Dying Alone, Friendless, Forsaken & In Prison, When I Might Have Been Honored-Forgiven- At Home & Free!

(Refused Canada's Pardon)

God Waits To Fill Your Heart With, Power, Hope & Joy!

You Must Choose!

*Dramatic final page from Word's sermon "Salvation and Damnation, All in One Text!"*

13

# THE MOST OFTEN PREACHED SERMON OF JESUS

*Originally published under the title "One Topic Jesus Repeated More Often Than Anything Else" in The Church Speaks, January 2, 1949. Later published in tract form under the title "The Most Often Preached Sermon of Jesus."*

In the scriptures the more important things are repeated. Jesus was laying the foundation for an eternal kingdom, so He made sure that certain foundational stones were laid deep and secure.

He knew that LOVE was an important thing in the lives of His citizens in this new kingdom, so He used the word "love" and teachings concerning love at least 61 times in the four gospels. He knew how love affects our lives, therefore He taught on this important subject often.

Jesus knew that STEALING would be one thing that would be detrimental to His kingdom, so He condemns stealing ***(klepto)*** at least eight times. He knew that a solid society cannot be built if there is no property protection.

Jesus knew that TRUTH was to be the center of His kingdom, so He emphasized truth in contrast to error at least 28 times in the gospel discourses. There is not a chance for stability in character without truth, so Jesus repeatedly elucidates upon "the truth."

These subjects, as important as they are, did not take up the major portion of Christ's time in His preaching, teaching and warning. Remember, Jesus knew men's hearts, weaknesses, temptations, desires, frailties and natural tendencies. He created men and had lived among them for 33 years. He saw the MOST COMMON AND MOST DEVASTATING SIN of man and constantly taught in order to help those who were overcome by it, or were being tempted to yield to it. It caused Him to be ridiculed and scorned. "Ye cannot serve God and mammon. And when the Pharisees, WHO WERE LOVERS OF MONEY, heard all these things; they scoffed at him" (Luke 16:13-14)

We know now that Jesus was right and that He was teaching the thoughts of God. The same doctrine that Jesus taught, when preached today, causes the preacher to be ridiculed. I've known preachers, who were bearing down on Christians to give at least as much as the Jews did for the support of their priesthood, to be visited by so-called elders (who were "God robbers" themselves), demanding that they shut up on teaching concerning stewardship. But remember this: ONE VERSE OUT OF EVERY SEVEN VERSES IN THE GOSPELS reveals Jesus' teaching on stewardship!

Brother, it must be important to demand that much of Jesus' time and teaching! It must be important for the Holy Spirit to write down that part of His teaching to such an extent! It must be important for Jesus to repeat that teaching from so many different angles!

## STEWARDSHIP

Why did Jesus talk more about STEWARDSHIP than He did about prayer? Prayer is important and it is one of the weak spots in the church today,[1] you can be assured of that, but Jesus talked MORE on stewardship than He did on prayer. Why? I think it is quite easy to answer. How can a man be a man of PRAYER while he is cheating the God to whom he prays? Would you want to be real friendly with me if you were deliberately cheating me? Suppose you KNEW that I knew you were cheating me. Do you suppose you would want to come over and visit me very often? Would you feel like asking favors of me under those circumstances? Neither does a "God robber" want to talk to God! Cheating God stops prayer! Quit robbing God and you'll feel more like praying. Honesty opens the gates to the place of prayer.

Why did Jesus emphasize stewardship above preaching? Do not forget it, brother! Preaching is important! If there is one weak place in the church today, it is in the pulpit.[2] But Jesus thought stewardship was of more importance than preaching. Why? The answer is simple. Preaching is lame without the preacher being SENT. He is either sent by faithful stewards of God or he is kept off the field by "God robbers" who profess to believe in God. "How shall they preach, except they be sent?" (Rom. 10:14). "God robbers" stop the preacher from even getting started. If he has to work as secular work to make his living, how can he give himself up wholly to his ministry?[3] How can he do "this one thing" if he has to make his living besides? Jesus knew that the "God robber" stops preaching—even despises preaching, especially when it gets near his pocket book! Therefore He emphasized stewardship above preaching.

Why did Jesus emphasize stewardship above repentance? We know that repentance is important. Without it we perish! If there is one weak spot in preaching today, that sticks out like a black eye, it is the lack of preaching on SPECIFIC repentance—naming sins that need to be repented of and forsaken![4] Jesus knew that no man has repented if he keeps on stealing. No person who steals from his father could be counted as a penitent believer, and NO PERSON WHO STEALS FROM GOD THE FATHER, HAMPERING HIS PROGRAM OF WORLD-WIDE

EVANGELISM, can be considered as a person who has repented! Jesus emphasized stewardship above repentance because no man has repented while he keeps on stealing from God.

Why did Jesus emphasize stewardship above baptism? According to the Word of God, the true believer, who has repented of his sins, is "born again" when he is baptized into Christ. Baptism was the PLACE of the New Birth (John 3:3-5; Mark 16:15-16). But it is better for a person to NEVER have been born, if he is BORN A THIEF! Just so, it is better for a person to never CLAIM to be born again, if he persists in robbing God. Should Christians think less of Christ than the Jew does of Judaism? They are still tithers! Should a Christian think less of Christ and His teaching than a Seventh Day Adventist does of his religion? They are tithers! Should a Christian think less of Christ and His teaching than the Mormons do of their *Doctrines and Covenants* and the *Book of Mormon*? They are tithers, too! We are to give our tithes (and our OFFERINGS), and anyone who does not do at least that much is a "God robber," no matter how many times you have been baptized.

Why did Jesus emphasize stewardship above the Lord's Supper? Do not get me wrong! The Lord's Supper is important. And the manner in which we partake of it is important too. And far more important than just partaking of the emblems is the condition of the heart when partaking (I Cor. 11:20). If a man is a traitor, enemy, misrepresenting Jesus in his daily life, and a God-robbing thief on top of that, how can he partake of the Lord's Supper in a "worthy manner?" We should be cleansed of the awful sin of robbing God just as much as the sins of shoplifting, auto parts theft, bank robbing or a Federal Post Office hold-up! Jesus emphasized stewardship above the Lord's Supper because the Lord's Supper, to a God-robbing thief, is damnation—double damnation to his soul!

Why did Jesus emphasize stewardship above fellowship? Fellowship means partnership. No person can have fellowship who does not have a PART in what is happening in the congregation. No person can have any FELLOWSHIP in the church if he is not doing his PART. Tithing is the minimum of giving, a starting place if you please. God expects every person to tithe to the spreading of the gospel, but that is not the end of our Christian obligation. Where there is no stewardship, there can be no fellowship! If you rob God, you put a double burden on your brethren in the church. How can you have fellowship with them?

Why did Jesus emphasize stewardship above Bible study? I am not minimizing Bible study. Bible study is important, but what good does Bible study do unless we OBEY? The disobedient student of the Bible is just as condemned as the ignorant church member, if not more, because he knows better! Anyone who has studied the Bible knows that the nation of Israel gave a tithe to the support of their priesthood–knows that a Christian should love God more than any Israelite ever did, because we have the fulness of God's revelation to man, whereas they had it only in part. We have a WORLD to evangelize, where they had only a nation to which to minister.

**OUR DUTY AS STEWARDS**

What is a steward? Taking all the definitions of Webster, it amounts to this: "A steward is one who takes care of another person's property for him, giving an accounting to the owner and seeing to it that the owner makes a profit on the good that he is entrusted to handle."

With that definition in mind, why did Jesus emphasize man's stewardship (proper use of God's money entrusted to him) so often? I think the key is found in Matthew 6:21, "For where thy treasure is, there will thy heart be also." If your money is invested in a riding academy, you will be interested in knowing how the riders are treating your horses, how the animals are fed, watered and housed. If you have an investment in the church, you are vitally interested in what goes on. No one will have to explain to you that it is necessary for you to come to both Sunday morning and evening services. They will not have to urge you to be in prayer meeting. Missionaries will not have to come like beggars to your door, because you will be interested in what goes on at church.

Tithers are the most consistent attenders at Sunday services and at prayer meetings. Where your treasure is, there will your heart be. Get your treasure in the house of God, working for the cause of Christ, and you will have no trouble in getting yourself there! Get Christians to invest in Christ's church and they will be faithful to it!

Christianity is not a cheap thing. Christ DIED for us. And He saves ONLY those who are willing to die for Him. "And he that does not take up his cross and follow after me, is not worthy of me" (Matt. 10:38). "Cross" meant DEATH in those days! You had better count the cost and pay the price instead of trying to cheat God, disgrace the crucified Christ, cause His church (that He purchased with His blood, that you refuse to support with your money) to be evil spoken of, and damn your own soul by hypocrisy.

The man who doubts God's Word, doubts God! Your faith in God is judged by your faithfulness to His Word. Where is your treasure? Show me where your treasure is, and I'll show you where your heart is! If your heart is in the church of the living God, you will not be deserting it, knocking it, nor fussing in it. If your investment is in the church, you will be wanting it to grow, thrive, be virile and strong.

Now let us notice some scriptures where Jesus deals with the subject of stewardship. In Luke 16:10-13, Jesus reveals a method of determining a man's trustworthiness. If a man is untrustworthy in the handling of money, you can not trust him anywhere. It is the easiest form of dishonesty. If you steal a horse, its markings will give you away. If you steal a cow, her brand will give you away. If you steal a car, the numbers and plates will expose you. If you steal a boat, its registration with the Coast Guard will bring your theft to light. But if you steal money, it is difficult to run down. Church members who would not think of stealing a chair from the church, nor the pulpit, nor even a light bulb out of the basement, think nothing of robbing God of money! A man's stewardship determines his trustworthiness. If I knew you were a God robbing thief, I would not let you behind my back because a man who will rob his Creator will rob any mere man, if he gets the chance to do it.

In Luke 14:33 Jesus teaches us that ALL WE POSSESS must be at God's disposal. I know a lot of preachers and church members that harp a great deal on this "all-belonging-to-God" doctrine, but you just try to get the tithe that God has demanded from them and you'll hear them holler from here to New York about tithing being for the Jews. Don't talk to me about "giving all" when you won't even give a tenth of the profits and blessings God has given you! "So therefore whosoever he be of you that renounceth not all that he hath, he cannot be my disciple." Do you believe that? If you do, it won't be hard at all to give God the tithe, plus good offerings from His blessings He gives to you! And if there comes a time when God needs ALL YOU HAVE, you will not wait for Him to take it all away from you through misfortune. You will gladly say, "Here, Lord, take it and use it for it is Yours anyway!"

You don't own a thing in the world–you just POSSESS it! When you leave this world you will leave everything behind that you THOUGHT you owned. God owned it before you got here. He allowed you to use it for a while and He demands a reckoning with you at the Judgment Bar for how you used it! You are only a STEWARD and it us up to you to determine whether you will be a GOOD steward or a BAD one.

In Matthew 22:21 Jesus says certain things belong to God. "Render therefore unto Caesar the things that are Caesar's (government taxes); and unto God the things that are God's." The Jews knew that the first tithe had always been dedicated to God and to his priesthood, for their living. We can refuse to pay to God that which He has always said was His "tax," just like we can refuse to pay our taxes to the state, with the same result–the loss of our property! Yes, and the loss of our souls and the souls of others we might have influenced with our money and example.

In Matthew 23:23, "Woe unto you, scribes and Pharisees, hypocrites! for ye tithe mint and anise and cummin, and have left undone the weightier matters of the law, justice, and mercy, and faith: BUT THESE OUGHT YE TO HAVE DONE, AND NOT TO HAVE LEFT THE OTHER UNDONE." We are to be faithful in the weightier matters, but we are NOT to overlook the tithe, either! Jesus did not relieve them of the tithe, but He condemned them for their laxity in other things. In Matthew 5:20 Jesus said, "Except your righteousness exceed the righteousness of the scribes and the Pharisees, ye shall in no wise enter into the kingdom of heaven." That is just as definite as John 3:5. If a man is not born again, he cannot enter into the kingdom of heaven; and if his righteousness does not EXCEED that of the scribes and Pharisees, he cannot enter in either. Jesus said the scribes and Pharisees were tithers (Matt. 23:23). We are to EXCEED them! Are you doing it? Can you expect to enter into the kingdom of heaven? If you've "trusted Jesus" you will obey Jesus.

Many times I hear good church folk say, "I wish our preacher would preach more like Jesus and act more like Jesus." I wonder. Do you want your preacher to preach and act like Jesus did? (Be real honest before you answer!) Turn to Mark 12:41-44. Would you like for your preacher to go back by the Lord's treasury[5] and watch to see just how much (or how LITTLE) you gave? And Jesus did NOT condemn the widow for casting in all that she had. He commended her for her gracious gift. Yet I hear preachers crying out to a gang of ungodly church members how unjust God would be if He demanded that the poor "washer woman" give her tithe unto her Lord!

Why shouldn't a widow be honest, just the same as any other member of the church? Why should she be deprived of the Christian joy of giving to her Saviour? Only the tight-wad, skin-flint, stingy-gutted, God-robber-in-heart would seek to plant covetousness in the heart of people like the widow.

Earlier in my ministry[6] before I saw the fallacy of having a "budget" and sending men out to solicit funds to "raise the budget," I was party to one of those scenes. One man I knew to be tighter than a Scotchman, so I told the men I would interview him personally. We came into his spacious front room, so luxuriously furnished, and were sweet-spiritedly seated in comfortable chairs. Before we could broach the subject of our visit, the man we had come to see said, "I know why you men have come, so I assure you I want to give my widow's mite." I said, "Brother ______, I will be delighted if you will give one-half as much as the widow did!" He laughed heartily and replied, "Brother Word, do you know how much the widow gave? Why, it took two times as much as she gave just to make a farthing!" "Yes," I answered, "But Jesus said she cast in ALL HER LIVING!" And I added, "If you will just give one-half of all you possess, this church will be able to build the new building we need so badly, send out at least three missionaries for 10 years, and have a nice "backlog" in the bank for any unforeseen emergencies!" Do you think he gave a "widow's mite?" No, he did not! What he had, he had stolen from God for years. He was well fixed. That was in 1928. From 1929[7] to 1936 he lost every cent he had stolen from God, lost his health, and his son (who turned out to be a drunkard) lost his life on one of the old man's fine farms! It never pays to cheat God! Jesus is still sitting by the treasury and He knows what you give, what you hold back, and what you SHOULD have given! He will be the final Judge; there will be NO appeal to a higher court, no polluting the jury or buying off the judge.

In Matthew 5:16 Jesus said, "Even so let your light shine before men: that they may see your good works, and glorify your Father who is in heaven." The world knows how much you really believe by the amount you are willing to invest in what you profess to believe. A true BELIEVER is a true GIVER. The average church member thinks more of his beer, whiskey, cigarettes, cigars, theater and entertainment than he does of his God! A whole week's religion costs him less than a trip to the theater. A sinner visiting in one of our services once cornered a deacon after a sermon on stewardship and asked him whether he really believed in the Bible teaching he had heard that night. The deacon emphatically said, "Yes, I do!" To which the sinner replied, "I know good and well you don't! You think more of that old bull of your's. You paid more money for him that you ever put into the church–and it costs you more to keep him up than you ever think of putting into the offering." He was a bull worshipper! The world is watching to see just where your heart is!

"Things" are not life. Do not think that by storing up things–bonds, papers, mortgages–you are going to have an abundant life. "Take heed, and keep yourselves from all covetousness: for a man's life consisteth not in the abundance of the things which he possesseth" (Luke 12:15). Notice that He says "possesseth," not "owneth!" You only possess things on this earth. God OWNS them! You are allowed to use them, and then you must give an account of how you USED them–to the OWNER!

Bishop Whipple came to town and told the story of an old Indian who came to him to get a two-dollar bill changed for two ones–one for himself to give to God and one for his wife to give. The bishop asked him if it was all the money he had. The Indian answered, "Yes." The bishop was about to tell him it was too much to give, when an old Indian missionary, with tears in his eyes, said, "It would be too much for a white man in Christian America to give. But it is not too much for an

Indian who has just this year learned of Jesus' love and seen His blessings. He appreciates Jesus and His gospel!" I wonder, sometimes, do we?

We call a man a hypocrite who prays, but refuses to pay his just debts. Jesus taught (and so did the prophets and apostles) that the tithe and offerings belong to God. Not paying them is beating a just debt. A debt to your God! You can pay it or beat it—but you'll have to give an account for your deeds!

*Still as of old, man by himself is priced.*
*For 30 pieces of silver Judas sold HIMSELF, not Christ!*

Can you now see why Jesus emphasized stewardship and reemphasized our duty to God as stewards? He loved us. So He warned us! Let us by God's grace bring at least the tithe to Him, and from His abundant blessings offer unto our God liberal offerings.

One of these days, when you are lying flat on your back, and life is fast ebbing from your body, you will have to trust God. Why not learn to trust God NOW?

"Whom am I, and what is my people, that we should be able to offer so willingly after this sort? For all things come of Thee, and of Thine own have given Thee" (I Chron. 29:14).

---

1. The *Christian Standard* once praised the Montavilla church for having over half its membership present on prayer meeting night. Word often cited a large church in Indiana he had visited that had less than five percent of its membership out for prayer meeting.
2. Word's famous "Jap Balloon Preaching" sermon would appear one month later in *The Church Speaks*, creating a controversy on the campus of San Jose Bible College.
3. Archie Word believed in full-time ministry. At a Centerville Rally he once took public issue with another speaker over the matter of preachers working part-time.
4. Word's watershed message "Repent or Perish!" (found elsewhere in this volume) was first preached at the Cincinnati (IA) rally in 1946.
5. Brother Word did not believe in passing an offering plate. Instead he had an offering box placed at the back of the church auditorium. The offering box is still used at Crossroads (formerly Montavilla) church in Portland, Oregon.
6. This incident took place in Toledo, Oregon.
7. *The year of the great stock market crash.*

Hear A. Word

Preach the Word

ARCHIE WORD, EVANGELIST, Formerly of Strathmore

**CHRISTIAN CHURCH, Lindsay**

*Beginning Friday, Jan. 16*

7:30 P. M.

**The Old Gospel**

**The Old Book**

**The Old Faith**

ROY B. SHAW, Minister, Song Leader

*Stirring Song Services*

*Solos, Duets Choruses*

*The Gospel in Song*

*The meeting that meant more to Archie than all others–136 converted in his home town of Lindsay, CA (1931).*

# 14

# THE HOPELESSNESS OF A CHRISTLESS SOUL

*Preached at the Sacramento Gathering, June 27, 1952. Reprinted from The Voice of Evangelism, November 22, 1952.*

Recently I purchased a second-hand La Salle automobile that had been cared for excellently. In the glove compartment was an original booklet that instructed the owner as to how he should take care of his La Salle. The makers of a car are more apt to know how to care for the car than any uninstructed new car owner. So it is with Christianity. God made us and He knows all about us. He gave us the privilege of running our lives, but He knew that we did not know very much about ourselves, so He gave to us a book of instructions called the Bible. We can follow its instructions and have the wisdom of God in our lives, or we can depart from its instructions and have the FOOLISHNESS OF OUR OWN DELUDED MINDS to guide us.

History is replete with instances of blind and foolish men thinking they knew better how to run things than God, and today we have millions who are trying to tell us there is no such thing as hell, no punishment for our sins, no retribution, no justice. Their lives usually show their beliefs, for men LIVE what they believe! God has spoken on the subject of hell in His manual of instructions. His Son mentioned hell twice to heaven's once. Any "hope" outside the everlasting Word of God is a false hope!

**DEAD HOPE**

"Having NO HOPE and WITHOUT GOD in the world" (Eph. 2:12) That was the condition of all the world outside of Israel when Jesus came to give a HOPELESS HUMANITY a genuine HOPE! The Jews were not without Christ, because "salvation was of the Jews." Abraham, the father of Israel, "saw the day of Christ afar off, and was glad" (John 8:56). The Jews drank of "The Rock" in the wilderness, which was Christ (I Cor. 10:4). But the Gentiles were "without God" because they had no knowledge of Him; they had no faith in Him; and they were, therefore, without pardon, life, grace, comfort or hope.

How dark was heathenism, even under its highest reign of philosophical culture! Education alone has never been able to find the everlasting, self-existent God. Brain-worshippers of today are no nearer God than the Greeks were 2000 years ago!

I quote from Alfred Edersheim's *Life of Christ.*[1] "One other mode of tracking the footsteps of the early Christians' wanderings seems strangely significant. It is by tracking their records among the dead, reading them on broken tombstones, and in ruined monuments. They are rude, and the inscriptions, most of them in bad Greek, or still worse Latin, none in Hebrew, are like the stammering of strangers. Yet what a contrast between the simple faith and earnest hope which they express, and the grim proclamation of utter disbelief in any future to the soul, not unmixed with language of coarsest materialism, on the graves of so many polished Romans. Truly the pen of God in history has, as so often, ratified the sentence which a nation has pronounced upon itself. That civilization was doomed which could inscribe over its dead such words as, 'To eternal sleep;' 'To perpetual rest;' or more coarsely expressed, 'I was not, and I became; I was, and am no more.' And adding as it were by way of moral, 'And thou who livest, drink, play, come.' Not so did God teach His people; and as we pick our way among these broken stones, we can understand how a religion, which proclaimed a hope so different, must have spoken to the hearts of many even at Rome, and much more, how that blessed assurance of life and immortality, which Christianity afterwards brought, could win its thousands, though it were at the cost of poverty, shame, torture, and the arena."

That is why Paul could say, "But we would not have you ignorant, brethren, concerning them that fall asleep; that ye sorrow not, even as the rest, who have no hope" (I Thess. 4:13). The world without Christ–those hopeless, Christless souls–have no hope beyond this life! The Christian has hope! Paul comforts those who mourned the loss of a Christian loved one. They had a hope. But consider how the old heathen world considered their dead!

Theocritus: "The living have hopes, but the dead are without hope."

AEschylus: "Of the once dead there is no resurrection."

Lucretius: "Nor does any one stand forth awakened, whom once the cold pause of life has found."

Catullus: "Suns may set and return; when once our brief day has set we must sleep one everlasting night."

Modern heathens are just as hopeless as the ancients. Strauss, not many decades ago, said, "Life beyond the grave is the last enemy which speculative criticism has to oppose and, if possible, to conquer." John Stuart Mill agreed. "Hope was only an earthly future, not for the individual, but for the race, created by Science, where all the greater of evils of life will have been removed." Mill said this concerning his mother: "Her memory is a religion to me."

Such is the hopelessness of Christless souls, no matter in what age they may have lived. The hopelessness of the

Christless soul is just the opposite of the hope of the Christian. The Christless soul has a "dead hope" while our hope has lived through one of the worst forms of death known to man—crucifixion! They hanged our Lord upon a cruel Roman cross by nailing His hands and feet to the hard wood. Not satisfied with that torture, they thrust a spear in His side. And while He writhed in agony they spit upon Him, plucked His beard out by the roots, and buffeted Him with their fists. They were sure He was dead, so sure that they placed Him in a tomb. And for good measure, they placed a guard of Roman soldiers on 24-hour duty to see that His body was not disturbed. But John the Revelator met Him some 60 years later on the Isle of Patmos, and the Risen Saviour said, "Fear not; I am the first and the last, and the Living one; and I was dead, and behold, I am alive for evermore, and I have the keys of death and of Hades" (Rev. 1:17-18). Because He lives, we have hope that through Him we shall live while the hopeless, Christless soul comes to the grave believing it will be the end of all things!

Early in my ministry I had this doubly and indelibly impressed on my mind. One of the ladies of the church was the only Christian in her entire family.[2] Her mother believed that Jesus was an illegitimate child.[3] Her father believed nothing except that a bottle was the panacea for every ill. The Christian lady died, and I was called to preach her funeral. A great crowd of neighbors and friends, both Christian and pagan, assembled for her funeral. The mother had to be revived three times with smelling salts. The father was sober but in misery beyond words to describe. After friends had viewed the body, the doors were shut and the family was ushered in. It was a large family. One after another went up to the casket, kissed the body, and screamed, "WE WILL NEVER SEE HER AGAIN!" After about 30 minutes of that kind of behavior, the undertaker finally got them to leave, and we took the casket to the cemetery. The family prevailed upon the undertaker to open the casket again, and they went through the whole scene over again. Oh, what crying, moaning, weeping and sighing! And with no way to comfort them, for they had a DEAD hope!

**A LIVING HOPE**

Just a few months later I was invited to preach the funeral of an old retired preacher.[4] His health had failed him, and he was living on a little farm in the community. He had raised one family, lost his wife, and remarried. To that union there had been born two children. The wife was a firm believer in the Lord. That day, in the same church building, with many of the same folk present, I witnessed a young mother, a believer, pick up her small children so they could see their father's face for the last time. She told them, "Don't cry, for we shall see Daddy again soon." We went quietly from the church to the place of interment, and after a brief service, they departed to their homes in the living hope of seeing their departed loved one "in the morning." The Christian has a hope that lives through the grave and into eternity, while the Christless soul has a hope that dies at the grave!

Max C. Fleischman, a multi-millionaire, committed suicide in October 1951. Why? He had millions of dollars, but he had no hope. His material things in which he hoped, and for which he lived, were going the way of all flesh. He had no pleasure in them any more, so he killed himself–the natural consequence of a Christless soul.

Christless souls see the setting of the sun, but no rising sun. They see the world becoming a dim reflection, with never a burnishing. There is only night for them, but the child of God looks beyond and sees the "eternal star of hope." They can say, with assurance, "I know him whom I have believed, and am persuaded that he is able to keep that which I have committed unto him against that day."

Richard Bacon, Jr., was a hopeless, Christless soul. He was a young American poet of much promise, but he rejected God. He died in 1841 at the age of 24. He had hoped to write a great poem, "The Deathbed of Hope," but in agony and despair, he exclaimed, "Strange! Was it not strange that I should have thought of that subject? Now I see it all: I am without hope!" While the hopeless sinner goes down with his corruptible inheritance, the child of God puts on immortality. "For me to live is Christ, and to die is gain."

A gospel worker in the Far East said, "We stand upon the threshold of the Buddhist temple, watching the lined face of the Buddhist priest, as with a dull and HOPELESS countenance he sweeps his hand along a row of prayer wheels. In the entry stands a heavy, chest-like wheel, six or eight feet high, with two iron projections, which ring a bell each time it turns. The old wheel turner sets it in motion with an indifferent face, chanting as it slowly revolves. We glance into the dark interior, and back at the monotonous grinding of the great wheel with its bell, and the sing-song mechanical functions of the priest. A sense of deep poverty and stark blindness of the faith which these represent comes over us, and we think of what it means that just such temples are the only houses of prayer to be found throughout Tibet, Bhotan, and Nepal."

But, according to I Peter 1:4, Christians have a hope and inheritance incorruptible, undefiled, that fadeth not away, reserved in heaven for them! We expect a new earth when this present earth is destroyed, a world renewed and perfected, a purified world in which righteousness is to dwell forever. No man can defile the Christian's inheritance, but the hopeless, Christless soul's inheritance is soon defiled and destroyed. What a pity to trade the eternal inheritance, undefiled by man, for that which is soon decayed and decomposed!

Oh, what a hopeless eternity for him who rejects the Lord of life! Alfried Krupp, the proud Prussian who was a manufacturer of death,[5] was one who feared death more than any other man. He never forgave anyone who spoke to him of dying. Every employee throughout his vast works was strictly forbidden to refer to the subject of death in conversation with him.

He fled from his own home when a relative of his wife suddenly died there, and when Mrs. Krupp remonstrated with him, he became so enraged that a life-long separation ensued. During his last illness, Krupp offered his physician a million dollars if he could prolong his life for 10 more years. But no amount of money could buy an extension of life or eternal life, not to mention the serene trust of the Christian who has hope in Christ.

I want you to compare Alfried Krupp, a Christless, hopeless soul, with that of John Bacon, the English sculptor of renown. He lived from 1740 to 1799, and in his will he directed that a plain tablet be erected over his grave at Tottenham Court Road Chapel, with his name, dates of birth and death, and the following inscription:

*"What I was as an artist,*
*seemed to me of some importance,*
*while I lived!*
*What I really was as a believer in Christ Jesus*
*is the only thing of importance to me NOW."*

This Christian has a living, undefiled, and eternal inheritance to which he is steadily going, while the Christless, hopeless soul has a dead, defiled, and short-lived inheritance that soon fadeth into an eternity of woes, sorrows, and eternal regrets.

---

1. Vol. I, p. 69
2. A Sister Stewart of the church in Crabtree, Oregon.
3. "Just a plain bastard" in Word's telling of this story in his book *The Other Day*.
4. This story also took place in Crabtree, Oregon.
5. Maker of Germany's guns, tanks, and ammunition in World War II.

# A Fighter for God!

EVANGELIST
WORD
AT THE
FIRST CHRISTIAN CHURCH, DUFUR

MR. AND MRS. A. WORD

Beginning His Third Week of Revival Meetings
Each Evening but Monday Starting at 7:30 p.m.

**Special--Friday Evening**
**Feb. 3—Childrens Boosters Services**

They come to hear the younger children, boys and girls, trained by Evangelist Word answer bible questions, and listen to a sermon prepared especially for boys and girls of today.

HEAR EVANGELIST WORD
Tonight with CHRIST
YOU HAVE NOTHING TO LOSE
Everything to Gain

THURSDAY EVENING FEB. 2—"Why I Believe in the Inspiration of the Bible." Evangelist Word speaking an entire evening explaining the great bible, how to understand it.

FRIDAY EVENING, FEB. 3—Children's Booster Service. Sermon "Why so Many Kinds of Churches."

SATURDAY EVENING, FEB. 4—"Shaking Out Snakes."

SUNDAY A. M. "What Does it Mean to be a Christian?

SUNDAY P. M. "God's Blockade on the Road to Hell."

MASTERLY SERMONS FROM A MAN WHO IS NOT AFRAID TO SPEAK THE TRUTH

*The great Dufur (OR) revival in 1933 saw 162 decisions for Christ, in spite of a terrible February blizzard!*

15

# OUR RECORDS

*The Voice of Evangelism,* December 15, 1956

"And I saw the dead, the great and the small, standing before the throne; and books were opened; and another book was opened, which is the book of life; and the dead were judged out of the things which were written in the books, according to their works" (Rev. 20:12).

Men are by nature creatures who desire to be remembered. History is replete with luminous illustrations of this characteristic of man. The Sphinx and the pyramids of Egypt stand as silent sentinels to tell the world of a departed race. Every archaeological expedition that leaves our shores returns with more artifacts and evidence that men make records of their achievements because they want to be remembered. Hammurabi's Code speaks of his wisdom and accomplishments. Temples of the great kings of Babylon recall their departed splendor. The Behistun Rock and the Rosetta Stone speak to men thousands of years after their creators have passed into oblivion.

Portions of Egypt are like covered libraries—the perfect climate for preserving the records has preserved these monuments to outstanding feats and skill that were (and are) unsurpassed. Even the priests were used by the kings (like Ptolemy Ephiphanes) to record their good deeds, that men might view them in the centuries to come.

Greece has left us its marvelous sculpture and beautifully adorned temples to remind us that great men once lived there. Homer's *Illiad* still speaks of the deeds of the past of men who wanted to be remembered. Xenophan's *Anabasis* is read by the succeeding generations of Greek students to call back the glories of the homecoming army.

Rome has made for itself a place in ancient history. Its columns, catacombs, Appian Way, and Gallic Wars speak to us of the records of departed men who wanted to be remembered.

Even our own United States is careful to record major events, that others might review their works and remember the outstanding geniuses who have done things to benefit us. The heroes of the Revolutionary War are honored today. The great leaders of both the North and the South are honored by statues. Congress has its records, not only for business purposes but that men might leave their marks on the minds of those who are to come after them.

All of these records grow dim with age, but time serves only to brighten the records that God has made of the doings of men. Every Christian's record is in the Lamb's book of life! Oh, that we might be as careful as to what goes on that eternal record as some men are as to what goes on some bronze plaque!

## WHAT I WANT MY RECORD TO SAY

There are some things I want indelibly entered on my record in heaven.

First, I want it written on my record that I was saved the Bible way. Not that I was hollered into heaven! Not that I was "prayed through" to get saved. Not that I was "altar- called," but that I was "gospel-called" (II Thess. 2:14).

I want it written that I was saved by grace through faith in the Christ of God. I would to God that we might be able to get this one idea across to men: that Scripture records no account of men praying for salvation under the dispensation of grace in Christ. They did not have to cry for His free gift of salvation. They did not have to beg Him who died for them to be saved. These things are unknown in the scriptures. Men did not cry themselves into Christ. They did not join the church on Easter Sunday morning just because the wife thought it was the respectable thing to do. They were not rounded up and herded into the church. They were not begged into the church. They did not have to sign a card and pay dues in order to be saved. They did not get baptized because of some girl friend. In the Bible, no church board demanded an experience. They allowed God to be the Judge. They were content to do as He had commanded and trust Him to vindicate them in that Great Day.

I want my record to say, "Word was saved according to the will of God as revealed in the Word of God, the Bible."

I want it recorded that I heard the Word from men who were sent to "preach the Word," and that it was such good news that they called their message "the Gospel."[1] I don't want that record to say Word listened to some man-made creed or book of discipline or denominational catechism. May God grant that I will not have on my record that I was influenced by some church council that was presided over by some uninspired man. May it never be recorded that I had some denominational groove of man-made salvation.

I want my record to say, "He believed in the Christ of God."[2] Not man's THEORIES about the Son of God, but GOD's record concerning His Only Begotten Son. Not man's theories, church traditions, nor doubting His Word and trusting my own weak and fallible feelings for salvation. May it be written that I accepted Jesus Christ as Deity; that I believed He was born of a virgin, lived a sinless life, and taught as only Deity could teach; that His death was for my sins; and that I believed He was the first to be raised from the grave, never to die again! May it be written that I, as a minister of His, did not subtract anything from His matchless teachings, nor did I think I could improve on His divine revelation.

I wanted it recorded that I repented of all my sins. That I surrendered my stubborn will to that of the Lord God and from that day[3] till I died I kept in His straight and narrow way. Not that I just gave up one or two sins that showed up too much, but that I "departed from all filthiness of the flesh and spirit and perfected holiness in the fear of the Lord." Not that I cut my drinking down a bit, but that I "abstained from the very appearance of evil."[4] Not that I quit telling such big lies, but that I "spoke the truth to my companions." Not that I quit running around with a dozen or so women, but I did not even "look upon a woman to lust after her."[5] Not that I became temperate in the use of such poisons as tobacco, marijuana, or "snoose," but that I "came out from among them and became separate." Not that I quit going to the "low dives" to dance, but that I came to the realization that "evil companionships will corrupt good morals," and that I left off all associations that would induce immorality.[6]

(Do you know why some churches have troublemakers in them? Someone got into the religious body without repenting of his sins! Maybe the preacher did not preach repentance. Some people do not know what repentance is. Repentance is being sorry enough for your sins to quit them! Crying over sins is not enough to please God! Good resolutions are not enough. I spoke with a man on his death bed this past week. I said, "Christ is willing to forgive our sins if we will confess our sins." He said, "If I leave them and mean it when I say so!" He was standing on the very threshold of death. There was no "wise cracking" or monkey business with him! What men thought did not matter to him then. And it won't matter to you when you face your God! Oh, that it might be recorded on ALL our records that we had a change of mind that worked a complete change of conduct! That we might cease our rebellion against God and our wise philosophies that are not in accordance with His revealed will and turn to God—every one of us! That we might have it recorded that we did a "right about face, forward march" toward God's eternal heaven! Forgetting what men will think, but only eager to know what God will think about our actions! That we might forget our "meal ticket," or our so-called "good times," and turn with all our hearts to live for God the way we will wish we had when we meet Him face to face at His judgment bar! REPENT OR REAP HELL!)[7]

I want my record to say, "Word had a faith in his heart that could not be kept there alone—he confessed with his mouth what he believed in his heart" (Rom. 10:10). I want it to be said that I was not ashamed of my Lord, but wherever I went that men learned from me that I had a Savior. Help me, O God, to remember that at first, when men went out to testify and confess Christ, it meant death to them—many times a terrible lot of persecution and torture before they died! But they did not waver. Help me, O God, never to fear to confess my love for You just as faithfully and as loyally as my wife and I said, "I do," at the wedding ceremony.[8]

I want my record to say, "Word was buried with his Lord in baptism, according to the command of his Lord."[9]

(Baptism is not a work of righteousness. It is an act of obedience to a divine command. Baptism does not earn salvation. It is an act of faith which shows confidence in the promises of Christ (Mark 16:16). I want my record to say, "Word believed his Lord and obeyed Him without trying to get by some other way."

Let us remember that Naaman did not earn his cure for leprosy, but he did obey the commandment of the prophet and received for his obedience his healing from that awful malady. Baptism no more earns salvation than the blind man earned his sight by washing his eyes according to the commandment of Christ.

Obedience is necessary to our salvation (II Thess. 1:8). Obedience is doing what you are told to do in the way you are told to do it. No one can know for sure that sprinkling will get by with God, but I do know that if anyone is "buried in water" (having faith which he confesses and repenting of his sins), he is baptized. I want it written down in my record that I took no chances with my soul.[10] That I obeyed the Lord without asking any questions!

Baptism (immersion) pictures before the waiting audience the death, burial, and resurrection of our Lord and Savior Jesus Christ. Baptism (immersion) pictures death to sin, burial of the old man of sin, and a resurrection to walk in a newness of life (Rom. 6:4). Baptism pictures our own ultimate end on this earth–death! It pictures our only hope of resurrection in Christ. "If the Spirit of him that raised up Jesus from the dead dwelleth in you, he that raised up Christ Jesus from the dead shall give life also to your mortal bodies through his Spirit that dwelleth in you" (Rom. 8:11).

I want my record to say that I became a "new creature in Christ" (II Cor. 5:17). That as a new creature, I loved God and loved His children. That as a new creature, I loved His Word, the Bible, even above some church doctrine. Above the traditions of the elders! Above state secretaries! That I loved His Word above a pension fund of a denomination.[11] Above church bosses and great religious syndicates. Above even my friends!

I want it recorded that I loved His commandments. Loved God with all my heart and loved my neighbor as myself! That I loved His church which He purchased with His own blood!

That I was a faithful Christian. That I "contended earnestly for the faith that was once delivered unto the saints" (Jude 3).

Oh, that we might remember that there is an Eye that is watching us! That a record is being made!

The only way your record can read as you would have it to read is for you to live as you want that record to read!

Man's records fade and fail...but the eternal record of God is unchangeable!

Help me, O God, that my record will read:

*He lived for Christ...and he died in Christ*![12]

---

1. Gospel preachers who influenced Archie Word's life included E. V. Stivers, Harold E. Knott, V. E. Hoven, Teddy Leavitt, James A. Pointer, and Garland Hay.
2. Word's favorite description of Jesus.
3. Archie Word finally made this "full surrender" in an upper room prayer meeting at Eugene Bible University on Nov. 11, 1925.
4. EBU student J. Willis Hale once encountered Archie with a whiskey flask in his hip pocket. Word swore, "Is every blankety-blank fool who comes here trying to be a preacher?"
5. In 1990 I interviewed several citizens of Word's home town, Lindsay, California. I decided not to recount most of the stories they told me about this aspect of his "wild life."
6. Word knew the dance business like few preachers could. Before his conversion he ran three dance halls in Fresno, California.
7. This long parenthetical thought was typical of Word's teaching and preaching.
8. Archie Word and Florence Procter were united in marriage at Linday, California, July 7, 1926, by Joseph R. Speck, minister of the Lindsay church.
9. In the four years of research I did for *Archie Word: Voice of Thunder, Heart of Tears,* I could not find any reference Archie ever made to his baptism. In *The Life Story of Archie Word,* Donald G. Hunt, Word's son-in-law, simply says, "He had been baptized when 12 or 13."
10. Which leads us to wonder if Archie Word was ever "re-baptized" after his long years in sin.
11. By "state secretaries" and "pension funds" Word was referring to practices of the United Christian Missionary Society (UCMS), which he viewed as unscriptural.
12. Archie James Word died "in Christ" on Nov. 17, 1988, at 11:10 p.m.

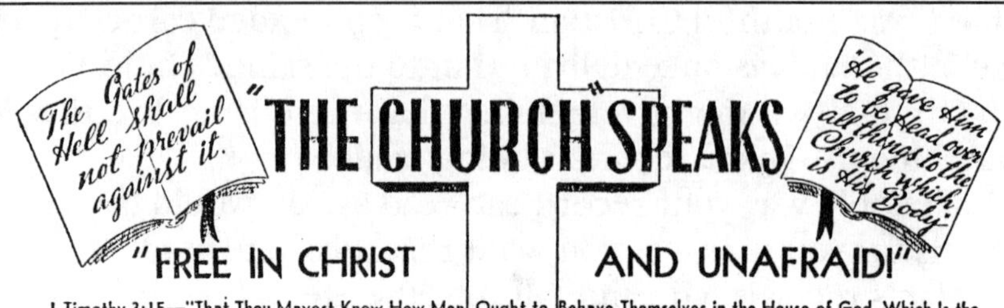


I Timothy 3:15—"That Thou Mayest Know How Men Ought to Behave Themselves in the House of God, Which Is the Church of the Living God the Pillar and Ground of the Truth."

Address All Communications to the Editor, A. Word, 550 N. E. Seventy-Sixth Avenue, Portland 16, Oregon ·

Published with the sole purpose of causing people to think about CHRIST'S TEACHING, especially relating to His church and holiness of its members

Volume 7 PORTLAND, OREGON, JANUARY 7, 1951 Number 1

## JUST TOO MUCH PANTS

*There may be some Christianity here, but the "Rents and Tears" show more to the World than does the "Unity of The Faith"*

We have seen some mighty funny spectacles walking down the streets in our cities, dressed in "Goon Suits" and "Zoot Suits" but when a couple of men try to put on ALL OF THE DIVISIVE HERESIES OF THE RESTORATION MOVEMENT, SPLITS AND CON-

(Continued on Page 6)

# UNHOLY ALLIANCE

God has always demanded of his people that they be SEPARATED people. This is a divine command of both the Old and New Testaments: *"Take heed to thyself, lest thou make a covenant with the inhabitants of the land whither thou goest, lest it be for a snare in the midst of thee: but ye shall destroy their altars, break down their images, and cut down their groves: For thou shalt worship no other god: for the Lord, whose name is Jealous, is a jealous God: Lest thou make a covenant with the inhabitants of the land, and they go a whoring after their gods, and do sacrifice unto their gods, and one call thee, and thou eat his sacrifices; And thou take of their daughters unto thy sons, and their daughters go a whoring after their gods, and make thy sons go a whoring after their gods."* (Exodus 34:12-16). As long as Israel heeded these instructions, as long as they maintained their integrity as the people of God, they were blessed abundantly. During the period when Israel's only attitude toward her religious neighbors was that of OPPOSITION and SEPARATION, God could work through them in wonderful ways, but just as soon as Israel began "letting down the bars" and began mingling and fellowshipping with the pagan nations around her, a spiritual blight fell upon her. When the religious leaders of God's people began to say by their actions, "one religion is just as good as another", God began to withhold His blessings and guidance. Surely, *"these things were our examples, to the intent we should not lust after evil things, as they also lusted."* (I Cor. 10:6).

When we turn to the New Testament, we see that exactly the same type of instruction regarding separation is given to the Lord's church as was given to Israel. Therefore, it is certainly a church-degrading sight to see professed preachers of the gospel entering into unholy alliances with Christ rejecting, Bible disregarding sectarians. Paul entreated, *"Now I beseech you, brethren, mark them which cause divisions and offences contrary to the doctrine which ye have learned; AND AVOID THEM."* (Romans 16:17).

For a long time, preachers in the church of Christ and Christian church have laid great emphasis upon such texts as Acts 2:38; Mark 16:16, etc. AND RIGHTFULLY SO, but have consistently refused to give application to such scriptures as Romans 16:17 and other Holy Spirit inspired commands and exhortations which will be dealt with in this article. For such preachers, Christ has the same denunciation as He had for the Pharisees: *"these ought ye to have done, and not*

(Continued on Page 2)

### THAT YOU MAY KNOW

I know that many of you folk who enjoy reading this paper will want to help us to publist it. We send it to nearly 9,000 people, with no subscription price. We depend entirely upon the LOVE GIFTS of those we serve, to make it possible for us to continue in this work.

You help us with your *"Money"* and we will help you with our *"Labors"*.

*Word's opposition to the Bill Jessup–Ernest Beam unity effort is seen in this 1951 cartoon*

# 16

# IF THE DEAD COULD SPEAK, WHAT WOULD THEY SAY?

*The Voice of Evangelism,* August 24, 1957

As far as I know, there is only one place in the New Testament where a record is given of a man who actually carried on a conversation after death.

"And he said, I pray thee therefore, father, that thou wouldest send him to my father's house; for I have five brethren; that he may testify unto them, lest they also come into this place of torment. But Abraham saith, They have Moses and the prophets; let them hear them. And he said, Nay, father Abraham: but if one go to them from the dead, they will repent. And he said unto him, If they hear not Moses and the prophets, neither will they be persuaded, if one rise from the dead" (Luke 16:27-31).

Jesus speaks of this as an actual experience of a man. The dead were actually speaking! A sensible conversation was carried on. Death does not end our existence–it only translates us from one world to another!

## IF THE DEAD COULD SPEAK

Just suppose that we could talk today to George Washington, to Abraham Lincoln, to Aristotle, to one of the Pharoahs, or to Julian the Apostate. I know there are some things I would like to ask George Washington. I cannot help but wonder how he would feel about certain "isms" from the old world coming in to invade this "sanctuary" that he was so prominent in founding.[1]

I would like to talk with Abraham and ask him what he thinks about weak-hearted, wobbly-jointed, nominal church people who are constantly pessimistic in their outlook–some of them even contemplating suicide because of a lack of faith!

I am sure that there are great scholars in the etymological departments of today's universities who would give thousands of dollars to have just one phonograph recording of a speech by Demosthenes, just to know the true accent of this old Macedonian Greek.

Certainly we would all like to ask the Pharoahs about the lost arts and how the pyramids were constructed.

To every person who is a Christian today, it would be interesting to speak with Julian the Apostate, who tried to obliterate Christianity. Wouldn't he be surprised to know that there are still those who are followers of Christ? I am sure he would see the futility of his great army fighting against God.

But if the dead could speak, there are some things they could not reveal to us any better. They could not reveal to us a better God than Jehovah, a loving Father and divine Creator.

They could not reveal to us a better Bible than the one we have–a book that is written for all classes of people, that answers the great questions of life, a book that is superior to all other books in its circulation, surpassing all other books from the standpoint of translation, a book that has been able to triumph over all its enemies, a LIVING book, the most practical book ever written, a book that reveals to us man's hope of salvation, truly "the Book of Books."

If the dead could speak, they could not reveal to us a better Christ than we know. His life fulfills the prophecies of the Old Testament. They could not tell us of a better character than Christ had. They could not give us better proof of the deity of Christ than His resurrection from the dead. They could not reveal to us a better plan of salvation that God has made known to us through His Holy Spirit–a plan based upon God's love in sacrificing His Son.

If the dead could speak, they could not reveal to us any higher system of morals than God has given. When we compare the morals of the modern dance, movies, television and commercialized amusements with God's great standards, we see how incomparably grand is the wisdom of God in His revelation to us (and how keen are the deceptive powers of the devil!).

If the dead could speak, they could not reveal to us a more perfect rule of conduct that Jesus Christ has given us in the "Golden Rule."

**THE DEAD ARE SPEAKING!**

But the surprising thing about all this is...the dead ARE speaking to us every day...by their influence!

Is Abraham, the father of the patriarchs, dead? No! He lives in the bosom of every Jew and Christian. Go to any great city and you will find men who are the direct descendants of Abraham. And they exalt him in their teachings! Every Christian knows the life of Abraham, and for 4000 years they have not ceased to exalt his great example of faith in offering up his only son!

Is Moses dead? No! Every judge on the bench is acquainted with the judgments given to Israel in the Old Testament through Moses. His great choice of serving God in preference to a life of ease and sin will live as long as man is living upon the earth. His prophecies concerning the fate of the Israelites who disobeyed God (Lev. 26:33) is being vividly portrayed before our very eyes to this very day.[2]

Is Celsus dead? No! His pre-digested skepticism has been the source of all the leading skeptics' harangues since his day. Voltaire, Holmes, Huxley, Paine, Ingersoll, Stalin,[3] and Marx were all mere reflectors of this blatant atheist of the third century. Surely Celsus speaks from his hollow dungeon and comes forth to wreck and ruin our morals and faith.

Is that kindly-faced, loving, dear old soul, your Mother, dead? No! Though she has been gone from this earth for years, your love for the right still lives in answer to her voice; your love for the truth, she instilled in you; your respect for God, your home, your children, and your country reflect a life of a mother who speaks from the dead.[4]

Are these characters of history dead? No! No! No! A thousand times, no! They live and work by their lives. Long after death has closed your eyes, so will you speak to those who live after you! What will your life say when you are gone? Will it say pride, jealousy, hatred, love of sin, cowardliness, love of money, or a genuine Christian who loved God will all his heart and loved his fellow man?

If the dead could speak, there could be only two classes reporting: the saved and the lost! Compare by contrast the words of dying saints with these words from men who had no hope in death. It reminds one of a story of Old England in the days when neighbors used to come around the newly-made graves and try to make some slogan for the tombstone of the one who had just died. One old scoundrel had just died, and the neighbors gathered around, but no one spoke. Finally one man said, "Some of us will go to heaven, and some of us will go to hell. But we all hope we will never see him again!"

Voltaire said, "Take that wretch away. I am abandoned by God and man. I shall go to hell!"

Paine said, "Stay with me, for God's sake! I cannot bear to be left alone."

Mirabou said, "Give me more laudanum. I don't want to think of eternity!"

Hobbs screamed, "I am taking a fearful leap into the dark!"

Newport said, "Oh, the insufferable pangs of hell, of eternity for ever and ever!"

The rich man said, "Father Abraham, have mercy on me, and send Lazarus that he may dip the tip of his finger in water and cool my tongue, for I am in anguish in this flame."

There are only two classes that are dead–the saved and the lost, and there are only two classes that are alive–the saved and the lost. Life is uncertain and death is sure! The young may die, but the old must! Today is the day of salvation.

*Oh why, oh why, will ye die*
*When the Rock of Hope is near by?*
*Oh why will ye die?*

Some day you will speak from the tomb.[5] What will you say? You are deciding your message today!

---

1. By "isms" Word may have had in mind Communism, of which he was an ardent foe in the 50s and 60s.
2. Word believed the scattering and persecution of Israel was fulfillment of this prophecy.
3. Stalin had been dead only four years when Archie wrote these words.
4. Though Word's mother (Maggie) was still living at this time, it is evident from these and other writings that he held her in high esteem. Not so, however, with his father (Luther), a hardshell Baptist, with whom Archie never got along.
5. At Archie Word's funeral, Don DeWelt said, "Archie Word is much more alive than we are! Do not tell me he is dead. I hear him from a hundred pulpits every Sunday!"

*Archie, second from left (hat in hand), during 1932 revival in Bakersfield, CA.*

17

# THE GREATEST SERMON THE WORLD HAS EVER HEARD

*The Voice of Evangelism,* September 21, 1957

"Ye men of Israel, hear these words: Jesus of Nazareth, a man approved of God unto you by mighty works and wonders and signs which God did by him in the midst of you, even as ye yourselves know; him, being delivered up by the determinate counsel and foreknowledge of God, ye by the hand of lawless men did crucify and slay: whom God raised up, having loosed the pangs of death: because it was not possible that he should be holden of it" (Acts 2:22-24).

The greatest sermon the world has ever heard is recorded in Acts 2:14-38.

This is a greater sermon that the Sermon on the Mount because it opened the new kingdom that Jesus Christ had taught His disciples to pray for! Matthew 5 predicts the coming kingdom while Acts 2 records the kingdom as an actual fact.

Why was this sermon the greatest sermon ever preached?

## THE GREATEST INTRODUCTION

It was the greatest sermon ever preached because it had the greatest introduction that any sermon ever had. It was a sermon that God had prepared! For a thousand years the prophets had been introducing the kingdom (Isa. 2:2-4). John the Baptist (whom Jesus said was the greatest prophet ever born of woman) had one outstanding message, and that was introducing the kingdom of God (Matt. 2:2-3).

The twelve apostles were sent to prepare the coming kingdom (Matt. 10:5-7). The seventy whom Jesus had chosen and sent (Luke 10:8-9), were sent to prepare for this kingdom. Even Christ Himself had promised the coming of this kingdom (Matt. 16:13-19), promising that in this kingdom there would be forgiveness, or remission of sins (Luke 24:46-49).

Just preceding the great day of Pentecost, Jesus had talked for 40 days, teaching His disciples about the kingdom that was to come (Acts 1). On the day of Pentecost, as recorded in Acts 2, the new covenant was ratified (Heb. 9:15-20). Christ had been crowned king, and His universal authority (which He had proclaimed in Matt. 28:18) became an actual fact. His chosen apostles, who were to be in the foundational part of the church, were baptized in the Holy Spirit. Why? Because they were to have the responsibility of revealing God's eternal will to man in the Scriptures. So we conclude that it was the greatest sermon ever delivered because of its elaborate preparation and introduction made by Jehovah God of heaven!

## THE GREATEST DATE

It was the greatest sermon ever preached because of the time in which it was preached. The date was planned by God. Scripture says, "But when the fulness of time came, God sent forth his Son, born of a woman, born under the law, that he might redeem them that were under the law, that we might receive the adoption of sons" (Gal. 4:4).

The Bible contains two major covenants. First, the covenant made by Moses, which was preceded by the Passover. When it was given from Mount Sinai, it was accompanied by a miraculous demonstration, a shaking of the entire mountain. Lightning flashed and thunder rolled as the awe-stricken people stood beholding in terror. The second covenant came to us preceded by the death of the Passover Lamb, Jesus Christ. On the day of Pentecost the new covenant was made known through the apostles. Their delivering of this sermon was demonstrated by another miraculous demonstration.[1]

This sermon was preached on Pentecost, which always came on the first day of the week, Sunday (Lev. 23:15). God gave a day of worship to the Jews in the Old Testament, and here He inaugurates a new and universal day for all mankind to use for His glory. It is not a rest day–it is a day in which to worship and serve the Lord God. This is the most important sermon ever preached in that God laid the plans for it to be preached on the "first day of the week" centuries before!

## THE GREATEST THEME

It is the most important sermon ever preached because Jesus Christ is proclaimed as Messiah and Lord for the first time. And for the first time His resurrection is publicly declared, a resurrection predicted by David! Here stood twelve men, whom the multitude recognized as Jesus' most intimate disciples, attesting to the fact that Jesus Christ had been raised from the dead. "This Jesus did God raise up, whereof we all are witnesses" (Acts 2:32). They were so bold as to say in the presence of several thousand people that Jesus Christ had been exalted, that He had been crowned king, and was seated at the right hand of the throne of God! When the sermon drew to a close, it is no wonder that this mighty man of God, Peter, who a few days before had been afraid to face a maid, now filled with the Holy Spirit, says, "Let all the house of Israel know assuredly, that God hath made him both Lord and Christ, this Jesus whom ye crucified" (Acts 2:36). This was the promise that God had made to Jesus – to make Him BOTH Lord and Christ (Messiah).

**THE GREATEST INVITATION**

It is the greatest sermon ever preached because the gospel invitation was proclaimed for the first time, and the promise of the remission of sins through Jesus Christ's shed blood was first preached (Acts 2:37-40). The baptism of the Holy Spirit which had come upon the apostles to qualify them as ambassadors for Jesus Christ caused the crowd to listen to these miraculously endowed men. The gospel was preached. Their sin was condemned. The evidence of Christ's resurrection was proclaimed. Great conviction came upon the audience. They said, "Brethren, what shall we do?" This inspired preacher, who had been given the keys to the kingdom, guided by the Holy Spirit, gives the infallible answer for all time to come! There is no misunderstanding his answer. There is no need to philosophize his reply. All we need to do is listen to his response and obey it! Peter said, "Repent ye, and be baptized every one of you in the name of Jesus Christ unto the remission of your sins; and ye shall receive the gift of the Holy Spirit" (Acts 2:38).

So many times after preaching this sermon that Peter preached on the day of Pentecost, people say to me, "Oh, Brother Word, that couldn't be right; this must be right or this must be right, because that has been my experience." I am reminded of a man who stopped to talk to a carpenter. The carpenter was building a house, and the man who passed by said to him, "Why, I am surprised at a carpenter making a building like that. Why, that couldn't be right." The carpenter stopped and said, "Sir, I am not the architect of this building. I am only the carpenter. Here is the blueprint. Look at it!"

Now that is my predicament. I am not the architect. I am not God. I am just the preacher. And what God has said on ANY subject is superior to what any man has said on that subject. There may be some things that God has recorded in His Word that are difficult to be understood, but whenever any statement is plainly given that I can understand, that I must preach! It is not for me to argue with God about His wisdom. It is for me to preach – and may God grant that every sermon I preach from the pulpit or on the street[2] be in accordance with God's divine will, just as much as this sermon which Peter preached on the day of Pentecost!

Have you heard the gospel–which means, "Have you heard that Christ died for your sins?" Have you heard the gospel, which means, "Have you heard that Jesus Christ was raised from the dead, and through His death for you, you can have your sins forgiven?" If you have, will you say today, "What shall I do?" And let me answer you in the words of the inspired apostle Peter, "Repent ye, and be baptized every one of you in the name of Jesus Christ unto the remission of your sins; and ye shall receive the gift of the Holy Spirit." Then the greatest sermon the world has ever heard will have a new meaning to you, and it will become the greatest sermon you have ever heard!

---

1. A rushing mighty wind, cloven tongues of fire, the apostles speaking in other languages as the Spirit gave them utterance (Acts 2:1-4).
2. Street preaching was still in vogue in 1957.

**Don't blame me**
**IF YOU GO TO HELL!**
**I WARNED YOU!**

A. WORD, West Coast Evangelist

Sunday night, December 1st
"The Conversion of an Anti-Christ"
Tues. Dec. 3
"How Is a Man Born Again"
Wed. Dec. 4
"What Are You Waiting for?"
Thurs. Dec. 5
"The Painted Face"
Fri. Dec. 6
"Christian Unity"
Sat. Dec. 7
"Heading for the Last Round-up"
Sun. Dec. 8
11 a. m. "One Who Never Forgets"
2:30 p. m. "Ten Rules for Making a Success of the Christian Life"
7:30 p. m. "Heaven"

**After all, it must be HEAVEN or HELL!**

• • •

*Christianity Without Denominationalism*

**Englewood Church of Christ**
**35th and Killingsworth St.**

*Revival handbill from 1935 meeting in Portland, OR.*

# 18

# WHAT SHOULD THE CHURCH BE PREACHING TODAY?

*The Voice of Evangelism,* November 2, 1957

We hear so much preached today that ought to be put in swill barrels, and we hear so little preached that really gets down to business and stirs folks for God and righteousness. Let us take time out to consider the highlights of what the church ought to preach today.[1]

**LOYALTY TO CHRIST**

I believe that one of the most prominent, conspicuous, and outstanding themes that the churches of Christ ought to be preaching today is loyalty to Jesus Christ – to His person, to His spirit, to His program, to His cause, and to His Word. This should be the first and foremost concern of any TRUE CHURCH that claims to be a part of the blood-bought audience that belongs to Christ. This loyalty should be uppermost and prominent always in the hearts of those who seek to evangelize the world. Of course, this applies only to those who love our Lord Jesus Christ with a deep sincerity and devotion!

Those who love the Lord and form His church on earth should be united in the bonds of entire Christian unity, with Jesus Christ alone as their Head and Center, His Word their rule, with explicit belief of and manifest conformity to it in all things. Nothing else will work.

As ministers of Jesus, we can neither be ignorant of nor unaffected by the divisions and corruptions of His church. Christ's dying commandments and His last ardent prayer for the visible unity of His professing people will not allow you to be indifferent in this matter of paramount importance. In this hour we cannot and we dare not be silent upon this subject so vitally connected with His glory. You lovers of Jesus and beloved of Him: you desire unity in Christ with all those who love Him, too. Don't you? An attachment to Christ that can be seen by our lives of holiness and charity is the original criterion of Christian character. That is the distinguishing badge of our holy profession, the foundation and cement of the unity that is in Christ.

If there is any high and holy eloquence in the preacher, it should come forth from the pulpit when he pleads in behalf of the honor and the glory of our Lord! We should, with all our hearts, be seeking to return to the simple apostolic Christianity of the New Testament. It should be every minister's ardent plea and the desire of his heart that the Lord Jesus Christ be honored in His rightful place of power, prestige, and authority in the midst of His people as the only head of His holy church! That would be putting proper emphasis on the proper subject. Every other item in the program of the church should be subordinate to this central plea of LOYALTY TO CHRIST! Christ must be made first, last, in the midst, and all in all if the church is to be what God expects it to be.

## NO CREED BUT CHRIST

The church should be preaching and professing no other creed than Christ. I do not hesitate to say that too much has been made of the human substitute creeds in the past centuries. There should be more loyalty to Him as the "Whom" we believe. It is not "in WHAT do you believe?" but "in WHOM do you believe?" This drifting away from loyalty to Christ and accepting Him as our only creed may not have been a premeditated act or a conscious disloyalty on the part of denominations, but it is no less a fact that Christ has been displaced by human councils and documents. We, as His church, should again emphasize that Jesus Christ is all and all, and that all party loyalty must inevitably be disowned, and a renewal of our vows to Christ Himself must take their place. The church should be exalting Christ and annihilating those divisive creeds and dogmas that have for centuries divided His professed believers!

Someone may say, "Well, Brother Word, that is my sentiment too, but just what do you mean by saying that loyalty to Christ and 'no creed but Christ' should be preached today? How can we do that?" My answer to you is not in the least bit hazy or befogged! I propose in that statement nothing but loyalty to His Word and to His gospel! "Christ alone being the head, the center; His Word the rule; and an explicit belief of and manifest conformity to it, in all things, the terms."[2] Christ supreme, His Word the standard, loyalty to it the condition. In exalting Christ we must not do as many of late years in the modernistic schools[3] have done – minimize His Word. No true leader for Christ should have any sympathy with any effort to belittle the authority of the Word of God! That almost threadbare platitude that "Christianity is not the religion of a book" should have a strange sound to our ears – ears that listen for His voice through His Word. We should be sounding out to an upset and confused world that Christianity is based upon and conditioned upon "The Book."

## THE AUTHENTICITY OF SACRED SCRIPTURE

Some of the so-called friends of Jesus have said that if every book of the Bible should prove to be a forgery, we would still have Christ – faith in Him would remain unimpaired. But that is not so! It would be just as impossible to have a beautiful rose while depriving it of the soil that keeps it beautiful. Truly, the only Christ we know is the Christ of the Book! The only authentic source of knowledge concerning Christ and His religion is found in a book – the Word of God. Our faith, if it is to stand, can never be independent of the Bible. If the records of Christ's life and works are spurious, then the only Christ we know is an artifical and make-believe Christ. THERE CAN BE NO CHRIST IN HISTORY IF THERE WAS NO CHRIST OF HISTORY! We can only know of historical events as they are preserved in records of some character. If we discredit the only history in which the thoughts, experiences and events of the life of our Lord have been recorded, we discredit Him and can never be sure of Him nor His teaching.

In order for the church to be loyal to Christ, we must be loyal to His Word. To be loyal to Christ and DISloyal to His Word is an utter impossibility. To proclaim the Lordship of Jesus and repudiate the Word by which alone that Lordship can be established is a manifest absurdity. The supremacy of Jesus involves the integrity of His Word. In exalting Christ, acceptance of God's authority in the divine revelation (known as the Bible) is imperative! The church today should be teaching loyalty to Christ, no creed but Christ, and forcefully proclaiming the authenticity of the sacred Scriptures.

## CONFORMITY TO THE TEACHINGS OF CHRIST

The church today should be teaching belief in and conformity to Christ's teaching as their central message. Closely related to this false assertion that the religion of Jesus is not the religion of a book (and apparently prompted by the same motive – that of disparaging the Word of God) is the demand that we preach Christ and not something about Him. If you want a brainstorm in the head of a preacher – and a vacuum in the heads of the listeners – try to preach Jesus without saying anything about Him!

Paul said to the Corinthians, "I determined not to know anything among you, save Jesus Christ, and him crucified" (I Cor. 2:2). In Paul's preaching, he must have said something to them about a Christ who was crucified! He reminded the Colossians that they had been "buried" with Him in baptism. Therefore, he must have said something to them about a Christ who had been buried! To the Athenians he preached "Jesus and the resurrection." He must have said something about a risen Christ! Paul would have made a sorry spectacle of himself in the Areopagus trying to preach Christ to the Greeks without telling them something about Him.

It is Paul who gives us an exhaustive analysis of the gospel that he had preached in proclaiming Christ. He said, "Christ died for our sins according to the scriptures; and that he was buried; and that he hath been raised on the third day according to the scriptures." Paul seems to say that it is the Christian's business to take the divine Word of God for our rule, the Holy Spirit for our teacher, and Christ (as exhibited in the Word of God) for our salvation.

The church today should be preaching as the early Christians preached! Preaching meant something very definite to the early preachers! It involved a faithful and loyal presentation of those great truths that radiate from Christ as the divine Son of God! It included the full exhibition of the facts, commandments and promises[4] of the gospel. They never once considered the possibility of preaching Christ to sinners outside of relation to these sacred oracles. They showed the world their undaunted loyalty to Him by their strict adherence to the teaching of the Word itself. The church today should be taking that stand which has withstood the assaults of 2000 years, and return to a "thus saith the Lord" position if we desire victory.

**A "THUS SAITH THE LORD"**

A return to a "thus saith the Lord" would naturally cause us to give a most conspicuous place to the Word of God, because only in it is to be found what God has said! The church should regard Christ as God's Incarnate Word. We should receive the Bible as His written word. We should appeal to each of these with equal confidence. Great sorrow should overwhelm us as we see the eclipse of Christ's glory in the mist of foggy old creeds and dogmas. We listen in vain amid the shouting of sectarian shibboleths for the precious name of Jesus. We should become sick and tired of the bitter jarrings and janglings of the party spirit, and with all our hearts seek to restore unity, peace and purity. In the midst of this turmoil and confusion known as denominationalism, let us turn to the Word of God as offering the only hope of restoring the glory of Christ and the unity of His professed followers. We should "speak where the Scriptures speak and be silent where the Scriptures are silent."[5] If you are a strong man, and you love Christ tenderly, the possibilities that are wrapped up in that statement should cause your breast to be filled with strong emotions. "Where the Scriptures speak, we will speak, and where the Scriptures are silent, we will be silent" would put an end to the strife over opinions, theories, inferences, and fanciful interpretations. It would put to rout the preaching of the opinions and inventions of men. The pulpit would have its apostolic assurance again, and every statement would be backed up with a "thus saith the Lord," either in expressed terms or in apostolic precedence.[6]

Therefore, I claim that the church ought to stand for the Bible as the inspired and inerrant[7] Word of God. They should let a "thus saith the Lord" stop all controversy regarding matters of faith. This will promote Christian unity better than all the super organizations that the wisest of theologians of this age, or any age past, can devise. In seeking to promote and encourage such unity, this basis will at once honor Christ and secure an answer to His prayer in John 17.

## THE NAMES OF CHRIST'S FOLLOWERS

A strict following of the Word of God would solve the question as to what names His children are to wear. The names worn by the followers of Jesus should be those that indicate the greatest esteem for Him personally. These are set forth in the Word of God and all of them are appropriate for the true followers of Christ.[8] Such names as we hear now applied to the various sects and denominations were not known in the days of the apostles. They always dim the luster of that Name that is above every name.

So long as these denominational substitute names continue, divisions will be perpetuated, for they were born in strife and applied for the purpose of differentiating those particular factions interested in perpetuating themselves. The church should be pleading with this divided condition to hearken to the abundant designations in Christ's Word for His people and His church.[9] These names beautifully suggest the relationship of the disciples to one another, to Him, and to His truth; names that none of His followers are willing to discard, but that all gladly recognize and gratefully accept; names that are unifying, that are the common property of all who love the Lord; names that will live when all of those human nomenclatures (so popular now) have passed into oblivion. For this reason, the true church today should be saying, "Let us call Bible things by Bible names."

## CHURCH ORGANIZATION

The church today should be preaching the organization of the church as it was in the beginning. Church figure-heads and denominational corporational machinery have been kicked out or killed in some totalitarian countries. The result is devastation when the movement depends on these supervisors, but if we should preach and teach the church as it is given to us in the Word, each congregation becomes an independent body, directing its own affairs, excercising discipline over its own members, subject only to the will of Jesus Christ as head and center to the teaching of His Word. No ecclesiastical tribunal is superior to the congregation.

**THE UNITY OF GOD'S PEOPLE**

The church today ought to be preaching the unity of the people of God, Jesus Christ being made the head of the corner, the basis of unity the New Testament church in its name, creed, ordinances, organization and life as set forth in the Holy Scriptures. This is what we need right now! Let the Bible be substituted for all human creeds, facts for definitions, things for words, faith for speculation, unity of faith for unity of opinion, the positive commandments of God for human legislation and tradition, piety for ceremony, morality for partisan zeal, the practice of religion for the mere profession of it, and the work is done!

We know there will never be a converted world until there is a united church.[10] Unity is set forth in the New Testament as a fundamental conception of the church. Christ prayed for it. The apostles strove to preserve it. Don't you think we should ever keep it before us, and that the church today should preach the unity of God's people based on the Word of God?

---

1. During 1957 Word wrote a tract, *Are Mr. Allen's Miracles From God?* This was to counter faith healer A. A. Allen, who visited Portland's Civic Auditorium. He also wrote a small booklet, *How, When and Where We Got Our Bible* to counter the popular newspaper ads taken out by the Knights of Columbus in the *Portland Oregonian*.
2. No source given for this quotation.
3. A reference that may have included his *alma mater*.
4. Word, like many Restoration preachers of his day, used these three points to illustrate the gospel: facts to be believed, commandments to be obeyed, promises to be enjoyed.

5. Though not much for promoting the Restoration Movement *per se,* Word here shows his admiration for this slogan that came from Thomas Campbell.
6. Notably absent are "necessary inferences," which, he has already inferred, gender strife.
7. This long before the controversy over inerrancy.
8. Word believed this to be true not only for individual Christians but for the corporate body of Christ as well. That is why, for many years, the sign in front of the Montavilla church building listed all the names of the church in the New Testament!
9. Word never contended for the exclusive use of "Church of Christ" as did some of his brethren and peers.
10. Precisely the reason why Don DeWelt, a Timothy of Archie Word, began the publication *ONE BODY* in 1984. DeWelt's "father in the faith" had an article, "How to Have Christian Unity," in the mint issue.

# YOU OUGHT TO BE THERE!

Every Evening Except Monday

*Miss*
ELIZABETH
HALL
Music
Director
*Conductor of*
Orchestras
Choruses
Quartettes
Trios
*and*
Duets

A Fine
Dramatic
Soprano
Voice
Graduate
*of*
Kentucky
University
*in* Music
New in
Portland

ARCHIE WORD, *Preaching*

BEGINNING AUGUST 13th A. M.

**THE CHURCH AT**

**550 N. E. 76th Ave.**

*Front page of 4-page handbill announcing Archie's 1939 revival–in his own church!*

# 19

# THE CHURCH JESUS SAID HE WOULD BUILD

*The Church Speaks,* January 1960, March 1960

There are so many different organizations on the earth today calling themselves churches that it is indeed confusing to the earnest man or woman who wants to know what kind of church Jesus did build. But if one will read the New Testament, he will find the church Jesus said He would build. It is not many different human organizations for "God is not a God of confusion, but of peace," and OPPOSING doctrines cannot be of God. Neither are there MANY gospels for Paul says, "I marvel that ye are so soon removed from him that called you into the grace of Christ unto ANOTHER gospel: Which is NOT another; but there be some that trouble you, and would pervert the gospel of Christ. But though we, or an angel from heaven, preach ANY OTHER gospel unto you than that which we have preached unto you, let him be ACCURSED"[1] (Gal. 1:6-8). So we must conclude that there is only ONE gospel.

Some preachers today preach "another Jesus" and mask their unfaithful teachings under the term "Modern Theology." Sometimes I am tempted to believe that we are living in the latter times that Paul spoke of in I Timothy 4:1-3, "Now the Spirit speaketh expressly, that in the latter times some shall depart from the faith, giving heed to seducing spirits and doctrines of devils; Speaking lies in hypocrisy; having their conscience seared with a hot iron; FORBIDDING TO MARRY, and COMMANDING TO ABSTAIN FROM MEATS,[2] which God hath created to be received with thanksgiving of them which believe and know the truth." And the descriptions of the latter times in II Timothy 3:1-5 could be called an epitome, or a brief resume, of the conditions displayed daily in the lines of newspapers[3] in America.

Where shall we go for a standard in judging the kind of church Jesus said He would build? Shall we go to the churches that men have built? Paul says, "For we dare not make ourselves of the number, or COMPARE OURSELVES WITH SOME THAT COMMEND THEMSELVES; but they, MEASURING THEMSELVES BY THEMSELVES, among themselves, are not wise" (II Cor. 10:12). Now we do not want to be like that, so let us go to THE WORD OF GOD, the only true source concerning the church Christ built, and see what it says concerning HIS church.

## CHRIST-CENTERED

First, we notice that it was a church that was centered in Christ. Christ was the creed of the church. God announced that creed at Jesus' baptism and at the Mount of Transfiguration. Moses and all the prophets predicted Jesus Christ, a prophet in whom all men would believe, for that is what the word "creed" means. "A prophet shall the Lord your God raise up unto you of your brethren, like unto me; him shall ye hear in all things whatsoever he shall say unto you. And it shall come to pass, that every soul which will not hear that prophet, shall be destroyed from among the people" (Acts 3:22). When the apostles went forth to preach, they preached Jesus Christ, and told men and women that they should believe on Him. More than that, Paul said that a public confession of their faith in Christ was essential to their salvation. "That if thou shalt confess with thy mouth the Lord Jesus, and shalt believe in thine heart that God hath raised him from the dead, thou shalt be saved. For with the heart man believeth unto righteousness; and with the mouth confession is made unto salvation" (Rom. 10:9-10).

The members of this church Jesus said He would build were baptized into Christ by command of His apostles. "And he (Peter) commanded them to be baptized in the name of the Lord" (Acts 10:48). This is also corroborated by the mighty apostle Paul: "Are ye ignorant that all we who were baptized into Christ Jesus were baptized into his death?" (Rom. 6:3). Paul also says that baptism (which all these Greek-speaking people understood as immersion) was the place where they PUT ON CHRIST (Gal. 3:27).

This church Christ said He would build was a Christ-honoring church. They bore His name, individually. "And the disciples were called Christians first in Antioch" (Acts 11:26). "Yet if any man suffer as a Christian, let him not be ashamed: but let him glorify God in this name" (I Pet. 4:16). They were proud to wear His name, collectively. "The churches of Christ salute you" (Rom. 16:16). They honored Christ by having His Spirit (Acts 2:38), and were told that without His Spirit they were none of His. "Now if any man hath not the Spirit of Christ, he is none of his" (Rom. 8:9). They honored Christ in their belief that He would come again, as He had promised. "This same Jesus, which is taken up from you into heaven, shall so come in like manner as ye have seen him go into heaven" (Acts 1:11). This doctrine of Christ's return became the greatest consolation to His persecuted saints.

## A GOSPEL CHURCH

Second, the church Jesus said He would build was a gospel church. Some people do not know what the gospel really is, so it is a comfort to know what the inspired apostle Paul tells us in I Corinthians 15:1-4. "Moreover, brethren, I declare unto you the gospel which I preached unto you, which also ye have received, and wherein ye stand; By which also ye are saved, if ye keep in memory what I preached unto you, unless ye have believed in vain. For I delivered unto you first of all that which I also received, how that Christ died for our sins according to the scriptures; and that he was buried, and that he rose again the third day, according to the scriptures." Here Paul emphasizes the death, burial, and resurrection of Christ. The members of this church believed the evidence they had been given and obeyed the commands of the gospel. They repented of all sin and became converted men and women, showing a new life to those among whom they lived. They publicly confessed their faith in Jesus Christ, believing His promise that He would confess them before the heavenly Father. Then they were baptized, buried with Christ in the likeness of His death, signifying by this act that they believed Christ had died, was buried, and was resurrected.

The act of baptism also taught the unbeliever that the one who was baptized believed that the old man of sin was buried, and that a new creature came forth from the grave to walk in newness of life. And to the skeptic they said, "We believe that some day we will die, but we who possess the Spirit of Christ will be raised up, even as Christ was raised up!"

They distinguished between conversion and salvation. Conversion, they taught, was the fruit of repentance. Paul, on the way to Damascus, gives us a living illustration of true repentance and conversion. He was actually sorry for his sins—so sorry that he quit them and became a man of prayer in the name of Christ whom he had persecuted! That was conversion. But when Paul had been three days and nights in Damascus, and had neither eaten food nor drunk water, there appeared unto him a man who was sent by God, Ananias, who said to Paul, "Why tarriest thou? arise, and be baptized, and wash away thy sins..." (Acts 22:16). This teaches us that salvation is not just a feeling but an edict of God: obedience to His commands of faith, repentance, and baptism. When Paul obeyed Christ as a believer, THEN he went forth rejoicing and preaching, blood-washed and Spirit-filled.

This church which Christ built rejoiced in the gospel promises of remission of sins, the gift of the Holy Spirit, and everlasting life.

## A PEOPLE'S CHURCH

The church Jesus said He would build was a people's church. It was not made up of the aristocracy only for Jesus had said, "Go ye into all the world and preach the gospel to EVERY creature." He also said, "For the Son of Man came to seek and save that which was lost." It was not made up of the learned only, but all creatures were admonished to accept eternal life in Christ. By coming into Christ they became members of His church. They did not have to know all about the Trinity. They did not have to learn 42 articles of faith. Nor were they required to memorize the small and large catechism. This church was complete in itself. Saved sinners made up its constituency. There was nothing to exclude the miserably poor and wretched of the East. They accepted Christ's motto, "Come unto me, all ye that labor and are heavy laden, and I will give you rest." Jesus was always poor, and the common people heard Him gladly.[4]

## AN OBEDIENT CHURCH

The church Jesus said He would build was an obedient church. Their lives in Christ began in obedience. "Then they that received his word were baptized: and there were added unto them in that day about three thousand souls" (Acts 2:41). In simple trust they believed, as Paul later described, "When he shall come to be glorified in his saints and to be admired in all them that believe in that day" (II Thess. 1:9). They continued obediently in the apostles' doctrine. "And they continued steadfastly in the apostles' teaching and fellowship, and in the breaking of bread and the prayers" (Acts 2:42).

They carried out the Great Commission by command. They obeyed is spite of prisons, floggings, threatenings and desertion. They obeyed in spite of hypocrites in the church and enemies out of the church. They obeyed in the face of false teachers, threats of expulsion, public beatings and ostracism. They believed–and they obeyed because they felt it was "better to obey than to sacrifice." Oh, how weak our love for Christ is in comparison!

## A FREE CHURCH

The church Jesus said He would build was a free church.[5] A diligent search of the Scriptures will reveal that the church in the Bible had no earthly headquarters. The church in Jerusalem was the "Mother Church" in the sense that it was the FIRST church, but as other congregations were established, the church in Jerusalem did not wield an official club over their heads. There were no church and state alliances; there were no presiding elders nor bishops in the sense that they are now referred to; nor do we find any general superintendents. Men had not invented denominational heads and bodies, state secretaries and regional directors. They were not slaves to a priestly clergy, nor to ignorance which gendered superstition. They were not bound by any man-made divisive creeds. They were not subject to fate, nor to the impotency of total depravity. They were free to receive (or free to reject) the gospel of Jesus Christ.

They were free to obey "the whole council of God." They were not bound by any denominational traditions. The preacher's bread and butter did not depend on higher officials over him. His "superior" could not say, "My dear brother, we will starve you to death if you do not get in line with our denomination!" The truth had made them free in Christ Jesus, and they stayed free for nearly 300 years!

**A PRAYING CHURCH**

The church Jesus said He would build was a praying church. "These all continued with one accord in prayer and supplication..." (Acts 1:14). "And they continued steadfastly...in the prayers" (Acts 2:42). The Holy Spirit came after 10 days of preparation in prayer. Christ Himself set the example, even to spending whole nights in prayer. I wonder what the Lord would think if He had come to your church prayer meeting last week! It is a matter of history that Peter was liberated from prison by prayer.[6] In comparison with these great examples of prayer, is it not a pitiful thing to look around today and see so many churches that dismiss their prayer meetings entirely during the summer? And in most cases can only scare up a dozen or so people to come to prayer meeting at any time? The early Christians prayed without ceasing. That was the kind of stuff those early Christians were made of! They believed God's ear was bent down to hear their prayers. "For the eyes of the Lord are over the righteous, and his ears are open unto their prayers" (I Pet. 3:12).

If you want to be sure whether the church you are attending is a church like Christ would have it, go down next prayer meeting night and take a look. See how many of the members are there to fellowship in prayer. Then go down to the next bazaar or party and see the numbers of "hangers-on" and the "dry rot" that has accumulated in the church!

We say that prayer is powerful, but the early church BELIEVED that prayer was powerful–and they used that power! If you want to make the church you attend a powerful church, YOU become a man or woman of prayer!

## A UNITED CHURCH

Seventh, the church Jesus said He would build was a united church. The church was built upon Jesus Christ and no other foundation (I Cor. 3:11). It was built upon the apostles and prophets, Jesus Christ Himself being the chief cornerstone.

It was the devil's business to try to cause division in the church. But it was the apostles' business to see that division was stopped. Men and women were called to follow Christ instead of following after great preachers (I Cor. 1:10-13). Paul did not want to the church to divide into the Paulites, Cephasites, or Apollosites;[7] he wanted them to follow Jesus only. They were not allowed to divide over human theologies or human opinions, nor to make their human opinions tests of fellowships.

Great men have advocated different forms of church government; other great men have made speaking in tongues a test of fellowship; while other great men have made foot-washing or no piano in the church a test of fellowship. The results today are many factions in the church and denominations instead of one great united church. In the beginning of the church, both Jews and Gentiles worshipped together. They were not divided over printing houses or missionary societies (things that had not been invented to cause division among God's people). But in the face of some false doctrine that was beginning to creep in among the Christians in Rome, Paul wrote, "Now I beseech you, brethren, mark them that are causing the divisions and occasions of stumblings, contrary to the doctrine which ye learned: and turn away from them. For they that are such serve not our Lord Christ, but their own belly; and by their smooth and fair speech they beguile the hearts of the innocent" (Rom. 16:17-18). If Paul's admonition had been heeded, there would not be the 400 different kinds of so-called followers of Christ today!

**A SUFFERING CHURCH**

The church Jesus said He would build was a suffering church. Its founder was crucified. Most of the apostles were murdered. The number of martyrs who gave their lives for the cause of Christ ran into the thousands in the first 300 years of the Christian era. The blood of the martyrs became the hot bed in which the Christian religion grew.

Paul told Timothy, "All that would live godly in Christ Jesus shall suffer persecution" (II Tim. 3:12). But those early Christians did not quit because they were not cordially received. They believed they were to suffer, yes, even to DIE in order to advance this faith in Jesus Christ! The church of the first century was not built around amusements, church socials or church suppers. They had business to attend to and it was important business–God's business! We can thank God today that they did not fail. What will our children think of us 100 years from now if we let this heavenly message die, refusing to suffer for it?

**A GIVING CHURCH**

The church Jesus said He would build was a giving church. From the very beginning men had been taught that one-tenth of their incomes belonged to their Creator. Abraham, the father of the faithful, observed the tithe 430 years before his illustrious family traveled down to Egypt. For 1500 years the Jews had been taught from Moses and the prophets that one-tenth belonged to God. When Jesus came, He commended them for tithing but condemned them for not keeping the weightier matters. Paul, the apostle to the Gentiles, said those who preached the gospel should live by the gospel in the same way that those who waited upon the altar lived from the altar (I Cor. 9:13-14).

The early Christians did not depend upon some beggar's system for supporting the church, nor did they have to be royally entertained in order to get Christians to give to the cause of Christ. They believed that one-tenth of their income belonged to God – that they were thieves when they took that which belonged to God. "Will a man rob God? yet ye rob me. But ye say, Wherein have we robbed thee? In tithes and offerings" (Mal. 3:8). And because they were GIVERS, they were "LIVERS," for Jesus said, "Where a man's treasure is, there will his heart be also." No treasure? No heart! This was one way they laid up treasures in heaven.

**A HOLY CHURCH**

The church Jesus said He would build was a holy church. The men who were preachers of the church Jesus said He would build were in earnest that Christian people should live differently from heathens and pagans with whom they were forced to do business and associate with. That is why Paul said, "Be not unequally yoked with unbelievers: for what fellowship have righteousness and iniquity? or what communion hath light with darkness? And what concord hath Christ with Belial? or what portion hath a believer with an unbeliever? and what agreement hath a temple of God with idols? for we are a temple of the living God; even as God has said, I will dwell in them, and walk in them; and I will be their God, and they shall be my people. Wherefore, Come out from among them, and be ye separate, saith the Lord, And touch no unclean thing; And I will receive you, And will be to you a Father, And ye shall be to me sons and daughters, saith the Lord Almighty. Having therefore these promises, beloved, let us cleanse ourselves from all defilement of flesh and spirit, perfecting holiness in the fear of God" (I Cor. 6:14-7:1). There is no mistaking Paul's teaching here. They were to be different from the people among whom they lived. They were to be so busy serving God that they would have no time to compromise with the devil. When they lived a different kind of life, the church went forward!

Today we have much talk about the "social gospel," a "new gospel," and "the spirit of the age,"[8] but if we really want to be practical, we will ask ourselves, "When did this church of Jesus Christ makes its most glorious advancement?" Go back to history and you will see that the church went forward when the church was pure and holy! The church has always gone backward when worldliness has come into the ranks.

## A TRIUMPHANT CHURCH

Last, the church Jesus said He would build was a triumphant church. Its members were not defeatists. Even in death Paul could say, "Henceforth there is laid up for me the crown of righteousness, which the Lord, the righteous judge, shall give me at that day; and not to me only, but also to all them that have loved his appearing" (II Tim. 4:8). There was no despondency here! Paul was looking forward to the time of his coronation!

This brave church overcame the hostility of both Jews and Gentiles. They overcame the opposition of the high priests, the Pharisees, and Greek philosophy. They overcame depraved humanity–and challenged the devil himself! They could not be stopped by Roman power or persecution. They conquered the known world without any modern helps. The Church stands today, victorious; and after 2000 years is proven to be an eternal institution, God-given and God-protected, made up of those who have joined Jesus Christ and have found peace in His salvation.

These Christians, members of the church Jesus said He would build, had their triumph in their death! Death is the one thing that breaks the skeptic–the one thing that makes infallible proof for the child of God. The death of Romaine is an example of the victory these early Christians had in death. During the seven weeks of his severe suffering, not one fretful word or murmur was heard from his lips. But often he would say, "How good is God to me. What entertainments and comforts does He give me. Oh, what prospect of glory and immortality is before me! He is my God through life, through death, and through eternity." When inquiries were made as to how he felt, his general reply was, "As well as I expect to be this side of heaven."[9] To a brother minister he said, "I do not repent of one word that I have printed or preached about Jesus, for I now feel the blessed comfort of that precious doctrine."

"I have lived," he said to another, "to experience all I have spoken, and all that I have written, and I bless God for it." Afterwards he observed, "I knew the doctrines I preached to be truths, but now I experience them to be blessings." As he lay waiting for his dismissal from this earth, a friend said to him, "I hope, Sir, you now find the salvation of Jesus inestimably precious to you." "Yes," replied Romaine in a feeble voice. "He is more precious to my soul." "More precious than rubies?" his friend asked. He caught the word and completed the Scriptural idea. "And all that can be desired is not comparable to Him!"

How could he thus go from this earth? Because he was a member of the church, Christ's body on earth. Death to him was only a release from this old body of pain and troubles–an entrance into an eternal home with the Jesus who had loved him and died for him.

---

1. The capitalization in the scripture text, as well as in the sermon text, was Word's way of making emphasis of the words he wanted people to take note of.
2. Without commenting on this section, Word was probably intimating that "forbidding to marry" and "abstaining from meats" were Roman Catholic doctrines.
3. In Word's case, the *Portland Oregonian*, which he would vigorously snap when he came across something with which he disagreed.
4. Brother Word's ministry was marked by his love for the common man, including the down-and-outer. He befriended and won to Christ many whom others could not (or would not) reach.
5. For many years the words "Free in Christ and Unafraid!" adorned the masthead of Archie Word's beloved *The Church Speaks*.
6. Word once joked that if he had to depend on the prayers of the church to get him out of prison, he would have to wait until the ants carried him out the keyhole!
7. Nor did A. Word appreciate those who dubbed members at Montavilla "Wordites."

8. Fascination with socialism in the 60s soon began to affect the church.
9. Brother Word's own final words were, "I will probably wake up in eternity–or, on the other hand, I may be better in the morning."

**REQUIREMENTS FOR SALVATION**

GOD'S PART

GRACE — Eph. 2:8-9; I Cor. 1:4; John 3:16

PREACHING — Mark 16:15; Acts 2:14; Acts 8:35; I Cor. 1:21

SINNER'S PART

HEAR — Matt. 17:5; Rom. 10:17

BELIEVE — Acts 2:37

REPENT — Acts 2:38; Acts 17:30-31

CONFESS — Romans 10:1; Matt. 10:32-3

BE BAPTIZED — Acts 22:16; I Peter 3:21

LIVE GODLY — I Tim. 6:11-5; Phil. 4:8-9; Gal. 5:21-22

HEBREWS 5:9

**No Book but the Bible!**
**No Message but the Gospel!**

Revised by A. Word and Lertis Ellett

**THE CHURCH REVEALED IN THE SCRIPTURES**

ORIGIN
TIME—A. D. 30. Acts 2: FOUNDER—CHRIST—Matthew 16:18.
PLACE—Jerusalem. Acts 2:5. FOUNDATION—I Cor. 3:11 and Eph. 2:19-20.

ORGANIZATION
HEAD, CHRIST. Eph. 1:2-23. "All Authority" Matt. 28:18. Legislative - Executive - Judicial.
OFFICERS: Evangelists, Eh. 4:11; Elders, Acts 20:17-28, I Tim. 3:1-7, Titus 1:5-9;
Deacon. I Tim. 3:8-13, Acs 6:18; Deaconesses, Rom. 16:1-2.
MEMBERS: Penitent Baptied Believers. Mark 16:16; Acts 2:41, 4:4, 5:14; Gal. 3:27.
GOVERNMENT: Congregaional. Acts 6:3-6, 13:1-3, 14:23; I Cor. 5:4-5; II Cor. 8:19.
WORSHIP: Acts 2:42, 20:
UNITY: Acts 4:32; Eph. 4:5-6 **ONE** Body. Spirit. Hope. Lord. Faith. Baptism. God. **Division Carnal** Roman 16:17-18; I Cor. 1-10-13, 3:1-3

NAMES
Of Individuals: Disciples Acts 6:1—Learners; Saints " 9:13—Character; Brethren " 6:3—Relationship; Christians " 11:26—Ownership
**The Gospel Only** Isa. 62:2; Acts 11:26; I Peter 4:16; James 2:7
**Makes Christians Only**
Of Churches: The Church — Acts 9:31 — Universal; Church o God — I Cor. 1:2 — Planner; Church of the first born — Heb. 12:23 — Honor; Body of Christ — I Cor. 12:27 — Activity; Churches of Christ — Romans 16:16 — Ownership; Churches of the saints — I Cor. 14:33 — Character

CREED
**Jesus Christ** Preached—Acts 2:2, 8:5; II Cor. 11:4.
Believed—John 20:30-31; Acts 8:12.
Confessed—Matt. 16:16; John 1:49.
I Tim. 6:12-13; II Tim. 1:12.
**Needs No Revision** Heb. 13:8, 7:25-28; I Cor. 1:24

MEMORIALS
The Lord's Day: Set Apart —John 20:26; Claimed —Rev. 1:10; Observed —Acts 20:7
The Lord's Supper: Instituted —Luke 22:19; Participation —I Cor. 10:16; Unity —I Cor. 10:17; Seal —I Cor. 11:25; Proclamation —I Cor. 11:26; Life Sustaining —I Cor. 11:30

DISCIPLINE
THE NEW TESTAMENT The Only Rule of Faith and Practice: Gal. 6:16; Phil. 3:16; II Tim. 3:16-17;
Every New Covenant Command is an Ordinance
Human Legislation is Sinful. Matt. 15:9; Mark 7:1-12; I Cor. 4:6; Gal. 1:8-9; Rev. 22:18-19.

FINANCES
Ordained—I Cor. 9:14; II Cor. 9:6-10; How Much? In Type—Heb. 7:1-10; Gal. 3:7-9.
Admonished—I Cor. 16:2; Gal. 6:6-8; Who? When? Why? How?
Blessed—Acts 20:35; Mal. 3:10; Luke 6:38; Luke 16:9; Matt. 6:19-21.

PURPOSE
Preach the Gospel—Mark 16:15. **"ALL THE NATIONS"** Luke 24:46-47 Baptize Them—Matt. 28:19.
Make Disciples—Matt. 28:19. Teach Them—Matt. 28:20.
Commit to Faithful and Able Men in Self-Governing, Self-Supporting, Self-Extending Churches!
II Tim. 2:28; Acts 13:3-4; Jude. 3.

**"MAKE ALL THINGS ACCORDING TO THE PATTERN"** *Hebrews 8:5*

NO ADDITIONS NO SUBTRACTIONS NO SUBSTITUTIONS
Rev. 22:18-19 and I Cor. 4:6.

**RESULTS OF SALVATION**

JUSTIFIED — Romans 5:1

SANCTIFIED — Acts 26:18

FORGIVEN — I John 2:12

RECONCILED — Romans 5:10

REDEEMED — I Peter 1:18-19

ADOPTED — Gal. 4:5

SAVED — Titus 3:5

**No Creed but the Christ!**

**No Names but those Divinely Given!**

E. P. S., San Bernardino, 10-M. 4-33

*Church chart used by Archie Word in his revivals. Word and Lertis Ellet revised V.E. Hoven's chart during 1933 revival in San Bernardino, CA.*

## 20

# I AM AN ADVENTIST!

*The Church Speaks,* July 1960

I am an adventist! This may surprise some of you folk who have known me for the past twenty-five years,[1] but if it does, it is because you do not know what an adventist is!

Jesus was an adventist. He said, "I will come again," and that is what "adventist" means. I believe that Jesus is going to come back to this earth again, and anyone who believes that is an adventist.

Because I believe that Jesus is coming again, I am an adventist–but NOT a "Seventh Day Adventist." Jesus is coming again, and that promise, in such trying times as these,[2] ought to make every child of God rejoice. It is a Bible doctrine, and to the Word of God I want to take you because "If any man speak not as the oracles of God, it is because there is no light in him."

I am not going to deal with WHEN Jesus will return. That is in the hands of God. I do believe that Jesus will not come back until this old earth becomes so exceedingly wicked, so frightfully ungodly, that it is not worth sparing any longer; and that time is in the hands and wisdom of God. He may not think as we think. The only reason this old world holds together (and the only reason God withholds His wrath from us right now) is because there are a few really godly and righteous people left. God considers that and in His judgment the world is still worthy to stand. All that we are enjoying right now is because of the godly people in this world. They are the ones who have saved it from destruction and preserved it for our enjoyment.

## FIRE AND BRIMSTONE SERENADES

God did not destroy the ancient world by water until it became so rotten there was nothing else decent to be done with it. It was Noah and his righteous family that stayed the hand of God for 120 years. Sodom and Gomorrah illustrate the same thing for they were destroyed only when there were not enough righteous people left to warrant their being allowed to exist. Not even 10 righteous people could be found in the city. Then came the explosion!

We are the "salt of the earth." Jesus said so. The earth is preserved because of God's righteous people. When it becomes just so wicked, then it will go up in smoke and Jesus will be revealed from heaven to wreak vengeance upon those who know not God and obey NOT the gospel. He is coming again to take vengeance upon His adversaries—"the day of vengeance of our God."

God is longsuffering and very patient, but one of these days it will all come to an end! Those who have presumed upon God's goodness and mercy will awaken to fire and brimstone seranades. God knows when you are warned, what you THOUGHT (as well as what you did). He will judge justly and that will be HELL for a vast majority of those living upon the earth right NOW.

The reason why most people do not come to the Lord for salvation is because they do not think very much about it. They think about wars[3] (both at home and abroad); about summit meetings[4] and world economics; fashions and making a living; sports, amusements and "controlling"[5] TV; but they seldom if ever give their souls a moment's notice. A little thought given to the second coming of Jesus our Lord (but then, JUDGE) would cause many a thoughtless soul to turn to Him.

Most people pay little attention to warnings. Just the other day[6] I picked up a young man from Johnstown, Pennsylvania, where several years ago the whole town was wiped out by a flood when a dam broke. He told me that to this day the old-timers recall how many warnings were given to them. "Oh, we have heard that before!" was the general response, and in their negligence most of them were lost. A few fled to the hills and were saved, while the vast majority either slept, played cards, drank their whiskey or amused themselves–until they were removed from the earth, SUDDENLY.

**GREAT GLORY!**

They could have been saved. They were warned, often. You CAN be saved now...if you want to be saved. If you are lost, it will be because you would not heed the warning: JESUS IS COMING AGAIN! Today, God's messengers and God's Spirit are warning every man, every where, of the destruction that is to come upon unbelievers. But there are those who stand back and say, "Oh, don't get excited. That is the part of the preachers and the fantatics, to get you to join up." Thoughtless souls pay no attention to the warnings and go on believing the devil (who is a liar) in preference to the sacred Word of God. The warning goes unheeded and destruction is certain. The fires are burning closer every day.

"I WILL come again...Let not your hearts be troubled," said Jesus to His disciples, who were heart-broken at the news of His going away. He said, "Ye believe in God, believe also in me" (John 14:1). WHAT A GRAND PROMISE! How comforting! Jesus is coming again!

When I go away in meetings, I bid my wife and family goodbye, but I remind them that I will come back again.[7] How anxiously they await my return. As the time wears on, they expect me the more. What a joy it is to surprise them by coming in a little ahead of time, because I know how glad they will be to see me. How glad it must make JESUS feel when He sees those who love Him, and earnestly desire His return, BUT how sad it must make His heart feel when He sees so many of His professed children making no preparation for His coming, not really caring whether He returns or not!

Some time back we had some sickness in our house. My mother, way down in central California, heard about it. She wired immediately that she would leave Fresno that night, but she forgot to say whether she would come by train, bus or plane. We made every effort to meet the right one by asking for the arrival time for trains, buses or planes out of Fresno. We met several wrong trains and buses, but thank the Lord we were PREPARED and THERE when the right bus did come in. How happy we were when she did arrive! How joyously we greeted her! But do you know there were a lot of folk at the bus station that did not seem to care anything about MY mother's arrival? That is the way it will be when Jesus comes. Some will be glad and some will be paying no attention at all. To them Jesus will come "as a thief in the night," unexpectedly. But to those who look for Him, "He shall appear the second time without sin unto salvation" (Heb. 9:28). Then we will have eternal salvation–salvation forever! That is just what God's people are going to enjoy. The dead shall be raised, and they will be redeemed from the grave. The bodies and spirits of the saints will be redemeed forever!

HOW is Jesus coming? He will come literally because the Word says, "This same Jesus which is taken up from you into heaven, shall so come in like manner as ye have seen go into heaven" (Acts 1:11). An angel said so! Paul adds, "For the Lord himself shall descend from heaven with a shout, with the voice of an archangel, and with the trump of God; and the dead in Christ shall rise first" (I Thess. 4:16). He will come in the clouds of heaven. Revelation 1:7 says so. Jesus promised, "And they shall see the Son of Man coming in the clouds of heaven with power and great glory" (Matt. 24:30). GREAT GLORY! "He shall come in his glory, and all the holy angels with him" (Matt. 25:31). When all the angels of God come with Him, He will be at the head of the greatest army this world has ever seen! It will be more glorious than the first angelic choir that ushered Him into this world the first time, when God prepared Him a body through Mary. His coming will also be with "ten thousands of his saints" (Jude 14). Who are they? They are the ones who have been redeemed by His blood–those who have already passed into the heavenly world, His chosen saints! Won't that be a glorious day? If we could roll all the Rose Festivals[8] and Mardi Gras into one big splurge, it would be nothing in comparision with that scene! Even a World's Fair would not compare with that colossal assembly.

## THE SINNERS' PARADE

All the atheists of this old world will be making confession on that day! Skeptics on high school teaching staffs and university professors who have robbed our sons of their faith in God will bow their knees and confess with their mouths that Jesus is Lord...but it will be too late! Can you see that long list of illustrious infidels approaching the throne of Christ–the Christ they have denied!–bowing and confessing that He IS and WAS (all the time) the Christ of God! Just count them as they pass by. There goes Celsus, Renan, Tom Paine, Bob Ingersoll, Rousseau, Hume, Owens, Darwin, Huxley, and Darrow. Men who lived on their pride and infidelity, but now have come into the presence of Deity. They liked the limelight while they were on earth, but now they are going to get the HEAT (but it will be in everlasting darkness). Bryan will be vindicated in that day as his notorious criminal defender[9] bows before God's throne, confessing his error and ignorance.

There is another prosperous group coming into view. Here on earth they used Jesus' name as a curse word, as they ridiculed religion and made their money selling booze and dope, cheating at games of chance. They now bow in fear and shame! Then comes the old self-righteous sinners, who were too good to suffer for Christ's church that He died for. THEN they said, "There are too many hypocrites in the church." NOW they will go down to the same hell with those very hypocrites, those they claimed to despise on earth! Oh, my sinner friend, if you have not humbly confessed the Lord to be the Son of God and your Saviour, the best time to do it is RIGHT NOW, while you have the opportunity! Confessing Him at the Judgment Bar will be too late!

## APPROACHING JUDGMENT

On that day, all the nations of the earth will stand before Him for judgment. Then the great judge will say, "Set the sheep on my right hand, and the goats on my left." To those on His left, He will say, "Depart from me, ye cursed, into everlasting fire, prepared for the devil and his angels." To those on His right, He will say, "Come, ye blessed of my Father, inherit the kingdom prepared for you from the foundation of the world."

When Jesus comes in His advent, "Then he will send the angels, and shall gather together his elect from the four winds, from the uttermost parts of the earth to the uttermost part of heaven" (Mark 13:27). I don't know HOW, but I know God is able to do what He has promised. He has never failed yet, and I know He will keep His promise on that day. He has power to gather His own from all the lands of the earth, out of every past century, from all the seas. Their bodies, thus resurrected, will be immortal, living forever in that eternal kingdom with the Eternal King.

"We shall not all sleep, but we shall all be changed; in a moment, in the twinkling of an eye, at the LAST trump. For the trumpet shall sound, and the dead shall be raised incorruptible" (I Cor. 15:51). "We know that when he shall appear, we shall be like him; for we shall see him as he is" (I John 3:2). "Wherefore comfort one another with these words" (I Thess. 4:18).

Oh, my friend, will you believe God at all? If you do, you must believe that Jesus is coming again, and that we should be anxiously looking for that moment when He will receive His saints unto Himself. Will you be ready when the archangel shall descend from heaven, and with one foot upon the land and the other upon the sea, shall swear by Him that lives forever and ever, "TIME SHALL BE NO MORE!" Oh, what a joyous day that will be for the one who has been a follower of the Lord Jesus Christ on this earth! The rebuffs and the heartaches that the unbelievers and sneering skeptics have heaped upon us will be as nothing then.

Do you believe Jesus is coming again?
Then get ready for it!
Be an adventist with me!

---

1. Archie Word began his work with the Montavilla church in 1935, twenty- five years before this message.
2. A reference to John F. Kennedy's (a Roman Catholic) bid for the presidency in 1960. Word devoted many articles to this subject in 1960.
3. Civil war broke out in the former Belgian Congo in mid-July.
4. A historic summit between West Germany's Konrad Adenauer and Israel's David Ben Gurion took place March 14, 1960.
5. Brother Word did not believe you could control a television set in the home.
6. The phrase "the other day" became the title of a book of illustrations authored by Archie Word in 1972.
7. Sometimes Word would be gone as long as six months at a time in his meetings.
8. Portland's biggest event, to this day, is the annual Rose Festival.
9. Clarence Darrow.

# THE CHURCH SPEAKS

Published with the sole purpose of causing people to think about Christ's Teaching especially relating to His church and the holiness of its members.

ADDRESS ALL COMMUNICATIONS TO THE EDITOR, A. WORD, 550 N. E. 76TH AVENUE, PORTLAND 13, OREGON

"Make All Things According To The Pattern"

VOL. 15, NO. 3. MAY 1963


## LIVING UNDER GRACE

By Larry Jonas

I SPEAK plainly, brethren. We who are stricter than other segments of the restoration movement are openly accused of legalism and Phariseeism. But worse yet, we have a current sore upon the body of Christ among ourselves which consists of calling one another "legalists". It is time we examined the scriptures to see what legalism or living under the law is really like in contrast with living under grace. For this purpose, I would like to present the highlights of Romans 7: 7 - 8: 6 for your consideration.

The purpose of the law was to name sin as sin. Every time you violated the law of God, the Law wrote you out a ticket, brought you to court and pronounced you guilty. It never had the power to pardon, only to condemn (7: 7). If there was no law against displeasing God, we could go right on displeasing Him without penalty (7: 9). Was the law then bad in that it condemned us? No, the law was good, and because sin could cause evil to come from a God-planned, good thing like the law, we learned how powerful and wicked

Continued to page 37

## STRANGE THINGS TODAY!

By A. Word

THE TEXT for this sermon is taken completely out of its setting, but by the grace of God, I want to use it to His glory, by applying it merely as it reads. "We have seen strange

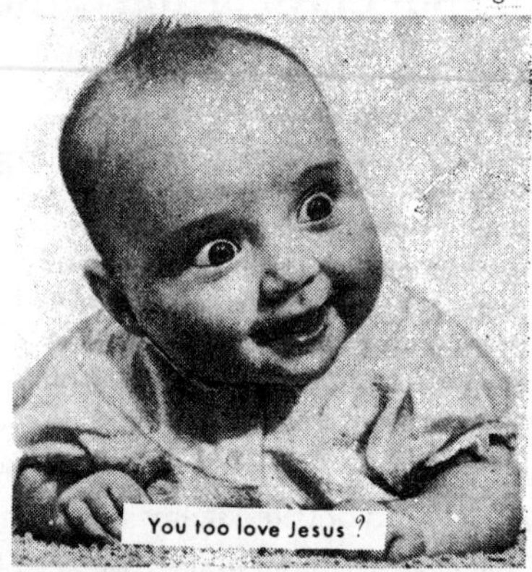


*Brother Word loved to use baby pictures in* The Church Speaks.

# 21

# WHY WE SHOULD ATTEND CHURCH

*The Church Speaks,* July, 1962

Down deep in the nature of every man is the need to worship. We cannot give God the honor due Him as we run after dollars and cents in our every-day life, so He has appointed a place where He will meet with us in the assembly; there we give to Him the honor, love and adoration, as well as thanksgiving, that He deserves. We know we owe it to Him, our ever-living God.

God made us, gave us a life, a soul, everything we possess; therefore every hour, every minute, every second depends upon His goodness and generosity in allowing us to continue to live. Why should we not spend time in a spirit of deep gratitude, worshipping so wonderful a benefactor? Certainly we would be (and many are) most ungrateful when we do not do what He has asked us to do in the way of expressing our gratefulness to Him in worshipping Him. We have so much to be thankful for: family, friends, forgiveness, country, education, guidance, food, clothing, and the knowledge of our God.

Why should we go to church?

## FOR SPIRITUAL STRENGTH

We should go to church for spiritual nourishment and strength. The church is the place God has appointed for the feeding of our souls. What good is a healthy body without a healthy soul to guide it? Jesus has told us, "Man shall not live by bread alone, but by every word that proceedeth out of the mouth of God" (Matt. 4:4). God has provided a place for the nourishment of our souls–the church. Here we can hear inspiring sermons that give us courage and power to live honorably. Through good sermons we receive help that undergirds and sustains us for the tasks we must do throughout the week. God instructs in humility, freedom from worries, love for our neighbors, and a determination to overcome our problems. In the church services there is a renewal and development of faith in God, and a power given to be examples to others. This day of worship and rest preserves the dignity of man in a day that is breaking into a faster and more demanding tempo.

## TO FIND PEACE AND SECURITY

We should go to church to find peace and security. In this day of domestic, national, and international troubles, we should remember that God will hear everyone's troubles, no matter what the color of the man or the deed.[1] It seems as though cares and hurt feelings melt away in God's presence, when the worshipper comes to God in sincerity. God's still, small voice makes all things right again. There is a comfort and a sense of peace that comes as we meet with the Lord in the place set aside for His worship. He seems to be just a little bit closer to us there than He is anywhere else. God gives peace when nobody else can. We go to Him as sinners; He takes us in, as a lover would. In sorrow He comforts us as no one else ever has. When we ask His forgiveness on bended knees for sins, offenses, and negligence, "the place of prayer" becomes more dear to us.[2] We come out of church feeling like we have a new start.

## TO UNDERSTAND THE BIBLE BETTER

We should go to church to understand the Bible better. In it are the words of life, but so few people at home study the Bible enough to understand it. The preacher is a specialist in teaching the Word of God, and hungry hearts are fed in the assembly. In church we learn how to pray for others and for ourselves, how to be obedient, and how to resist temptation. We yearn to have a better understanding of God, His church, and our Saviour, and it is in the assembly that our spiritual understanding is deepened. Surely in church, under the teaching of Christ, our perspective of life becomes clearer.

## OBLIGATION

A very practical reason for going to church is because it is our obligation to go. God has said for us not to forsake the assembling of ourselves together (Heb. 10:25). It is an "ought to" then for the "easily to be entreated." Jesus once asked, "Could ye not watch with me for one hour?" God knows the power of example, and every person who attends church sets a godly example for others (possibly not so strong) to follow. Every Christian wants his children to have the same rich heritage which he had–a deep reverence for God and a vital interest in things eternal–and the church is where that is cultivated.[3]

## ENJOYMENT

We ought to go to church for the sheer enjoyment of being there. The beauty of the surroundings gives one peace. Sunday is not complete unless the child of God has been to church. The quiet atmosphere is impressive to the thoughtful. We can pray more fully in church than at home, where the noises in the house distract our attention when we see to talk with

God.[4] The singing of the hymns helps me to express my heart's desire to please God.[5] Actually, if we did not go to church but for the singing (and that singing were from our hearts) we would be much better off than staying at home. Those hymns help to lift the true worshipper to higher realms of thought.

**TO PLEASE GOD**

All of these reasons ought to spring from one source: I want to please God! Our attending the church for which Christ died is an evident sign to God and man that we love HIM. When we love a person in this life, we desire to be near him, or to visit him. So it is with Christ!

**FOR FELLOWSHIP**

We ought to go to church for the fellowship with others of like faith and mind! Fellowship is much to be desired. It was one of those things in which the early church continued steadfastly (Acts 2:42). We love the music and harmony of kindred spirits as we join with others in singing praises to our Lord and Master. It thrills my soul to know that I have a fellowship that reaches around the world, and from eternity past into eternity that lies ahead. In the house of God every many can feel equal to his neighbor and his brother–just children of God!

**THE WORLD'S CONDITION**

We ought to want to go to church because of the chaotic condition of the world at present.[6] We see the results of wars past and wars cooking, and we know the sorrows that they all plant, nourish and reap. We need to pray for all people. We cannot have much of a voice now in the United Nations, but we can speak with the God who rules the nations! We can know that the God who heard the prophets of old has promised to hear us! We can go to Him, especially in the church, and pray that He will spare this old wicked world, allow us to set an example before the heathen, and make a place that is blessed for our children. We cannot bring about anything that is really good without the help of God. If there ever was a time when we need His help, it is now. In going to church, we are making a contribution of good in a fight against much evil.[7]

**THE LORD'S TABLE**

Let us be faithful to God and His church as He has been faithful to us, never failing to assemble with the saints around the table of the Lord, communing with Him.

(Author's note: Here the article ends, rather abruptly. But on the very next page of *The Church Speaks* in which this essay appeared, Word ran a piece by Charles Spurgeon, "Why I Come to the Lord's Table," which seems appropriate to conclude the closing paragraph of Word's message.)

"I come not because I am worthy; not for any righteousness of mine. For I have sinned and fallen short of what, by God's help, I might have been.

"I come, not that there is any magic in partaking of the symbols of Christ's body and blood.

"But, I come because Christ bids me come. It is His table. He invites me.

"I come, because it is a memorial to Him as oft as it is done in remembrance of Him–His life, His suffering and death. I find myself humbling myself in His presence and bowing before Him in worship.

"I come, because here is portrayed Christian self-denial, and I am taught very forcibly the virtue of sacrifice on behalf of another, which has salvation in it.

"I come, because here I have the opportunity to acknowledge my unworthiness and to make a new start.

"I come, because here I find comfort and peace.

"I come, because I rise from this place with new strength, courage, and power to live for Him who died for me."

1. Moves toward integration in the early 60s brought increasingly strained race relations in America.
2. One month earlier, June 25, 1962, the Supreme Court banned prayer from public schools.
3. The Word's six children are all faithful members of the Lord's church.
4. Word would not tolerate distractions in the church service. Often he would "invite" mothers with crying babies to take them to the nursery. Youth who whispered risked incurring his wrath from the pulpit.
5. His favorite hymns included "Shall We Gather at the River" and "I'll Live For Him."
6. Word probably had the Vietnam War in mind. A few months after this article was published, tension gripped the world during the Cuban missile crisis.
7. James Matthew Alley, a revivalist who visited Montavilla, once gave high praise to the worship services Brother Word conducted at Montavilla: "For the best possible description of the service I refer you to Pendleton's *Memoirs of Alexander Campbell* in which he describes the Lord's Day services in the days of Mr. Campbell's greatest triumph as a preacher at the old Bethany church" (*Voice of Thunder, Heart of Tears,* p. 419).

22

# HOW TO BE HAPPILY MARRIED

*The Church Speaks,* March, 1964

"Marriage is honorable in all, and the bed undefiled: but whoremongers and adulterers God will judge" (Heb. 13:4).

"Whoso findeth a wife findeth a good thing, and obtaineth favour of the Lord" (Prov. 18:22).

"Therefore shall a man leave his father and his mother, and shall cleave unto his wife: and they shall be one flesh" (Gen. 2:24).

The God who ordained marriage for people is the same God who desires happiness for those people. He uses the marriage relationship as a picture of the relationship that exists between Christ and Christians (Eph. 5:22-23).

There are some basic laws of marriage, and upon them, largely, depends the happpiness that will pertain to that home–as they observe His laws of GRACE for the marriage relationship!

## GOD-ORDAINED

First, realize that marriage and the home are God-ordained. From the very beginning (Gen. 2:18-24) marriage was divinely prepared for and instituted.

Entering into the marriage relationship is a covenant, or contract. God wants a godly seed, so He intended that marriage be an honorably kept covenant, with no "putting away" (divorce). "And did he not make one?...and wherefore one? He sought a godly seed. Therefore take heed to your spirit, and let none deal treacherously against the wife of his youth. For I hate PUTTING AWAY, saith Jehovah, the God of Israel...take heed to your spirit, that ye deal not treacherously" (Mal. 2:15-16). This marriage was designed for our happiness, but broken covenants–broken contracts of marriage–become one of the most bitter roots of unhappiness known to man!

When the Lord Jesus came, He made it evident that this marriage contract is to last until death separates the marriage partners (Matt. 19:6). Paul confirms Jesus' teaching in Romans 7:2-3. Any person who knowingly and wilfully breaks this contract will break ANY OTHER contract if he thinks it is to his gain, because there is no contract on earth more sacred than wedlock! Remember this, however. People can always rationalize the position they have placed themselves in, or the deeds they are doing; so do not be surprised if people excuse their breaking of the marriage covenant, and do it with no shame at all. (But they cannot find happiness in so doing!)

Keep your marriage covenant inviolable if you want to have a happy married life. Make it "Until death do us part..."

## ONLY IN THE LORD

If you want to be happily married, marry "ONLY IN THE LORD" (I Cor. 7:39). That Scripture applies specifically to widows seeking remarriage, but God does not have one standard for them and another for the single person. It is always "IN THE LORD" when Christians marry!

Be careful to choose a person of genuine Christian character to begin with. Make up your mind you will marry only in Christ. Don't let the idea of an "unequal yoke" in marriage even enter your mind (II Cor. 6:14). When you choose a mate, do not marry a "doll" nor a "dolled-up clothes-horse." Look for character! This is good advice for both the boy and the girl contemplating marriage. It can save a lifetime of regret! Remember, marriage is for LIFE! Until death! Trials are going to come as certain as "the sparks fly upwards." Paint and polish will rub off quickly–it is awfully thin. (Observe how it works in Hollywood divorces and suicides.)[1]

The woods are full of divorcers and divorcees who did not have character enough to make a success of marriage. (Even with all of our modern conveniences they could not make it! Just remember, in the generation past many women washed on a board, carried their own water from the well, and made their own soap. Many of them lived on homesteads, cooked on wood stoves, cut their own wood, and had to WALK to the store over country roads, while their husbands suffered the hardships of labor without modern implements.)[2]

A wedding between two Christians will overcome difficulties, so marry "IN THE LORD."

**BUILD ON CHRIST**

If you want to have a happy married life, make it a Christian home from the beginning! Build your home on the teachings of the Lord!

Start off by going to church on Sunday and worship God in the place He has APPOINTED, and in the manner He has ordained. Act like Christians all week long, day and night; in business, at home, in school, while visiting, in public and in private, in the daylight or in darkness.

Treat each other with Christian grace. Be Christian toward your children–and if you have step-children, treat them like a Christian should too! Teach and live Christ in your home. Let the husband be the loving head of the family. He should be one who knows the way and leads the family in it. If he is a Christian, he will have character—even though he may sometimes fail. Still, he is the leader in the Christian home. The wife should be in submission to her husband, with a "meek and quiet spirit," not bossy nor a whining nagger. In a Christian home the children give loving obedience, because they have been taught to obey from earliest childhood (Eph. 6:1).

A home built on Christ is a happy home and will give deep satisfaction all its days. The Christian family is headed for a joyous golden anniversary in the future!

## WATCH CHILDREN'S COMPANIONS

If you want to have a happy home, with future happiness assured, watch out WHO your children "court" or keep company with. If they make the right choice, it will make them happy and give you happy grandchildren.[3]

Parents should be informed enough about Christianity so that when their children are old enough to think about marriage, they are able to help them make wise decisions and Christian marriages. If you live your Christianity in your home, your children should love you and respect you for what you are.

People of the world are wiser than many church people. They know that if you want to have pure-bred dogs, you must have a pure-bred father and mother dogs. Dogs produce after their kind...and so do people! If we want Christian children, we must have Christian parents. The proper choice here makes for happiness all the days of marriage, and will make for the progress of Christianity by the example you have set.

## GROW OLD GRACEFULLY

If you want to have a happy home, grow old gracefully! Don't try to be a kitten when you are an old cat! Is there anything sillier than to see some old woman trying to paint her face and frizzle her hair and wiggle along like some 16-year-old girl?

You can spend your life trying to fix up your face and figure (refusing to have children because it will "ruin your figure"), but know this: you will not be young very long! Age is coming on as relentlessly as winter in Alaska. Wrinkles will appear as sure as clouds in the tropics. Your steps will become slower and more awkward, no matter how much "charm schooling" you take. The mind will become less active and the body weakened, and infirmities will be your lot as age comes on. There will be more loneliness because those you have known have "gone on before" you. Eyes will fail and ears become muted with the passing of the years...but if Christ has been your LORD, RULER and GUIDE in getting married, in making a home, in rearing your children, in seeing your grandchildren and possibly your great-grandchildren, you will not only have had a blessed marriage and home, but you will know you are headed for that ETERNAL HOME that Jesus has gone to prepare for you! You will have a happy consumation of your married life!

**"LITTLE HEAVENS"**

Home should remind us of heaven. A number of years ago, some skylarks were brought over to this country from the United Kingdom. They were turned loose in the eastern section of the United States, where they soon made themselves at home and began to multiply. One day a research student was listening to their song with scholarly interest. But as he listened, he saw an Irish laborer suddenly stop, take off his hat, and turn his face skyward, a look of surprise and joy and memory on his face as he listened, entranced, to the song of the birds he had heard sing in his native land as a child. For the bird-expert it was only a scientific observation, but for the Irishman, it was the sacred memories of his long-desired HOME.

So, through the gospel of Christ, there comes to us hope, as it tells us of our heavenly home, "The Eternal Homeland of the Soul." It is a home that will last forever, and our homes here on earth can be a preparation for that eternal home.

My heart longs for all homes to be "little heavens,"[4] filled with the joys that only God can bring, surrounded by obedient children of God who will grow up to make "heavenly homes."

(Editor's note: The essay ends at this point. But in another message on the home, "A Christian Marriage and Home" *The Church Speaks,* March, 1965, A. Word included a list of 19 rules for a successful marriage. We include that list, and his concluding comments.)

**RULES FOR MAKING A SUCCESS OF YOUR MARRIAGE**

1. Never be angry at the same time. Always control your temper. Keep it to yourself, if possible.
2. Never talk AT one another, either alone or in company. Don't take advantage of company to say what you are afraid to say when alone.
3. Never speak LOUDLY to one another...unless the house is on fire!
4. Let each one strive to yield most often to the wishes of the other! Never let the other be more kind than you are!
5. Let self-denial be the daily aim and practice of each partner. Never be selfish! (The very nearest approach to domestic happiness on earth is in the cultivation, on both sides, of absolute unselfishness.)
6. Never find fault unless it is absolutely certain that a fault has been committed, and always speak lovingly in your correction.
7. Never taunt one another with a past mistake. Forgive, forget, and HOPE that it will never happen again.
8. Neglect the whole world, if you have to, but don't ever neglect each other!

9. Never allow a request to go unnoticed! Answer all requests in some way.

10. Never make a remark at the expense of the other. It is ugly.

11. Never part in anger, but with loving words remember the absent one. You may never meet again!

12. Never meet without a hearty welcome and an expression of love.

13. Never hold grudges against each other nor let the sun go down upon your wrath.

14. Never let any wrong you have done the other go by until you have frankly confessed it, and, in sincere repentance, asked for forgiveness.

15. Never forget the happy hours spent together. Talk about them often.

16. Never sigh over what might have been, but be content with what you have and try to make things better every day.

17. Never forget that marriage is ORDAINED OF GOD, and that His blessings and your cooperation can make it what it should be.

18. Never be contented to walk anywhere except in the straight and narrow way!

19. Never stop working, praying, and hoping for a home in heaven!

What kind of home will that make? That will help to make a home where the father is KING, the mother is QUEEN, and the children are their HAPPY SUBJECTS. THERE WILL BE NO PLACE ON EARTH LIKE THAT HOME! It is a place where father, mother and children can live, learn, love and be genuinely happy together! It is a place where they can invite their friends and loved ones, and enjoy God's blessings together! We pray God that the home that is started tonight will be that kind of home, in all sincerity. It will be a home where, in all the world, hearts are sure of each other. It will be a place of confidence. It will be a place where the mask of guarded suspicion and coldness (which the world forces us to wear in self-defense) will be discarded, and where we pour out the unreserved communications of full and confiding hearts. It will be a place where expressions of tenderness gush out without any cessation or awkwardness, and without any dread of ridicule! It will be a hilltop of cheerfulness and serenity, so high that no shadows rest upon it; where the morning comes so early and the evening tarries so late, that the day has twice as many golden hours as those of other men–twice-filled with joy and happiness!

Friends, let's allow nothing to break our homes. Let us work to build more homes and better homes. Christian marriages are the foundation of Christian homes . . . godly homes . . . happy homes . . . lasting homes!

---

1. Word may have had in mind the recent suicides of Marilyn Monroe and Ernest Hemingway.
2. Here Word had to be thinking of the hardships of his own parents (Luther and Maggie Word).
3. The Word children presented Archie and Florence with 15 grandchildren and 27 great- grandchildren.
4. Brother Word was probably most tender when preaching on the subject of the home.

## 23

# THE AMERICAN CRISIS AND HOW TO MEET IT

*The Church Speaks,* September 1965.

An essay marking A. Word's 30th year with the Montavilla church.

This prophet of God lived in the eighth century before Christ, and he faced a very critical time in the history of Israel. He warned...and they paid no attention to his call. God always warns before He strikes! Every prophet of God was a warning messenger from the heart of a loving father (God) to His wayward children (Israel). God had called Israel. God had saved and blessed Israel, and now–like so many other people who are well-fed–she had left her God and gone into sin.

God was reaching the saturation point with Israel's blatant hypocrisy. He was gorged with their "whited-sepulchre" appearance. He had had enough of their sacrifices with no heart! church services with no heart! oblations with no heart! holy days with no heart! and a priesthood with no heart! There is a fundamental law of God that runs from Genesis to Revelation–"The wages of sin is death." And they were about to be paid off! It was a time of CRISIS and the did not know it, even though warned! "Prepare to meet thy God, O Israel" (Amos 4:12).

This universal and eternal law works on individuals as it works on nations. Remember though, when nations suffer for their sins, the individual sinner suffers too! When the nation goes up in smoke, we will go "BOOM!" too. Study history and you will see that no nation has ever gotten by with sin! "Be sure your sins will find you out" is just as true with nations as it is with individuals. There is a coming day of reckoning. Judgment, just and awful, is going to be poured out! God's law regarding the wages of sin does not change. Ever!

**NATIONS WHO FACED CRISIS**

Look at a few instances with me. The Antedeluvians lived in their wickedness . . . until God had His fill of them (Gen. 6:5-7). Then, with the power that God alone could use, He struck. They were facing a crisis, but they did not believe Noah when he told them of their impending jeopardy.

Look at Israel. She became a great nation, powerful in war, under David. She enlarged her borders under Solomon. But then Israel wandered into sin. Soon she was divided, and in a matter of a short time she was taken into exile, national shame, and disgrace.

Take note of "Babylon the Great," located on the Euphrates River, surrounded by walls 300 feet high at places, wide enough on top to race four 4-horse chariots, side by side. Babylon was known as the "Mistress of the Plains," the capitol of the known world. But sin came in and while her king and his lords drank themselves into a senseless stupor, the Medes and Persians marched in to slaughter them without mercy.

Greece also illustrates "the wages of sin." Established by Philip of Macedon, she was made into a universal empire under Alexander the Great. Greece became the greatest center of learning, arts, sciences, philosophies and languages; but she also became wicked and licentious . . . and Rome rose to crush her divided and deteriorating forces into a miserable mass of beautiful ruins.

Let Rome speak from her depths! Mighty Rome, sometimes referred to as "The Eternal City." She lasted for about 1200 years. Her capitol was built on seven hills, on the Tiber River. Rome ruled more land than any other empire ever had . . . but Rome fell in A.D. 410 without a single battle of note. Sin had done its work . . . eating out the very vitals of her national life! The Goths, Vandals and Huns plundered her art treasures and trampled her courts of law. Edward Gibbon *(The Decline and Fall of the Roman Empire)* lists five reasons why Rome fell:

1. The rapid increase in divorce.
2. The mad craze for pleasure.
3. Building gigantic armaments (while their real enemy was within).
4. A decadence of the people's morals.
5. The decay of religon.

(It is interesting to look back and note that every one of these national errors was fed by the theater of their day. They went to the theater once a week, but we have it in our front rooms eight to twelve hours a day...and our's is more subtle.)

## THE AMERICAN CRISIS

The wages of sin was death to the Antedeluvians, Israel, Babylon, the Medes and Persians, Greece and Rome–and if we do not have sense enough to see and face the crisis of OUR day, we will be just another nation in the junk yard of history. The very same things that specifically ruined Rome are eating away at our American way of life, RIGHT NOW! Like a cancer, unseen, but malignantly eating away (as it has always been), "the wages of sin is death." It has ALWAYS been death, and God has not changed His mind about it now.

Right now we face, nationally, a tremendous critical hour. The world of nations is standing at a giant crossroads. Krushchev's successor[1] and J.F.K.'s successor[2] plan to meet in conference to try and iron things out . . . but they will not deal with the root of all the trouble, SIN! How can an atheist (Brezhnev) and a professed "Disciple"[3] (Johnson) ever iron out the sin question? It is an hour of crisis. As a nation, we have never faced a more critical situation nor a darker hour. We have never needed God so desperately as we do right now.[4]

## A PHILOSOPHICAL CRISIS

I know something of the educational world, having taught for some 12 years at college level,[5] and having been associated with students from colleges and universities in this city.[6] By and large, God is almost entirely left out of the curriculum. If God is ever mentioned, you would think He was riding on the exhaust pipe. We are feeding at the table of gross materialism in the realm of philosophy. Paganism is in the saddle and riding hard. She has her roots sunk deep into two miasmic marshes: Evolution and Naturalism.

People say to me, "Brother Word, don't you think evolution is a thing of the past?" I cannot help but answer, "NO!" It is not a thing of the past! It is now being taught in our grade schools, high schools, colleges and universities–not as a theory or an hypothesis, but as a FACT! In reality, it is an unproven postulate–an assumption and a supposition. I am against any sort of Church and State union, but with the educational systems of our nation so completely dominated by these evil philosophies, I can see why some people have a strong case for institutions of learning where some of the teachings of Christ can be taught without having the sheriff knocking on the doors.[7]

Evolution is a denial of the God of the Bible, and the institutions supported by the taxes of the citizens are turning out infidels by the hundreds of thousands. In a few short years they will be the instructors and professors who will be teaching our children this amoral doctrine of the "survival of the fittest."[8] Evolution is a false philosophy that acts as a foundation for almost anything else that the devil can invent.[9]

## A MORAL CRISIS

We are facing a moral crisis, and it is due, to a great extent, to the teaching of the false philosophy of evolution. As a nation, we were taught the 10 Commandments as a basic moral code. But now we are told that morals have changed! What was wrong a few years back is now perfectly all right. People living together, unmarried, is not frowned on any more; they are "just doing what comes naturally" and we should not do anything to frustrate them. Now each man is a law unto himself and he does what is right in his own eyes. We have a nation of moral anarchists built on behaviouristic philosophy! Nothing is absolutely right and nothing is absolutely wrong. We live in a nation of different shades of gray, morally speaking.

According to the *Chicago Tribune,* a professor from the University of Wisconsin was arrested for stealing. She was taken before a judge. He remonstrated with her and gave her a lecture on right and wrong. She said, "There is no such thing as right and wrong. Things are either stupid or intelligent. I was stupid; I got caught." Can you see why so many of our young people have no standard for life?

A young university student said to me the other day, "I am tired."

"Tired of what?" I asked.

"Tired of expressing myself. Tired of doing as I please. There is nothing to live for, nothing to strive for, nothing to die for. I am tired of it!"

Do you know what that leads to? Suicide![10] Surely a large group of our young people are tired of psychiatry! tired of new psychologies! tired of present-day "isms," schisms and spasms! tired of expressing THEMSELVES! There is no challenge, no battle, no conflict, no sacrifice! They want something to challenge them! Hitler saw this need. So did Mussolini and Stalin. And they capitalized on that desire while we present a mush-headed, mealy- mouthed, namby-pamby, panty-waisted religion that says, "Do nothing or do anything. Be nothing or be anything. Say nothing or say anything." And on that diet our young people are deserting the church of the Lord! Naziism, Facism, and Communism demand the last ounce in men–and so does TRUE CHRISTIANITY.

Surely we have a moral crisis in our nation! Thirty years ago we had one divorce in 30 marriages. Last year (1964) we had nearly one out of three marriages end on the rocks,[11] and in some counties there were more divorces granted than there were marriage licenses issued. Marriage is the UNIT of society. When the home breaks, the nation is doomed. Right now, the homes of America are cracking at the seams from one end of the nation to the other.[12] It would be God's blessing if He should rain hell-fire and brimstone on Reno and Las Vegas,[13] as well as any other easy divorce-mill center! And I would include lawyers and judges who aid and abet in this national tragedy!

The crime wave in America has become a permanent wave! According to the FBI, we had nearly two million crimes committed in the USA last year (1964)–major crimes! Our crime bill is now $20 billion per annum.[14] We have had a 98% increase in crime in the past 13 years. (And it is the 17-year-olds that lead in crime–kids whose parents should have been home, taking care of them.)

Prostitution is increasing at the rate of 40% in some of our cities. Drunkeness has increased 70% in five years. Sixty per cent of high school kids are drinking some form of intoxicants. The liquor business (through magazine advertising) are making a bid for the teen-agers. Unless God intervenes, our next generation will be a gang of softies, pagans, drunks and punks. We now have 750,000 saloons in America. They are called everything else but saloons, but they smell like saloons! Calling a skunk by another name does not change its odor! Actually, they are worse than the old saloons (women did not hang around them).

Illegitimacy has increased 300% in 10 years. Pornography has become a $500 million business.[15] For every dollar the nation spends on churches, we spend $1200 on crime. We have 175,000 more places to buy booze than we have places to go to worship.

We are headed straight for God's judgment unless we repent and turn to God. We gambled away four billion dollars in 1963 and our "soul mate" and companion in the "dirt shoot," Great Britain, gambled seven billion dollars. Gambling is always a sign of national deterioration.[16] Remember, they were shooting craps at the foot of the Cross!

**A POLITICAL CRISIS**

Worse than the philosophical problem or the moral problem is the political problem facing us. But I am not merely talking about "party politics." God knows that is rotten enough. This political problem is world-wide in scope. It is a clash between East and West. The war we face, growing out of this antagonistic political situation, is stoning, arrests, imprisonment, or death. In China, no signs are allowed on the buildings to tell people it is a place of worship. Christians in Spain are compelled to meet "underground." What are we doing about it? NOTHING. People are deserting the Lord's church. Sunday evening services are suspended in most churches across the land. Prayer meetings are dead. Religion is decaying in the USA. Sixty million Americans profess NO religion at all. J. Edgar Hoover said recently, "All other conditions are secondary in importance to the disastrous decay of religion." The World Council of Churches is no help. They could not evey agree on a definition for the word "church!"

There is only one cure–a return to God; a genuine, old-time, Holy Spirit, Bible-revival of Christianity! It was Christianity that made America to begin with. Christianity gives a moral standard that makes for national integrity. A Christian behaves himself! Christianity builds homes and

Christians keep their marriage vows. Christians are law-abiding citizens. Christians are not prostitutes or whoremongers. Christians are sober and truthful. Christians are not out stealing. Christians are not gambling. Christians are not drunkards. Christianity is the ONLY religion that has build a decent place to live on earth. Compare by contrast Russian standards with ours.[17] You will notice they did not please Lee Harvey Oswald.[18] He came back to America so filled with their hatred that he dared to risk his life to kill our president. (And any Catholic-dominated country is just as bad.) Our only hope is a return to God.

It is estimated that 100,000 Chinese Christians were martyred in China between 1948 and 1960, while we have had our comforts, yes, our luxuries. We have prospered through two wars, but the time to "pay up" is coming, unless we repent. God is giving us our last chance! Today, Jonahs, Elijahs, Nathans and John the Baptists are crying, "REPENT!" and God is waiting to see what we will do about their call. If we repent, we will be spared; if we do not repent, we will PERISH. Judgment is on us.

Sometimes it takes a great tragedy[19] to awaken a community. It may be the same with nations. Are we going to wait until we see the flames of hell searing our faces before we will turn? Or will we be warned of God and seek to do His will?

What will YOUR answer be?

---

1. Leonid Brezhnev.
2. Lyndon Johnson.
3. President Johnson, a member of the Disciples of Christ, incurred Word's wrath for drinking, playing poker, and attending Catholic and Episcopal churches while in the White House.
4. 1965 was marked by growing opposition to Johnson's escalation of the war in Vietnam, the assassination of Malcom X, and race riots in the Watts district of Los Angeles.
5. Archie Word, Lee Turner, and Warren Bell founded Churches of Christ School of Evangelists (today Northwest College of the Bible) in 1952.

6. Portland has a number of liberal arts colleges, including Portland State University, Lewis and Clark College, the University of Portland, Oregon Health Science University, and Reed College. It is also home to Multnomah School of the Bible.
7. A reference to Catholic parochial schools. A few years after this article was written the Montavilla church, then known as Crossroads, started a Christian school which continues to this day.
8. Thirty year's time has proved Word to be prophetic.
9. Evolution has paved the way for abortion, euthanasia, racism, secular humanism, and the New Age movement.
10. Suicide is now the leading cause of death among university-age young people.
11. Thirty years later (1994) the national average is one out of two.
12. Studies have since shown that the breakup of the nation's homes began in the mid-60s.
13. A sentiment the faithful in those cities might not agree with!
14. Now over $900 billion!
15. All these figures pale in comparison to today. There are more stores selling hard-core pornography in America than there are McDonalds.
16. What would Archie think of today's state-sanctioned casinos and riverboat gambling?
17. But today, 30 years later, Russian educators are passing out Bibles to school children while American educators pass out condoms!
18. Oswald, JFK's assassin, defected to the USSR in 1959.
19. Word may have had the Kennedy assassination in mind here.

My last letter to Bro. Word

205 N. MAIN • P.O. BOX 1132 • JOPLIN, MISSOURI 64802 • 417-623-6280

September 20, 1988

Dear Brother Word,

I was visiting with Don DeWelt on the phone and he tells me that you have not been well as of late. He was out in Gresham for a revival and had lunch with Tom one day. There were 40 responses to one of his messages. He said Brother Strubhar had done a good advance job of preparing folks for the meeting.

Anyway, I was sorry to learn you were not feeling well and wanted you to know we are praying for you. Evelyn and I have fond memories of your three-week revival meeting with us in Lexington back in the early 1970's. What a good time we had calling, traveling the countryside, having services each night. There aren't too many three-week meetings anymore, are there? More like three WEAK night meetings. We did have Tom here for five nights of preaching last spring and are gearing up for another five nights next month.

Brother DeWelt is writing his autobiography and I'm helping him a little bit on it. Do you still have records of when he and Dave were baptized? He isn't clear on the date. Also whether you immersed his parents or not. If you feel up to including any statement about Don I'd be glad to use it (I haven't told Don I'm asking you this). He speaks very highly of you in the forthcoming book. You are his "hero."

May the Lord give you strength and health, if it be His will. I know all of us are pulling for you, but if the Lord wants to take you like he did Enoch of old, that will be alright with us. You have been a good example to me in Word and doctrine. I thank God for the opportunities we have had for fellowship and work in the gospel.

In Jesus' Name,

Victor Knowles

Victor Knowles

*Last letter from author to Archie Word.*

24

# FIRST INSTRUCTIONS FOR THE NEW CONVERT

*The Voice of Evangelism,* January 1966

Now, my dear young brother or sister in Christ, you have been born again, born into the family of God, and there are some very necessary and essential things with which I want to acquaint you relative to your growing up in the Lord's family. We want to see you grow, and as a new babe has an appetite for milk, naturally causing him to grow, so you will have a desire to grow up, develop, and become a full-grown man or woman in Christ as rapidly as you can. It is natural to want to grow!

Do you remember how long it seemed for you go get to be 16? Why? You were anxious to reach that age. You did all you could to hasten the day, even trying to appear that old when you really were not. We want you, just as anxiously, to seek to be grown up in Christ. Here are some things that will help you develop mature Christian character.[1]

**READ YOUR BIBLE**

If you would make fast growth and be sound in spiritual life, read your Bible regularly, every day. Set aside a certain time when you make it a practice to meditate upon God's great revelation, the Bible. Remember that without it there is no way for man to know the mind of God concerning all the mysteries that surround us. Listen to God speak to you from its pages. Pay attention! Never read God's Word thoughtlessly or with indifference as to what it says to you. Be a ready learner and doer.

The Word of God is soul-food, and there is no substitute anywhere that will take its place. Do not trust in church papers,[2] Sunday lesson materials, or even commentaries. Go to their SOURCE! Drink from the fountainhead. Don't be like the old man who was being taught by a preacher how to read. They were using the Bible as their textbook. One day the preacher came by and asked the man's wife how he was getting along with his reading. She answered, "He's done graduated from the Bible to the newspaper!" Such a "graduation" would be a demotion in one's spiritual life.[3] "As newborn babes, long for spiritual milk which is without guile, that ye may grow thereby unto salvation" (I Pet. 2:2). This is a never-to-be-forgotten truth for you as a young convert.

If you come into a room where a small infant is crying and try to console him, you may rock him for a moment or so, but if that baby is hungry there is only one person who can satisfy him and that is his mother. She has the milk that he longs for. Be like that baby–desire the Word and be satisfied with nothing else.

Paul gave wonderful instruction to a young evangelist–learn to handle the word of truth (II Tim. 2:15). The only way you can "rightly divide the word of truth" is by studying it. By studying and doing you will grow and not backslide.

## PRAY

God has stipulated another source of Christian growth: prayer. "In nothing be anxious; but in everything by prayer and supplication with thanksgiving let your requests be made known unto God" (Phil. 4:6).

Prayer is the Christian's breath. Do not suffocate yourself. "Continuing steadfastly in prayer" (Rom. 12:12). Remember that we pray unto Him who is "able to do exceeding abundantly above all that we ask of think" (Eph. 3:20), so do not be afraid to ask and trust. Pray about everything that comes into your life–joys, sorrows, victories, defeats. God wants to help us in all our problems in life. "But if any of you lacketh wisdom, let him ask of God, who giveth to all men liberally and upbraideth not; and it shall be given him" (James 1:5). God has promised this!

You will find, in a short time, that you will have enemies, even when you are a Christian, trying to do your dead-level best. What should you do about your enemies? Jesus said, "Love your enemies, and pray for them that persecute you" (Matt. 5:44). It will take genuine God-given grace to do this at first, but in time you will be grown up enough to do God's will, even in dealing with your enemies.

## STAY AWAY FROM BAD PEOPLE

A third piece of instruction needed in successful living for Christ is staying away from bad people. Remember, "Ye are an elect race, a royal priesthood, a holy nation, a people for God's own possession, that ye may show forth the excellencies of him who called you out of darkness into his marvelous light" (I Pet. 2:9). Discard everything you know to be sinful or will lead to sinning. Evil companions certainly will act as a weight (Heb. 12:1-2), holding you back and retarding your progress for God. "Be not deceived: evil companionships corrupt good morals" (I Cor. 15:33). Always remember this verse when you are choosing your friends and associates.

Not only should one be careful about selecting his companions, morally, but watch out for religious scoundrels and apostates too. Paul pleaded with the Roman church, "Mark them that are causing the divisions and occasions of stumbling, contrary to the doctrine which ye learned; and turn away from them...they beguile the hearts of the innocent" (Rom. 16:17-18). Watch out for this "any old church will do" doctrine, now so rampant in the world.[4] False religions can damn your soul if you succumb to their heresies. The best way to deal with them is to dissassociate yourselves from them. Cut them off.

One of the best standards by which to judge the company you keep is this: if they keep you from praying or cause you to lose your firm convictions relative to a "Thus saith the Lord," get away from them–far away!

**TRY TO WIN SOULS**

Here is another asset to Christian growth for the new convert–try to win some other soul to the Lord, and begin working on it right away.[5] Christ expects you to be a worker for Him. How were you converted? Did not someone speak to you, either privately or from the pulpit? Most people who become Christians are won by some person caring enough for their souls to talk with them. The early church, when they were "scattered abroad," carried out the Lord's commission (Acts 8:4). Christianity is like measles–keep it well broken out on your tongue, feet and hands. Remember that every person outside of Christ is lost. Jesus said, "Go ye into all the world, and preach the gospel to the whole creation. He that believeth and is baptized shall be saved; but he that disbelieveth shall be condemned" (Mark 16:15-16).

We, as His disciples, are to be His workers. "Ye shall be my witnesses both in Jerusalem, and in all Judaea and Samaria, and UNTO THE UTTERMOST PARTS OF THE EARTH" (Acts 1:8). Though this was spoken to His apostles, that last part certainly takes us into acccount. We are to be "fishers of men." A fisherman who does not fish never catches any fish! The purpose of Jesus' coming to earth was to save the lost (Luke 19:10), and through us He is still seeking and saving others. In saving others, you save yourself–and you become strong in the Lord.

## DO WHAT GLORIFIES GOD

Another important factor in the new convert's successful growth is seeking always to do those things which will glorify the Lord. "And whatsoever ye do, in word or in deed, do all in the name of the Lord Jesus, giving thanks to God the Father through him" (Col. 3:17). Allow nothing to come into your life that will in any way jeopardize your own soul or the souls of others. Never take a chance with your own soul in doing anything that might cause some weaker person to stumble. A growing Christian seeks to be a Christian seven days a week.

After studying the sinless life of Christ, one of the best rules of conduct (when any doubtful thing comes up), is to ask yourself, "What would Jesus do?" For example, would He watch Hollywood's productions–made by wicked people, which appeal to wicked people, causing wicked people to become more wicked and ungodly? Would Jesus be attending the modern dance, where they twist like sex-driven maniacs?[6] Would Jesus be attending the race track (either dogs, horses, or automobiles)? Do these things build up the kingdom of Christ or tear it down? Judge your actions accordingly.

## ATTEND CHURCH REGULARLY

If you would succeed in your Christian life, this is very important: do not miss the Bible school hour, the Lord's Supper, the preaching, or the prayer meeting. You won't either –if you have the interest of the Lord and your soul uppermost in your mind. Can you imagine Jesus staying home from the church for which He died? Remember, sinners are watching you. They read you instead of the Bible. Let them have a genuine impression of what it means to be a washed-in-the-blood, Holy Spirit-filled-Christian.

We rightly preach, "Forsake not the assembling of yourselves together as the manner of some is" (Heb. 10:25). Should we not practice what we preach? We know from Acts 20:7 that the early church met together on the first day of the week to break bread and listen to the Word. Strive to be like those early followers of Christ, who were under the direct leadership of the apostles.

In all my long life's ministry,[7] I have never spoken to anyone on his (or her) deathbed and had him tell me how sorry he was that he had lived a godly life, faithful to the Lord and His church! It is the safe side–and it is the only one that will build you up in Christ. Nothing can take the place of love and loyalty to Him who died for us. This love and loyalty are shown by how we treat His church, His body on earth. Love and loyalty grow a fine type of Christian. We should all try to be "blue ribbon" Christians, not content just to be a little stunted "runt" on display.

## GIVE TITHES AND OFFERINGS

Another facet of the Christian life, so essential to growth, is giving regularly to the cause of Christ. "Upon the first day of the week let each one of you lay by him in store, as he may prosper..." (I Cor. 16:2). This denotes the regularity with which the Holy Spirit-inspired apostle expected Christians to assemble and to give their offering for the service of Christ. Every young Christian ought to form a habit of systematically giving the tithe to the Lord, plus an offering.[8] Surely no Christian should even consider giving less to Christ, our Saviour, than the Jews did under the Law. Christians should give to the local church where they attend. Suppose everybody decided to give whenever and wherever they pleased? There would be no way of telling whether there would be enough in the local treasury to pay the bills or not. Then the church would have a bad name in the community and the Lord would be disgraced.

Every Christian should give cheerfully (II Cor. 9:6-7). No true and loving father ever has to be begged to support his family. Why not? Because he loves his family! It is just as true among Christians. We give in appreciation for Him who died for us, with a desire that we might help take the gospel to others. Beware of covetousness, because if you covet long enough, you will soon steal. Coveting precedes the stealing of the tithe that belongs to God! You can steal from the Lord, but you cannot be a strong, growing Christian while you steal from God. Remember, there is a final reckoning–and there will be no evading the consequences then!

## COOPERATE WITH THE LEADERSHIP

Another important phase of Christian growth is cooperating with the preachers, elders, and fellow-Christians. Don't be always criticizing them–pray for them! If you need help, come to the leaders in the church and ask for help. They will be more than glad to assist you. They will prove to be like the Lord who did not come to be ministered to, but to MINISTER! Let them in on your joys and sorrows. You will need them very badly one of these days, so be a friend to them now. Funerals, disasters, and other sorrows come; then we will stand in need of Christian help. Be on good speaking terms with the officers of the church. In unity, there is power.

## NEVER BECOME DISCOURAGED

Above any other temptation the devil will throw at you, the temptation to become discouraged is about the tops. A man said he dreamed that he died and went to hell. When he came in, he saw they were having a bargain sale. He saw all kinds of tools the devil used to kill off Christians. Among them was a long, sharp "splitting wedge." It was marked the highest of all the tools. The man asked what made that old wedge so high-priced. The devil said, "That is the wedge of discouragement. If I can get the sharp edge of that wedge into a Christian's heart, I can split him wide-open!" It is true! So, trust in the Lord and never become discouraged.

Expect temptations. Jesus had them. He was tempted immediately after his baptism (Matt. 4). Persecutions will come (II Tim. 3:12). Trust in the Lord. He has promised to help you (I Cor. 10:13). God will make a way of escape. Endure temptation (James 1:12). Temptations that we overcome make us stronger. Be strong in the power of His might! Act like men! Be strong! And every victory over temptation will make a better man of God out of you, will mature you.

**REMEMBER: THIS IS NOT OUR HOME**

Finally, keep in mind that this is not our home, but that we are on our way to heaven. It is better to go to heaven alone than to go to hell with a great crowd! It is better to go to heaven from a shanty than to go to hell from a palace.[9]

"Eye hath not seen, nor ear heard, neither hath it entered into the heart of man the things which God hath prepared for them that love him" (I Cor. 2:9). Truly our salvation down here, revealed from God, is wonderful; but just think what it will be to be in the place Jesus has gone to prepare for us!

Jesus' regard for us is something like the little boy who worked so hard to build a small sailboat. Finally, his Daddy helped him out, and together they had a nice two-mast sailboat to be sailed on the city park lake. The boy set it out and watched it go sailing out to the center of the lake. But the wind died, and the boat sat in the middle of the lake until it grew dark. The boy went home, anxious for the safety of his boat. Early the next morning he returned, only to find someone had taken the boat. A few days later he saw the boat in a store window. He rushed in and asked for his boat. The proprietor said, "I paid so much for that boat. If you want it back, you will have to pay me." The little fellow went home crying to his father, and told him the story. The father was touched by the tears of his son and gave him the money to buy it back. The lad hurried back to the store and paid the amount asked. Then, taking the little boat in his arms, he walked home crying for joy, "Little boat, you are twice-mine. I made you, and I bought you back!"

Friend, that is what Jesus has done for us. Never forget it! And as you grow with this ever in your mind, there will be success written in your part of the Book of Life!

---

1. The following 10 instructions are taken from A. Word's 4-page circular which he gave to new converts during his revivals on the West Coast (1930-1935). They are nearly identical to a circular used by Billy Sunday. For a comparison, see pp. 181-183, *Voice of Thunder, Heart of Tears.*
2. Here Word would have included his own beloved *The Church Speaks.*
3. Not that Word was against reading newspapers. He was an avid reader of the *Portland Oregonian,* getting many illustrations from it for his preaching.
4. Perhaps a reference to the popular slogan, "Go to the church of your choice."
5. Don DeWelt recalls that he witnessed to a Catholic friend right after being baptized by Brother Word. Why? "Because our Lord, through Brother Word, told me to! The emphasis I have consistently placed on winning the lost...to a large extent came from A. Word!" *(Happy On My Way To Heaven,* pp. 43-44).
6. Word, who once ran three dance halls in Fresno, came down hard on "The Twist" craze of the 60s.
7. Word was ordained to the ministry in 1927.
8. Word became sold on tithing when he gave $33 to the church when he got out of the Navy. Ten days later he received ten times the amount in back pay!
9. The year A. Word died (1988), he said, "We'll just take off for heaven from Gering. Heaven is better than Nebraska."

Star-Herald, Sunday, November 20, 1988

# Word lived life the way he taught it

By TED BROCKISH
News Editor

SCOTTSBLUFF — Archie Word's life was the Word.

Word, an associate minister and professor at the Scottsbluff School of Evangelism, died of natural causes Thursday in Regional West Medical Center here. He was 87.

A traveling evangelist during the 1930s, Word "preached longer than anyone in my acquaintance," said Don Pinion, the pastor of Bluffview Church of Christ where Word served in recent years as an associate minister. Pinon will officiate at a funeral for Word at 2 p.m. Monday at the church.

Another funeral will be held Friday at Portland, Ore., where Word founded Northwest College of the Bible. Word taught for 16 years at the college and preached there for 32 years.

Margaret Hunt of Ottumwa, Iowa, the oldest of Word's five daughters, said there would be people from all over the Northwest at the Portland service.

ARCHIE WOOD

Both Mrs. Hunt and Pinon said Word's influence touched the lives of thousands of people across the United States.

More local, region news, page 5

"He was the most dynamic preacher I've ever met," said Pinon. "He has probably placed more men in the ministry than any man I know."

From 1930 to 1935 Word traveled throughout the country, leading revival services that each lasted six days a week for six weeks. Pinon estimated that Word converted from 35 to 165 people at each stop.

He settled down in Portland to raise his family and continue ministering through the college he founded. He stayed there until 1969. From his marriage to Florence Procter in 1926, six children were born — daughters Barbara Brink and Esther Burgess, both of Portland, Jenelle Green of Gering, Anna Jean Rodda of Mishawaka, Ind., and Mrs. Hunt and son Archie Jr. of Portland. All survived Word, as did sister Nellie Arnold of Brownsville, Calif., 10 grandchildren and 27 great-grandchildren. His wife currently resides at Heritage Health Care Center at Gering.

As a father "he was very firm yet kind," Mrs. Hunt recalled. "He never, ever punished us without crying."

Word came to the Scottsbluff area in 1969, and was invited by Pinon to teach at the Scottsbluff School of Evangelism.

On Labor Day 1976, Pinon recalled, Word and his wife were involved in a car-train collision east of Scottsbluff that almost completely severed one of Word's ears.

"Two days later he was back in class wearing a turban," Pinon said. "That was the kind of determination this guy had."

Spreading the word of Christ was his life.

"He ate it, slept it and rested on it," Pinon said.

Word's life didn't start out that way, Mrs. Hunt said. He quit high school and lied about his age to join the Navy during World War I, she recalled, and was a prizefighter during his days in the service — "not the kind of life you put before people as an example."

*Front page story announcing Word's death in the* Scottsbluff Star-Herald, *Nov. 20, 1988.*

# 25

# INFALLIBLE PROOFS OF THE RESURRECTION

*The Church Speaks,* March 1967

Several years ago I was preaching in a small town in Indiana.[1] One morning two cars collided head-on and some people were killed. At once the crowds began to assemble, hurrying to the scene of the accident. In a short time that little village was a teeming mass of interested humanity. Why? Because an extraordinary event had taken place. That is what people do when there is an extraordinary event–ANYWHERE and in ANY AGE. They run together! Every square inch is examined again and again with a fine-tooth comb. Every detail of the event is discussed a thousand times over.

Why do I make reference to this NOW? Because at Easter the whole world is thinking about an event that took place 1900 years ago that was VERY MUCH OUT OF THE ORDINARY. A man who had become famous for his preaching RIGHTEOUSNESS for three years, now hung on a cross. The hands that had healed the lepers were pierced with spikes. The feet that walked the waves of stormy Galilee were nailed to a hard-wood Roman cross. His head (where the Spirit of

God once descended as a dove) was crowned with a crown of Palestine's sharpest thorns. All nature seemed to recoil in horror. The sun refused to shine, hiding its face from the awful scene. The earth beneath quaked and trembled, while men smote their breasts in fear. What was it? Certainly it was an extraordinary event!

Let us imagine ourselves in that community at that time. After the crucifixion we would have returned, no doubt, to our homes, just as the vast throng did. Our hearts would have been heavy because of the terrible miscarriage of justice. We would have been enraged at the Invader[2] who had allowed the life of this Righteous Man to be publicly taken. Within our very souls, no doubt, we would be thinking, "God will somehow act on behalf of this Righteous Man!" Anxiously we would watch His disciples, as many others did, to see what they would do. Would they return blessings for the bestiality that had been heaped upon their Lord...as He had taught them to do? Any rumors concerning them would have brought the whole community together in haste.

The whole city would be in a terrible state of tension. Early on the third morning, we rise and eat our breakfast. We have visited the tomb before. We have seen the guard and the Roman seal. Suddenly, the dishes begin to rattle and the table to shake with an earthquake! In wild panic we rush out, mutely gazing at one another. Perplexed, we re-enter our home. But INSTINCTIVELY we feel that the solution to our problem somehow lies in that tomb of the Righteous Man.

An hour later our neighbor, in great excitement, rushes in and shouts, "THE STONE IS MOVED! THE TOMB IS EMPTY! HE IS RISEN!"

What would happen? When that word was spread about the community, what would people naturally do? Every camel, every donkey, every means of travel would be pressed into service as every last man, woman and child able to walk would hurry to the scene of this extraordinary event! A thousand times every square inch would be examined, souveniers would be chipped from the sepulchre, and every detail would be discussed again and again.

Suppose weeks pass and we hear rumors that the Righteous Man has been seen ALIVE in the country! The whole community would be in a state of excitement–almost a state of shock! Every movement of the disciples would be carefully noted. Suddenly, the word is noised about that something has happened to the lowly disciples. Every heart is alert, and by the thousands the people run together...

Peter stood up in the temple on the day of Pentecost and preached the sermon recorded in Acts 2:14-41. The result was 3000 Jews being CONVERTED to Christ and baptized. We cannot help but ask, "Why?" Why was the testimony of Peter and the rest of the apostles so readily BELIEVED AND ACCEPTED on that day?

The answer is obvious: There were MANY INFALLIBLE PROOFS[3] that could not be resisted by any honest, truth-seeking man!

What testimony did they have?

**IRREFUTABLE TESTIMONY**

1. They had the testimony of the LIVING (John 20:25). The disciples saw Him! (Remember, they had nothing to gain by telling this.)

2. The testimony of HEAVEN (Acts 7:56). Stephen saw the resurrected and exalted Christ...in heaven! (And he was killed for his testimony!)

3. The testimony of ANGELS. "Why seek ye the living among the dead? He is not here, but is risen..." (Luke 24:6-7).

4. The testimony of DEMONS (Acts 19:14-15). The seven sons of Sceva took it upon themselves to try and cast out demons. The evil spirit answered and said, "JESUS I KNOW, and Paul I know, but who are ye?" Notice the PRESENT TENSE.

Jesus was alive in heaven, but these demons knew Him and His power.

5. The testimony of the ROMANS. The silence of Rome about the broken seal (that represented Rome's power and authority) bears mute evidence that she had, that day, grappled with a power beyond her strength! When completely licked, men do not talk!

6. The testimony of PSYCHOLOGY. It is contrary to human nature and mind patterns for men to turn about and instantly love what they hated before, WITHOUT SUFFICIENT EVIDENCE upon which to base their CONVERSION! Yet Saul, a persecutor, was suddenly changed into Paul, the apostle of the Lord. What caused the change? He had seen the resurrected Lord–the only adequate cause for such a complete change!

7. The testimony of ETHICS. Men of all ages have wrestled in vain with their carnal natures, but the chains have snapped when they have submitted to the power of the RESURRECTED LORD![4] Ethical science stands dumb before the miracle of twice-born men!

8. The testimony of REASON. The tomb was sealed and guarded by Roman guards. Three days later it was empty! What became of the body? There are two possibilities. (1) Friends could have taken it...but could a few defenseless disciples overpower the Roman guard? Why would they want to? So they could be killed for a fraud? (2) Enemies might have taken the body. But why would they want it removed? They were doing everything in their power to keep the body IN the tomb! Therefore, friends COULD NOT and enemies WOULD NOT! Who DID remove the body? Only GOD can answer!

9. The testimony of MEDICAL SCIENCE (John 19:34-36). A few days later, Simon saw Jesus alive and well...yet with a gaping hole in His side, big enough for a man to place his hand in it (John 20:25).

10. The testimony of HUMAN NATURE. The first law of human nature is self-preservation. Thousands of early

Christians, with the first-hand information, held to this doctrine in the face of loss of all that life holds dear—houses, lands, loved ones, LIFE ITSELF! They MUST have had EVIDENCE upon which to base their actions or they would not have given up life!

11. The testimony of EXPERIENCE. Almost every home has its vacant chair.[5] Death has made its fearful visit, and hearts are left bleeding. The weary hours drag wearily by; days and weeks give place to months, and the wound is scarcely healed. Here was One dearly loved, mourned and wept; some even brought spices to embalm Him. But, observe: three days after His death, their sorrow was turned to great joy and public rejoicing! There is only one answer. Jesus was resurrected! Jesus was alive!

12. The testimony of the FIVE SENSES. (1) Sight. When the body was laid away, they saw it! They saw the dead body, shrouded in linen. Later, Peter and John SAW those clothes, but the BODY had slipped out and left the clothes undisturbed. They immediately believed—because of what they SAW (John 20:6-8). (2) Touch. "Handle me and see; for a spirit hath not flesh and bones as ye see me have" (Luke 24:39). (3) Hearing. Jesus said, "Mary," and Mary replied, "Rabboni!" (John 20:16). IT WAS THAT OLD FAMILAR VOICE! (4, 5) Taste and smell. After Jesus mentioned food, Peter said, "It is the Lord" (John 21:1-14).

13. The testimony of the 500. For some 25 years, half-a-thousand men mingled with their fellowmen, bearing witness to the fact that they had seen the Risen Lord! (I Cor. 15:6).

14. The testimony of the 3,000. Many in the crowd at Pentecost acted upon the EVIDENCE presented. They were there in the very same city where the events took place! No one denied the statement of the resurrection of the Lord! Three thousand acted upon the message of a Resurrected Christ!

Now, 1900 years of victory marks the history of the Resurrected Christ. He is our Saviour now, but soon we must meet Him as our Judge! "The times of ignorance therefore God overlooked; but now he commandeth men that they should all everywhere repent: inasmuch as he hath appointed a day in which he will judge the world in righteousness by the man whom he hath ordained; whereof he hath given assurance unto all men, in that he hath raised him from the dead" (Acts 17:30-31).

Consider your relationship to Him, the Son of God, the Resurrected Christ!

---

1. This month-long meeting took place in Washington, IN, in October, 1945.
2. Probably a reference to the last enemy, Death.
3. Acts 1:3.
4. A few weeks before his own conversion to Christ, Archie Word had said he would "bow down to nothing but God and His power."
5. Archie's own mother had died just two years previous to this message.

# 26

## THE CASE FOR APPLIED CHRISTIANITY

*A sermon preached at The Centerville Rally, Centerville, Iowa, August 1967.*

I have thought many times, as I have stood before large audiences, that if a preacher could know all the ungodly and impractical and hypocritical and deceitful things in the hearts of some people, how he would preach! Well, I try to preach just like it. You might be just as free from guilt as a pig is from feathers, but brother there might be somebody present with a few feathers! So I want to make this message just as practical as I can.

James 1:22 says, "Be ye doers of the word, and not hearers only, deluding your own selves." If you are only a hearer and not a doer, what are you doing? You are deluding yourself! The church, from very early times, has had an amount of people who have heard but have not done. That was why James wrote as he did. And it is still true today. Some people have been going to church from one to 60 years and have heard sermons, sermons, sermons–and they go out and do just exactly as they did last week, doing nothing about what they heard! Some of these people have heard a thousand sermons on the plan of salvation, but to save their lives they couldn't teach an outsider the steps of salvation. Do you know why they can't? Because they have never taken the Scriptures out and put them to work. APPLIED CHRISTIANITY!

A faith that is needed today to confront this world is a faith that shows itself in the actions of the membership in its obedience to the will of God. You don't have to go out calling very long to find somebody who says, "Oh, that bunch down there." Or, "Oh, that church member!" What is wrong? Some church member heard but did not do! And the man on the street says he is a hypocrite.

A legend is told of a Japanese who died and went to heaven. On the outside of heaven he saw a long row of shelves, and on those shelves were ears and tongues! He asked the angel in charge, "What do these mean?" The angel replied, "These are the ears of those who heard what to do but didn't do it, and these are the tongues of those who told others what to do, but didn't do it themselves." The part of them that was good entered heaven, but the ears and tongues had to stay outside!

There is no doubt but that the church has people who can tell other people what to do better than they are doing it themselves. That is why I am preaching this message on APPLIED CHRISTIANITY. Here are some places where many church people need some practical Christianity, some applied Christianity!

## CONTROLLING THE TONGUE

James 1:26 says, "If any man thinketh himself to be religious, while he bridleth not his tongue but deceiveth his heart, this man's religion is vain."

Over and over people hear about the need to control the tongue, but when it comes to a practical application, it is seldom really kept in control. Keep in mind that any church member, any preacher, and any weak-kneed, wobbly hypocrite can hold his tongue–when there is no stress! Anybody can hold his tongue–when there is no trouble! A fellow can even drive horses and mules without cursing–when they behave themselves, but it is an awful temptation to fly off the handle when things don't go right!

I was in a meeting[1] years ago, and a woman had told the people there that when our second child[2] was born, I wouldn't speak to my wife for six months because the child wasn't a boy! She told this all over town–really great advertising! You say, "How did you find out about it?" I didn't...until 15 or 20 years later when her son in Portland recognized me and said his mother was very sick and wanted to see me. I went to see her, and I found she had been paralyzed on one side of her body. As I stood there by the side of her bed, she poured out her heart in contrition and told me the ungodly thing she and done–and why it was that the meeting in Carlton had only a few converts.[3] I was a lot younger then than I am now, and if I had known about it at the time, I would probably have lost my temper and told some people off around there! When somebody hits you in a tender spot, it is easy to lose your temper–and your tongue! And when somebody has wronged us, when we have been insulted, or when we have been falsely accused, this is when we need to apply our Christianity.

The thing that hurts is when there is just a little bit of truth in it...when it gets right close. Some church people (and even some preachers), when this happens, revile their foes, lay them low, become abusive, lose their tempers, show a devilish disposition. They will use unchristian lanuguage as they call the person any kind of a name that will qualify. They will upbraid, speak profanely, threaten harm...and this often leads to downright fist-fights and shame! Everything was going along fine, and you would think the person to be a real Christian...until such a test came.

I used to carry a rope in the back of my car. One night I got stuck, and when a trucker tried to pull me out, the rope broke right in two. It was a nice looking rope—as long as there was no tension applied to it. But when we put the pull on it...SNAP! The church has people in it like that.

James 1:19-20 puts it this way: "Let every man be swift to hear, slow to speak, slow to wrath: for the wrath of man worketh not the righteousness of God." The wrath of man is contrary to the teachings of the Word of God. Practical Christianity is to take what you hear and APPLY it—use it in your everyday life!

I came to preach to the church in the Montavilla district of Portland, where I am still preaching.[4] At the time, a preacher friend[5] said, "Arch, don't take that Montavilla Christian Church." That is what it was called when I went there, and it had one of the biggest kitchens in the city. After we began there we stored the plates in the furnace room for 10 or 12 years and finally gave them to the Goodwill. The basement partitions dividing the Bible school rooms had been slid back during the week so the kids could roller skate. "Don't go to that church, Brother Word. It has been known as 'the fightingest church in the Northwest' for years." I went anyway—for if anybody needed the gospel, those people did! My preacher friend wrote me a letter and said, "You won't last six months. If you do, I'll send you one of the best ties in town!" So after I had been there a year, I wrote him, "I've been here six months and haven't got that tie yet." I wait another year and wrote him, "I've been here two years and haven't got kicked out. WHERE'S MY TIE?" At the end of the third year, I wrote him again. Back came a box with a note in it: "Here's your tie—I'm tired of being dunned!"

But the thing that really made me begin to wonder was when Bert Knight[6] told me, "Brother Word, this church is just exactly that (a fighting church), and has been through the years. It has split twice, disfellowshipped I forget how many people at one time, and in one ordeal that took place, one of the deacons knocked the preacher (or the preacher the deacon, I don't know which) clear down the basement stairs. They exchanged reviling words such as, 'I'll ruin your ministry;' 'I'll close every pulpit in the land against you;' 'I'll expose you;' not realizing they were exposing themselves."

What am I talking about? Applied Christianity! And the use of our tongues from the standpoint of control. But there is another way not to control the tongue besides flying off the handle in a rage and saying things a person shouldn't. I think it was General Sheridan, of Civil War fame, who said, "There is a set of malicious, prating, impudent gossips, both male and female, who murder character and kill time, and will rob a young man of his name before he has years to know the value of a good name." And that kind of a tongue is just as bad as the man who gets mad and flies off the handle and cusses! Yet, in spite of the Scriptures' prohibition of gossiping, cursing, and reviling, people go right on doing this very thing.

Turn to Psalm 50:19-21. "Thou givest thy mouth to evil, and thy tongue frameth deceit. Thou sittest and speakest against thy brother: Thou slanderest thine own mother's son. These things hast thou done, and I kept silence; Thou thoughtest that I was altogether such a one as thyself: but I will reprove thee, and set them in order before thine eyes." God here condemns this use of the tongue–not just losing your temper, blowing up, and going crazy; but this business of subtly figuring out how you can ruin the other man by telling stories on him.

Proverbs 20:19 says, "He that goeth about as a talebearer revealeth secrets; therefore company not with him that openeth wide his lips." Watch out for the person who always has something to tell, and is always wanting to mow somebody down. I think it was Einstein who said, "I think I have found the best formula for success in life." They said, "Put it on the board. We want to see it." Einstein wrote, "Let 'A' represent success in life. I would make my formula like this: 'A' plus 'Y' plus 'Z' equals 'A' (success). 'X represents work, and 'Y' represents play." Someone asked, "Professor, what does 'Z' mean?"

Einstein said, "That means 'keep your mouth shut!'" Work and play and keep your mouth shut! It is better not to say too much.

Proverbs 10:18 tells about people who do things like this: "He that hideth hatred is of lying lips; and he that uttereth a slander is a fool." But do you want to know something? There is just a lot of this that goes on in church! People know these Scriptures. They have heard them a thousand times. They have been told, warned, and admonished; yet this business of slandering and gossip (tools of the devil) affect every congregation that I have ever had anything to do with (sooner or later). You learn of a new congregation coming into existence, and everybody thinks they have a group of real Christians. You know what happens? Just about the time they think they have everything under control, they find out (when their backs are turned) that the devil is not dead yet!

I took a tire with a slow leak in it to a service station. The man put air into the tire. It got bigger and bigger and bigger—and my eyes did the same! I backed up a little—then a little more! You think you have everything under control, and the work is getting bigger and bigger. Watch out! For everything can go "Pshsssssss!" Just like that tire! There is a devil, and he uses people's mouths—gossip and slander!

I think it was Shaeffer's fountain pens that used to have these words on the box: "When this pen flows too freely, it is almost empty." Let me tell you something. A tongue flowing too freely is a sign of an almost empty heart—empty of the love of God!

As you look back on your life, how many instances have you known where gossip and slander have had results too terrible to write in a book? I have seen people (who were friends for years and years) split apart because of an ungodly tongue. What a shame!

I spoke on a conference in Cincinnati, Ohio, years ago.[7] A preacher from Winchester, Virginia, had brought a delegation. I had preached something about tobacco. There was a woman in that delegation who used tobacco. Back home, when the preacher announced they were going to have me for a revival meeting, the woman went up and down the streets of that town, telling everyone she could find, "Don't go hear that idiot preach!" She went to her children, to all her grandchildren, to all her aunts and uncles, cousins, and everyone else – but it backfired! Any preacher who was supposed to be so brainless as I was represented to be, they wanted to hear preach at least once! So they did. And they came again and again!

When the meeting got underway, some of the woman's relatives, including her own grandchildren, were converted. The last Sunday of the meeting, while we were waiting for some people preparing to be baptized, a man came in and said, "Brother Word, there is a woman outside who wants to see you." I went out to her car, and there sat a woman who was practically bent double. Her face was covered with a handkerchief, her nose was red, her eyes were nearly swelled shut. She had been crying and crying. She sobbed, "What in the world am I to do?" (She told me what I have already told you.) The fact that some of her relatives were being baptized in spite of her had broken her down. Now she was thinking of others whom she may have kept away with her gossip. She said, "What can I do?" I said, "You can come into the church this afternoon, or you can wait until tonight, and tell the people what you have told me." She did so that night when more people were present. Only God knows how many people were affected in that city because of gossip, slander, and an ungodly tongue.

Revivals are hindered by tongues! Hearts are broken! Divorces come about because of gossiping and slander! Evangelists are driven from their ministries! Men have resigned the eldership because their names were ruined in the whole community because of slander and gossip! Whole neighborhoods have been thrown into uproars! APPLIED CHRISTIANITY would have avoided this! From a practical standpoint, one way to kill gossip is to refuse to listen to a gossiper. Tell him, "I am going to take you to the person you accuse and make you face him." If that doesn't work, say, "I want you to write that down." That usually stops it.

## MANIFESTING CHRISTIAN MORALS

Every person here knows what the Bible says about morals. "Thou shalt not steal." "Thou shalt not commit adultery." "Thou shalt not...thou shalt not...thou shalt not!" We know all of these—but you don't have to go far in religious work until you find people who have no more morals than a dog.

Do you mind, Brother Reyman, if I retell the story you told at Rushville last week?[8] A couple had come to church, and brought some children with them. Brother Reyman went to see them one morning. Everybody should have been up, but the couple was still in bed. The children were running around the house, so the couple got up, got dressed, and Rodney talked to the woman about their church relation. She said, "I hope we can get him converted so we can get married. It would be wrong for me to marry him before he becomes a Christian." In bed with him...and not married! Had she ever thought about the morality of it? Well, certainly she must have sometime in her life. Applied Christianity means you live like a Christian is supposed to.

When I was a boy I went to school one morning, and a bunch of kids were talking. I asked what was the matter. A girl had given birth to a baby the night before. She was the daughter of a deacon, and sang first soprano every Sunday. What was the stir all about? Her brother and father were going to the next town, where the boy lived, and were going to kill him! Did she know it was wrong? Did he know so too? Of course. Everybody knew it was wrong, but applied Christianity was not there.

I would like to read Romans 12:1 and ask how many people have heard this: "Present your bodies a living sacrifice, holy, acceptable to God, which is your spiritual service." Yet, how many church people ruin their bodies year in and year out?[9] Some church-goers stand right outside the church building and light up cigarettes. Some of them can't wait to get out of Bible School to smoke before they come back in for Communion! (I'm surprised some churches don't have a tobacco break!)

Years ago I held a meeting in Wichita, Kansas.[10] The church janitor said, "Brother Word, I'm surely glad you came and held this meeting. It surely has helped me. It used to be that the church foyer and sidewalk and steps were just like a carpet lined with cigarette butts. It surely has cleaned things up around here." And it stayed that way as long as the preacher was there with whom I was working.[11] But when the next preacher came along, he had to bring along his private secretary from his previous field of labor. (Nobody in Wichita, of course, had sense enough to be a secretary!) He was caught in immorality with her and is now completely out of the ministry.[12]

There are many preachers today who would preach about these sins, but they are afraid somebody will stigmatize them.[13] For instance, a man recently said to me, "You believe in faith, repentance, confession, baptism, and no T.V. as the plan of salvation. You are with the anti-T.V. church, aren't you?"[14] Do you know what I told him? (It is very seldom that I have enough sense to think on my feet. I usually think of it next week. I'm real smart next week! Well, aren't you?) But this time it was different. I said, "So we have the T.V. church and the anti-T.V. church? Do we have the tobacco church and the anti-tobacco church? and the card-playing church and the anti-card-playing church? and the dancing church and the anti-dancing church? and the booze-drinking church and the anti-booze-drinking church? and the theater-going church and the anti-theater-going church? and the liar's church and the anti-liar's church? T.V. promotes everyone of these ungodly things. Why not just say you have Christianity?"

I want to tell you, brethren, that the 21 epistles in the New Testament were written to help the church go straight, to give it a practical rule of conduct and life–and the Christians weren't called "anti-this" or "anti-that" by others who claimed to be Christians! They simply took the Word of God and went by it, and every one of these verses that God has given should help us live like God would have us to live. And, friend, until we get to the place where we say, "Lord, I just want to live for You; I want my life, my soul, my influence–everything I do–to count for Jesus Christ," we are going to have this unapplied, impractical churchanity with not genuine Christianity in it at all!

I appeal to you, friend, that if you have been guilty of these ungodly things; if you have been letting the devil run your life instead of God; even if you go to church every Sunday; even if you are a preacher; you don't have practical, APPLIED CHRISTIANITY, and as you are, you are not going to heaven! The Bible says you must be "born again"–born of water and the Spirit. And the Spirit produces fruit: love, joy, peace, goodness, kindness, longsuffering, meekness, faithfulness, and self-control. Friend, get right and stay right. Be a doer of the Word and not a hearer only, and God will bless you!

1. This meeting took place in Carlton, Oregon, July, 1931.
2. Barbara Word Brink.
3. The Carlton revival resulted in "only" 14 conversions; a lot by today's standards, but the fewest number of conversions in Word's storied five years of revival work on the West Coast (1930-1935).
4. The Words left the field of full-time revivals late in 1935, to take the Montavilla church. At this point in time Archie had been preaching there for 32 years.
5. James Matthew Alley.
6. A retired railroad man who's son, Elston, later became a preacher.
7. Word was a featured speaker at the annual Conference on Evangelism, sponsored by Cincinnati Bible Seminary, in the early-to-mid 1940s.
8. Rodney Reyman of Reno, Nevada. The Rushville Rally, smaller than the Centerville Rally, was an annual summertime gathering for people in the Mideast.
9. In 1994, 27 years after this sermon was preached, the FDA declared that nicotine was an addictive drug.
10. This revival, held in 1944, resulted in 177 conversions.
11. Word's lifelong friend, Russell Boatman.
12. Throughout Word's long and busy career, he never had a secretary. He preferred to personally answer all his mail, make all of his appointments, etc.
13. Early in his ministry a Baptist preacher asked Archie to preach his famous sermon, "Merrily Goint to Hell," in his church. Word asked "Why?" The preacher replied, "Because if I preached it, I would be fired!"
14. It is not for sure who first began calling the Portland-Ottumwa churches "anti-T.V." Vernon Newland went on record with this charge in 1974.

### Deaths

*"Blessed are the dead which die in the Lord from henceforth . . . that they may rest from their labours; and their works do follow them" (Revelation 14:13).*

**Archie Word**, 87, one of the restoration movement's foremost evangelists, died, at Scottsbluff, NE, Nov. 17. Word was born near Glasgow, KY, but was raised in Lindsay, CA. After stints in the Navy and the boxing ring, he enrolled at Eugene Bible University where Harold Knott's class on Christian Evidences convinced him once and for all about the inspiration of the Scriptures. He did student preaching at Crabtree and Toledo, OR.

The years 1930-1935 saw brother Word and his wife, the former Florence P. Procter, travel the United States from coast to coast in revival meetings. His first meeting in Coos Bay, OR, ran six weeks and resulted in ninety-three conversions. His next meeting was at Elmira, OR, and lasted "only" three weeks with sixty-three conversions. His third meeting was in his hometown of Lindsay. The six-week meeting saw 136 hometown folk converted to Christ. His longest revival was thirteen weeks in Pomona with more than 100 souls saved.

More than 3,000 were converted during this period of time. Russell Boatman was a teenage boy when Word came to San Bernadino. Boatman testifies, "To hear A. Word preach the Word was to hear preaching at its best. I was a teenager when Evangelist Word came to my home congregation in San Bernadino. To this day that was the greatest revival and evangelistic campaign that congregation has ever experienced." During this time Ripley's *Believe It or Not* carried Word's famous advertising slogan: "Hear A. Word Preach the Word."

With four children now in tow the Words settled in Portland, OR, and began a long and fruitful thirty-three-year ministry with the Montavilla church (Crossroads today). Standard Publishing presented the church with a special recognition in the 1940s for sending forty-six young people into full-time Christian service. Before the Words left in 1968 more than 100 young people had entered the ministry. In 1944 he began editing *The Church Speaks* and continued the publication for twenty-six years. In 1952 he founded a Bible college, Churches of Christ School of Evangelists, along with Lee Turner and Warren Bell. During this time his family grew to six children and he continued to hold revivals across the country, Mexico, and the British West Indies.

In 1969 he and Florence moved to Scottsbluff, NE, where he taught in the Scottsbluff School of Evangelism and served as associate preacher for the Bluffview Church of Christ until his death. His life-long wish to die in the pulpit was not granted, but he was working on a sermon just a few days before his death.

Funeral services were held at the Bluffview church Nov. 21, and the Crossroads church, Portland, OR, Nov. 25. Don DeWelt was among the many who gave tributes. DeWelt said, "One day you will read in the CHRISTIAN STANDARD that Archie Word is dead. Don't you believe it! In the hearts of thousands there is a warm memory of that day and hour when they stepped across that line of decision and came down the aisle to see brother Word waiting for them, hand outstretched in welcome. As long as these people are alive and can remember, he is not dead!"

Surviving in addition to his widow are children, Arch Word, Jr., Esther Burgess, Barbara Brink, Janelle Green, Anna Jean Rodda, and Margaret Hunt. Memorials may be sent to: Archie Word Memorial Prayer Chapel, Crossroads Church of Christ, 2505 Northeast 102nd Avenue, Portland, OR; Northwest College of the Bible; or Scottsbluff School of Evangelism.

for January 15, 1989 CHRISTIAN STANDARD

*Obituary of Archie Word as reported in* Christian Standard, *Jan. 15, 1989.*

## 27

# WHAT SHOULD WE DO UNTO JESUS?

*The Church Speaks,* September 1967

"Pilate saith unto them, What then shall I do unto Jesus who is called Christ? They all say, Let him be crucified" (Matt. 27:22).

There are only two classes of people to whom this question can be addressed: the saved and the unsaved; and those are the ones to whom I will be speaking today.

To the professed followers of Christ, it is the duty and privilege to give themselves to the work of calling on the unsaved in the name of Christ.[1] We should religiously give ourselves to religious calling! In that Great Day, we will see how glorious it really is to work for the Lord (and how INglorious the lazy church member is). Calling is constructive, especially in the midst of so much DEstructive work from the devil's camp. Surely calling is right–and the lack of calling is genuinely wrong.

Moses gave Hobab a beautiful invitation: "Come thou with us and we will do thee good." Christians ought to repeat it often—and at the same time examine themselves to see if they would be doing the stranger good if he did come his way!

It is a wide field, this calling business. The lost are all about us; our neighbors, loved ones, friends, visitors in our homes. And they come in all classes. They are rich, poor, high and low, backsliders, lost and drifting into eternity without any hope. Millions in our very day are ensnared in heathenism.[2] They need Jesus! What should we do? We should tell them about HIM by our words and our deeds. We should urge them to seek the Lord while it is possible to find Him!

Now, to the UNsaved people, my text is of the greatest import. Every person out of Christ, small or great, old or young, should carefully listen, because this question is personal, spoken by Pilate and recorded in Scripture to help all who will hear and heed.

"What then shall I do unto Jesus who is called Christ?" Pilate had to face the question—and he trifled with it, making shipwreck of himself because he did not handle it right. Every person who trifles with this question will eventually make shipwreck of himself for time and eternity!

I want to ask and answer four questions about this one question in this sermon to the unbeliever.

## WHAT CAN YOU DO WITH JESUS?

You cannot evade the question! You must do something with Him. You cannot avoid the question. You cannot escape it long. You must do something with Jesus because neutrality concerning THIS question is impossible; God will see to that!

What can you do with Jesus? You can accept Him as your Saviour, or you can crucify Him, morally, in your heart! Pilate tried to wash his hands of the blood of this Innocent Man. (He was afraid of the people.) You can crown Him as your Saviour, or you can reject Him as Pilate did. HELL IS GOING TO BE FILLED WITH MORAL COWARDS! You can cling to Him as your only hope, or you can put Him away and refuse to have anything to do with Him here.

There are not three things to be done with Jesus; there are only two. You can obey Him or rebel against Him. You can be for Him or against Him. You can say "Yes" to Him or "No." You can follow Him or turn away from Him and His company. You can accept Him as your Saviour or reject Him. You must do ONE of these TWO things. There is no third choice open to you.

## WHO IS TO DECIDE THIS QUESTION FOR YOU?

Consider, unsaved friend, what are YOU going to do with Jesus? Who is to decide this question for you? There is only one person in all the world who can decide this question for you! There are no substitutes! Your foes cannot answer this question for you (and you have some enemies if you have ever accomplished anything for God that is worth mentioning). The Lord Jesus had enemies! If you love your enemies to death, you can save the funeral expenses. Jesus died for His enemies. However, enemies cannot decide this question for you.

Your friends cannot decide this question for you (and you, no doubt, have many good friends). If you had a million friends, and all of them true to you, they could not decide this question for you.

You will not be forced, coerced nor compelled to decide this momentous question. You must meet it as a man! Remember, questions bring out the highest dignity God has bestowed on humans–and their greatest danger, decision! God has given you this terrifying gift, the power to make decisions–the right of choice. You can say "Yes" or "No"–even to God! But you must, in finality, answer to God for your decision. There is no greater dignity bestowed on man.

Jesus comes asking, "What will you do with Me?" God calls and man MUST use his highest honor, the right of choice. You must choose "Yes" or "No." This highest honor brings the greatest danger—the wrong choice. No danger can compare with it! You can ruin yourself forever with the wrong choice: ruin your life here, ruin your soul, ruin your friends, ruin all that pertains to you, ruin your health, ruin your hope and ruin your family! The right of choice is God's highest crown. Don't blame God for your mistakes or losses.

"As I live, saith the Lord Jehovah, I have no pleasure in the death of the wicked; but that the wicked turn from his way and live: turn ye, turn ye from your evil ways; for why will ye die, O house of Israel?" (Ezek. 33:11). You cannot blame God if you are lost. He has suffered for you and invites you to come unto Him with your burdens and labors, promising you rest. Jesus wept over Jerusalem, calling her people back to Him (Matt. 23:37). You cannot intimate that Jesus is at fault.

If you choose wrong; if you miss the upward way; if you miss salvation and heaven; boy or girl, man or woman, aged or infirm, it is nobody's fault but your's. You, alone, must decide. No one but YOU can decide your salvation and determine your destination. You are using your God-given privilege of choice. Choose Jesus and be sure. Tonight!

**DOES IT MATTER WHAT YOU DO WITH JESUS?**

Does it make any difference if you choose the world instead of Christ? How does it matter? Wherein does it matter?

It matters vitally to you—in your own life. Your salvation depends on what you do with Jesus. "And in none other is there salvation: for neither is there any other name under heaven, that is given among men, wherein we must be saved" (Acts 4:12). Your meeting God satisfactorily depends on how you have dealt with this question. "I am the way, and the truth, and the life: no one cometh unto the Father, but by me" (John 14:6). Your receiving of strength to overcome depends on your relationship to Jesus. "Ye are of God, my little children, because greater is he that is in you than he that is in the world" (I John 4:4). Your philosophy, so dear to you now, will not count then!

Your influence on others depends upon what you do with Jesus. Every life affects some other life. Some one has said, "You can shroud, coffin and bury the body out of sight, but not your influence. It has set in motion agencies which you are powerless to arrest. Influence! There is no shroud, coffin nor burial for it. It walks the earth like a pestilence; or an angel of death if it is wrong, and if it is good, if flows on like healing waters, blest of God, until the hand of God arrests and chains it."

God said influence is like yeast (Luke 12:1; I Cor. 6:7-8). It works silently, but will in time reach all. Influence is like salt, preserving and seasoning, if good (Matt. 5:13). Influence can be a root of bitterness or a poisonous herb (Heb. 12:15). It is like gangrene (II Tim. 2:17), fatal if it is not halted. Your influence can be like a viper's nest (Psa. 58:4; 140:3), if it is wrong.

What you do with Jesus now, determines what God will do with you then. What you do with Jesus will determine where you will spend eternity. It matters for life HERE. It matters for influence NOW. It matters...for your eternal welfare is dependent upon what you do with Jesus. You will spend eternity (and I will spend eternity) in accordance with what you and I have done with Jesus. "And the witness is this, that God gave unto us eternal life, and this life is in his Son. He that hath the Son hath the life; he that hath not the Son of God hath not the life" (I John 5:11-12).

Our eternal destinies rest upon Jesus, God's dividing line! One of our down-town missions[3] has a sign over the door,

"IF I SHOULD DIE TONIGHT, WHERE WOULD I GO?"

Ask yourself, "If I should die tonight, where would I spend eternity?" The answer is (and I answer with fear and trembling), "You will go into eternity according to your decision relative to Jesus!"

What then will YOU do unto Jesus, who is called Christ? It is the most important question you will ever face.

Jesus is the only window of hope in this life's dungeon through which we look into eternity.

**WHEN SHOULD YOU DECIDE THIS QUESTION?**

It is your question and my question. It is an inescapable question. It is an unyielding and unrelenting question. When should you decide it? Yesterday? It cannot be, now. Yesterday is gone, never to return. Tomorrow? Tomorrow is unborn. We know nothing of tomorrow. We have no promise of tomorrow. The Bible distinctly prohibits tomorrow. "Boast not thyself of tomorrow, for thou knowest not what a day may bring forth."

When should you decide? TODAY! "Today is the day of salvation...Today, if ye hear His voice, harden not your hearts!"

Teddy Leavitt[4] used to tell of a logger who accepted Jesus on Sunday evening. The logger was hurt in a logging accident in the woods on Monday. He died on Tuesday–but in the meantime, he kept repeating these words: "Isn't it wonderful I found Jesus Sunday? Isn't it wonderful I found Jesus Sunday?"

Won't you find Jesus tonight?

---

1. The editor well recalls three weeks of intensive door-to-door calling with Brother Word in a revival in Lexington, Nebraska, in 1970.
2. At this point in time the Montavilla church was sending mission support to Alaska, Jamaica, Mexico, Puerto Rico and Rhodesia (now Zimbabwe).
3. On notorious Burnside Street, often visited by Brother Word.
4. Teddy Leavitt was a rough-and-tumble revivalist who would challenge the toughest man in a lumber camp to a fight. After defeating him, all the men of the camp listened to Teddy preach!

# 28

# FIRST CENTURY PEACE IN THE CHURCH

*The Voice of Evangelism, June 1970*

"Then had the churches rest throughout all Judea and Galilee and Samaria, and were edified; and walking in the fear of the Lord, and in the comfort of the Holy Ghost, were multiplied" (Acts 9:31).

When there is trouble in the church, there is usually a reason; and when there is peace, there is a real reason too.[1]

Peace like a shaft of light lay across the land, and the big reason was that Saul of Tarsus, who had been the leader in the persecution of the church, had been converted. No one seemed ready to pick up the work that had been so completely taken from Saul's hand. Apparently the whole persecuting party of Jews was without a leader, depressed and disorganized. That was one reason why the church had peace, but what stymied them worse that that was the threat of Caligula to put his image up in the temple in Jerusalem. This turned the heads of the persecuting Jews from the new-born church to an older and stronger enemy – Rome (with a crazy emperor).

God's ways are far above our ways. He gave the early church an intermission of peace in this peculiar way.

This was so different from the immediate past with its stimulating activities, spreading the Word in the face of blood-letting persecution – even the death of one of their outstanding preachers – and threats of further trouble to anyone who dared oppose them. However, excitement and extreme activity can check growth in character, and God would give His church a better opportunity to grow by converting their worst opponent, making of him their chief exponent of THE WAY he had so forcefully sought to harm.

It was rest from the blows of the persecutors. It was rest from the writhing anxieties of not knowing what type of persecution might burst upon them next. (Worrying about trouble kills more people than actual persecution.) It was a rest from fleeing from place to place, from one hiding place to newer and better places of refuge. The early Christians had to elude their persecutors or take the consequences! But Christ in His mercy is mindful of the needs of His church. They needed some peace and tranquility, so the Lord gave it to them.

Every person needs some repose in the midst of storm, trouble and conflict. Although such tests of character and faithfulness are said to add strength to the one passing through the storm, rest is needed. In fact, it is imperative. God knew this, so He gave them peace.

If they were to be edified, it was mandatory that they have peace from intruders. One of the evident attributes of the Lord's church is spontaneous love among the saints and a spirit of cooperation. The conditions which had prevailed where all had been having similar wants, fears, dangers, sorrows and anxieties would be conducive to making for harmony among them, drawing them together in the sweet spirit of brotherhood.

It is good for us to take note of the various things that go into Christian character, making us pleasing to God. We do not need a hard, stiff, unbending, harsh treatment. We need variety, and God gives it for our benefit. Christians need different seasons. Real Christians[2] can profit by the changes. We need the cold blasts and the tempest as well as the summer evening's soft sigh. to every Christian there will come times of caution, anxious watching and heart-searching times of anguish, but we also need the times of rest, happiness and calmness of peaceful days.[3]

No doubt some of the older ones in the faith looked for the persecutors to come upon them while they were at rest, but the persecutors left them alone, and like the church in Corinth, they "had peace, as in all the churches of the saints" (I Cor. 14:33).

This peace was a welcome watchword for these who had been so harried by their relentless foes. But times of peace from the outside are often just the time for the devil to bring confusion and discord on the inside! Discord that is brought on by a common enemy that we know to be near and strong is so different from the peace and harmony that comes from genuine love among the brethren. This can only make us feel the satisfaction we hope for when we reach the other side and rest with Him in glory. This peace must have been a pleasant experience among those who had experienced the many trials and disappointments from their former brethren (the Jews). How gratifying it must have been to introduce the followers of the Lord to their first set of new ideals and affections.

How wonderfully delightful this peace – if for nothing else the communication with fellow Christians and visiting between the churches of the area! Possibly they had known something of each, and no doubt they had wept together over their trials and persecution, but now they could have their "conversation in heaven," and they would no doubt find that an edifiying time – walking in God's fear and praise, enjoying the comfort of the Holy Spirit as they developed His fruit.

"The fellowship of kindred minds is like to that above..."

...And they had it abundantly during this time of peace throughout Judea, Galilee, and Samaria.

Until one has sorrows, he does not know how to appreciate comfort! And when that sorrow is so terribly deep that no one can prove efficacious, then the comfort of the Holy Spirit is deeply appreciated.

Their past experiences and circumstances would cause these disciples to walk in the fear of the Lord circumspectly, different from the Jews, as examples of their forgiving, crucified Lord. The church should always walk this way, having love, trust and joy in the Lord, ever remembering that He deserves our deepest reverence at all times. We should walk in fear, realizing that we are constantly under His surveillance, and that He is a God of righteousness and purity. We walk in fear as we remember we are individually accountable for the extending of His kingdom. We should remember we are God's converters, and if we lose our sanctified relation there is no way for it to be restored, humanly speaking (Matt. 5:13).[4]

We should walk in the fear of the Lord, realizing we need to be constantly sustained by divine influence. There is nothing that can replace that divine power! We cannot depend upon organized perfection in denominational machinery or in some grand preacher's eloquence or oratory. No human authority can take HIS place in the church! We must be empowered by the Holy Spirit – and the Lord only is the dispenser of His Spirit to us! He gives the doctrine that is our heavenly message. Without it there is no salvation. Our Heavenly Benefactor gives the ever-living power that makes all the functions of the church operate effectually. This will contribute to our being edified (built up like a building rises from the basement through its superstructure). We are built up gradually, with proper proportions, if we are fearing God and letting Him build us up.

It is no wonder this church was "multiplied." They took advantage of the opportunity to grow numerically as well as being edified individually. The only way a church can multiply is to have its members edified – settled, established, strengthened to be deep, solid, firm. Then people go to work and multiplication takes place naturally![5]

There is no doubt from the New Testament account that the church grew tremendously during times of the severest persecution. People were added to the church, and no amount of trouble could cut off its growth or cut down its rolls. Recruits kept right on coming into the fellowship, even as others were imprisoned or killed. This, to my mind, sets forth Christianity better than anything else. The consistent walk of the church at all times, and the heartfelt experience of all Christians as they are impelled by the Holy Spirit, are the best human means for the increase of the church, for a great impression on the ungodly world, and for the conversion of sinners. Under every circumstance the power must be of God!

This is made known by God's method of preaching the gospel (which to the world seems mere foolishness). But it works! After hearing the gospel and being empowered by the Holy Spirit, the convert makes an impression on others by walking in the fear of the Lord.[6] The world sees the change, hears his testimony, and takes note of the way he lives. The consistent Christian life speaks for itself and calls others to walk in this new life and new way. This has always been a powerful and irresistible argument. The absence of the changed life by the power of God is one of the most condemning accusations against the worldly church. The person who makes a hollow profession never makes converts to Christ. The world condemns him for his hypocrisy, and the church condemns him for his backslidden apostasy!

(The world will put up with hypocrisy and hollowness in everything else on earth except religion! They speak out against the hypocrite quicker than church members do!)

Edification and multiplication are closely connected and intentionally placed close together in our text. One actually causes the other! One of the inescapable products of edifying is multiplying. The well-nourished and truly spiritual church is a growing church. It witnesses by life and expression, and the truth is evident to all. It is inspired to active labors at all times. By its holy walking and heart-joy in God it attracts men to join their company. A godly church says, "Come thou with us, and we will do thee good; for verily the Lord is with us."[7]

A revival meeting may bring on a spasmodic fluctuation for a while, but if the members are not edified, there will not be a consistent growth that is steady.[8]

This early church, by its doctrine and life, soon grew to 5000 men (and if the proportion between men and women in the church was as it is now, there must have been several thousand members!). They were at peace in all Judea, Galilee and Samaria, and they were being edified, built up in the most holy faith; and as they grew, they walked in the fear of the Lord, as an example of their doctrine. They were comforted by the Holy Spirit. And as a result of all this they were multiplied, locally and abroad.

Would to God that the churches of our era could be patterned after the same blueprint...and experience the same progress and growth!

1. Brother Word ended his long 33-year ministry at Montavilla in 1968. It was a ministry, for the most part, marked by peace.
2. Word had a 4-part sermon he often preached on "Real Christians." Educated, consecrated, separated, dedicated.
3. Few days like this existed in 1970, a year marred by the trial of the Chicago Seven, Weathermen bombings, Kent State, Angela Davis, and the deaths of Jimi Hendrix and Janis Joplin.
4. "If the salt have lost its savor...it is thenceforth good for nothing, but to be cast out and trodden under foot of men."
5. this was Word's plan for "church growth" (a term not in vogue then). Strong edification (preaching that stressed every-member evangelism) led to natural multiplication (numerical additions).
6. Word's straight preaching converted prostitutes, drunkards, dance band leaders, etc., who became powerful witnesses for Christ after their conversion.
7. Numbers 10:29. Actual rendering, "Come thou with us, and we will do thee good; for Jehovah hath spoken good concerning Israel."
8. In 1968 Word re-entered the field of full-time revival work.

# CROSSROADS Family Circle

Crossroads Church of Christ

2505 N.E. 102nd Ave. • Portland, Oregon 97220
(503) 257-9193

VOL. 11 NO. 46 NOVEMBER 23, 1988

A. Word 1988

## All Things Considered... by Tom Burgess

In Memory

ARCHIE JAMES WORD

April 21, 1901 — November 17, 1988

Preacher of

"THE WORD"

Archie Word grew up in Lindsay, California, joined the Navy after a year in high school, was discharged two years later, finished high school and business college, and was working for Standard Oil Co. when W.S. Lemmon persuaded him to go to Eugene Bible University. Until this point in his life he had seen the inside of the liquor industry, had been in prize fighting and in general had been around seeing sin first hand. Now he was on the threshold of new living - college days of Bible study, student preaching at Crabtree and Toledo, Oregon, and five years in the evangelistic field with an estimated three thousand converts, among them 38 ministerial student, a college president and a college professor.

When A. Word spoke he made it clear what he meant; no one was left wondering what he said. Personally he was 100% business and solicited the same from the Christians.

continued on page 2

## Events Next Week...

In the U.S. Navy when 16.

Memorial Services to be held on November 25th, 1:00 pm Crossroads Church of Christ

A graduate of Strathmore High School.

*Front page of special issue,* Crossroads Family Circle, *Nov.23, 1988, announcing Word's passing.*

# 29

# OVERCOMING OUR SINFUL PAST

*A sermon preached at the Holgate Rally, August 1975, Portland, Oregon*

"Let us walk becomingly, as in the day; not in revelling and drunkenness, not in chambering and wantoness, not in strife and jealousy. But put ye on the Lord Jesus Christ, and make not provision for the flesh, to fulfil the lusts thereof" (Rom. 13:13-14).

This topic is very Scriptural! Paul dealt with the subject at hand. And this subject is appropriate for Christians today.

You may be asking, "Do you mean that this topic applies to US? Do you mean we have been sinful–that we need to overcome our sinful past?"

Yes! I mean that every one of you who are now Christians have had a sinful past! We all need this sermon, and usually those who think they need such a message the least usually need it the most! Maybe some of you have not yet overcome your sinful past. You, then, especially need this message.

Too many church people are like a little boy riding with his father when going past a drive-in movie theater. The little boy asked his father, "Do you know what that thing is?" The father asked, "What?" And the boy said, "The devil." They rode on a little way, and the child added, "But I like the devil a little bit."

Too many times we look at the bootlegger, the gambler, the tobacco slave, the dance hall manager, the T.V. "slop-fed" person, the one on LSD or other drugs, and we smugly say, "Isn't he or she terribly sinful!"[1] God knows they are bad enough, but I want you to read your Bible and notice that not one of these sins are mentioned by name in any of God's lists of sins. They are known to be sins because of Christian PRINCIPLES–principles set up by the Lord in His Word to cover every doubtful and dangerous innovation that the devil can invent to entice the unwary and foolish ones into his pit! God has laid down such Christian principles to guide and protect His children as long as the world stands. But the Bible does speak explicitly about our "little" sins: being liars and cowards, fearful and unbelieving (Rev. 21:8); being covetous (Col. 3:5); envious (Rom. 1:29); backbiting, being boastful and haughty (Rom. 1:30); being unmmerciful (Rom. 1:32); and Galatians 5 lists enmities, strife, jealousies, and wrath. All of these we have all been at one time or another. In these we have all sinned and come short of the glory of God (Rom. 3:23), so we all need this sermon!

In overcoming our sinful past you must...

## SEE YOURSELF AS ONE WHO HAS BEEN A SINNER

When I was drinking and selling it, it was not bad to me.[2] The dance hall[3] did not seem like sin to me; nor gambling, lying, cheating in business, etc.,[4] because I was making money on these things. When I was chewing and smoking, it was not a sin to me because it was popular to do so, so it could not be too bad.

A sinner is like an alcoholic–he must admit he is in trouble, or he cannot be helped. Sinners cannot be helped as long as they keep saying, "I'm o.k.–it is the preacher who is the sinner."

I had to be convinced of my own sinfulness by straight Bible preaching, applied to me, before I could overcome my sinful past.[5] You, too, must do this, or you will never overcome your sins—past, present, or future. After I was converted,[6] someone who at that time was not at all religious, wrote me, and said, "If you had not been so wicked, mean, and ungodly, you would not have become a preacher"—inferring that I was an awful sinner. He was blind to his own sinfulness.

You must become convicted of your sins if you want to overcome your sinful past. And unless you are willing to yield to God's leading in your life, you will never be saved, you will not overcome your sins. In your decision, you are choosing your destiny—for Jesus said it is "Repent" or "Perish" (Luke 13:3,5).

**YOU MUST BECOME CONVERTED**

Conversion is the result of repentance. It involves a whole change in the purpose of your life. Paul's case aptly illustrates this. On his way to Damascus he repented—and the purpose of his life was completely changed. He didn't kill any more Christians—he didn't want to or intend to! In Texas they have a saying, "You are so wrong, brother, that you couldn't be wronger!" When you see you are wrong and you are converted, you have a change of purpose, and it makes you so right that you could be any "righter." Then you are on your way to overcoming your sinful past. Conversion will put sin out and righteousness in. Then you can sing (and mean it),

*"What a wonderful change in my life has been wrought,*
*Since Jesus came into my heart.*
*I have light in my soul for which long I had sought,*
*Since Jesus came into my heart!"*

When you really get converted, the Word of God will fill your heart instead of the smoke-filled pool hall, dance hall, dirty magazines, lascivious stories, cursing, lying, cheating, covetousness, gossiping, hatred, envy, backbiting, jealousies, anger, or any other sin.

After I was converted and was back in my home town, I passed the "Yaller Dawg" saloon.[7] From way back inside a voice yelled out, "Hey, Word! Where is your Bible?" I did not say anything then, but later, when my Dad and uncle were with me, and the same thing was said, I walked into the "Yaller Dawg," stepped up to the bar, and said, "I notice you still have a healthy respect for Old Word by hollering at me from a distance!"[8]

Then I added, "I have been what you are, but you have never been what I am."

That summer I went back to work with the same old gang, fumigating citrus trees with hydraynic acid. They saw the difference–and later three of them were converted! You must be converted (changed from the inside out) or you will never overcome your sinful past.

## GET INTERESTED IN OTHER PEOPLE'S SOULS

A soul winner has no time to gossip, play cards, or watch television. I went to work for God and believe me, after 50 years of serving Him, I can tell you it is a very satisfying life to live. I went to college, took voice lessons and song leading, and sang solos for my newly-found Lord. In a short time we had a great group of singers in the church at Dallas, Oregon. Then I got into a quartet, and we sang for revival meetings all over the state. Then I learned how to preach and went to work at it.[9]

Nothing will help you overcome your sinful past like living and preaching righteousness (because you are interested in other people's souls), and nothing will condemn you more surely and more quickly than not caring what happens to others. You will be hated by rebels, but loved by the Lord. And He will help you to overcome!

## GET YOUR POCKET BOOK CONVERTED

"Where your treasure is, there will your heart be also" (Matt. 6:21).

Too many church folks have an investment of $70.00 in Christian equipment (Bible, etc.) and $700.00 in a color television. They give the Lord two hours a week and 20 hours a week to watching T.V. Doing what? Watching the world that they love so much! If you want to get rid of your T.V. and set a good example for others, promise God you are going to give Him ten times as much time as you have given to T.V.

Get your heart right with God–and your pocket book will be right too. Invest your money, your time, and your talents in an effort to save souls, and you will not slide back and fall into the pit from which you were dug. Buy books to use for God–and study them. Get your heart into God's business, and you will overcome your sinful past.

## GET YOUR GIRL FRIEND, BOY FRIEND, WIFE, OR HUSBAND CONVERTED

I married the finest Christian girl in all the world.[10] But thank God she was smart enough NOT to marry me until I showed the fruits of genuine conversion. I loved her for her fine self, and she loved the "new" me. We set out to build a Christian family–not on abortion or the pill. We gave our lives in total commitment to the Saviour of souls, and there was no desire to go back into the sin that we had left behind. Jesus Christ, God's Son, saved us, made us overcomers, and we will praise His name forever!

How have I been helped to overcome my sinful past? By being convicted of my sinfulness, being converted, becoming interested in others, and putting my money into God's work.

God can change your life too–if you will really let Him. Why don't you let him?

1. Of this list of six sins, A. Word had practiced the first four in wild-oats years: bootlegging, gambling, tobacco, and managing dance halls.
2. Word became a bootlegger in the San Joaquin Valley after his graduation from high school in 1922.
3. Word operated three dance halls in Fresno from 1922-1925.
4. What lurid sins are probably included in this "etc." Late in life Word testified he had committed every sin except murder.
5. Word began to hear "straight Bible preaching" when he enrolled at Eugene Bible University in 1925. Preachers like E. V. Stivers, Harold E. Knott, V. E. "Daddy" Hoven, and Teddy Leavitt helped in the conversion of A. Word.
6. Word's conversion took place in an upper room prayer meeting at EBU on Nov. 11, 1925.
7. A notorious bar in Lindsay in Word's day. It has been replaced by slightly more "upscale" drinking establishments today.
8. Archie left the Navy undefeated in the boxing ring. For a time he continued a career as a bruising prize fighter in and around Lindsay.
9. Word's "baptism of fire" in preaching happened in Toledo, OR, in the summer of 1928, when Garland Hay's voice gave out and Archie had to finish the revival.
10. The Words were married July 7, 1926, about 8 months after Archie's conversion.

# 30

# THE BIBLE'S FINAL CALL

*The Voice of Evangelism,* September, 1981

"And the Spirit and the bride say, Come. And let him that heareth say, Come. And let him that is athirst come. And whosoever will, let him take the water of life freely" (Rev. 22:17).

Invitations are important.

Do you remember how you felt when you were not invited to a party when many of your friends were?

I have known men and women who had never drunk to become so discouraged by not being invited to a function that they started drinking to forget their misfortune and unpopularity! Our text contains the last of God's invitations and the greatest of His biddings to wayward men and women–to come and find safety in Christ!

## THE SPIRIT'S AND THE CHURCHES' INVITATION

"The Spirit and the bride say, Come." The Holy Spirit of God and the church (the bride) invite all to come to salvation–

to prepare for citizenship in heaven! It is a call to all to leave the low road of sin and walk the high road of holiness.

The overall objective of this verse is to show the freeness of the offer. It impressively sets down for the last time (as God closes His Book) the greatness of the provision that He has made for all to come to Christ and be saved! Can you see the appropriateness of this invitation to close this Book and to seal the Sacred Volume in this way?

The Holy Spirit was back of every invitation to wayward Israel to come to God and be saved. God inspired those Old Testament invitations just as He inspires this one. But this one is the greatest of them all! The Holy Spirit was back of every messenger proclaiming mercy through the gospel. He is saying "Come!" as friends invite friends, neighbors invite neighbors, and strangers invite strangers to accept the Lord and be saved!

It is the business of every member of the church to be inviting every person to find safety in Christ. It is the chief business of every preacher to extend God's great invitation.[1] Baptism and the Lord's Supper are saying that we died to sin and have been raised to walk as saved souls. The Lord's Supper also reminds us that when we fail, the blood of Christ can cleanse us if we confess our sins to God and walk in the light.

Every consecrated Christian life depicts before the world the excellency of his new life after he has answered the invitation to come to Christ. Every new convert filled with Christian zeal is a living invitation to all those who have known him before his conversion to answer the same invitation to this feast of salvation. The world sees the change!

Every Christian parent should be inviting his or her children to walk in the light of God. Every brother should be inviting his brother, and every sister should be giving this urgent invitation to the feast to her sister. Every Christian employer should be inviting his employees to come to Jesus and be saved. The memory of mothers and fathers "gone on before" should call to mind God's invitation by loved ones to accept heaven's invitation and be ready to meet them around God's throne.

**THE HEARER'S INVITATION**

"Let him that heareth say, Come."

Anybody who hears can give God's invitation to others! What can you do on earth that is of more value than this? This is a universal invitation–no one is too poor or too ugly to be left out![2] Preachers are not to monopolize this privilege. It is EVERY Christian's privilege!

In fact, if every Christian would get out into the field and earnestly give God's invitatiion as recorded in our text, there would be no need for a bus ministry. The bus ministry personnel are now doing what every child of God should be doing–working to get this last invitation from heaven out![3]

**AN INVITATION TO THE THIRSTY**

"Let him that is athirst come."

Have you ever been thirsty–really thirsty? Thirsty people can be downright rude in getting to the drinking fountain. Thirsty people won't be particular about how clean or pure the water is either. They know it will quench their thirst–and they want it! Thank the Lord, this water is from heaven's pure fountain, and thirsty souls are invited to drink of the water of life.

Anyone and everyone who desires God's salvation will find the fountain is open to him with the assurance that it will give him eternal life! It is not asked of him, "How worthy are you?" No matter what sin he or she may have been in, God does not ask how far you have strayed or how far you went in open rebellion. If you are thirsty for God's salvation, you are welcome!

There is no age limit! You can come, even in old age, if you are willing to believe in Christ and trust His Word! The Lord tests our professed faith by demanding that we turn from all known sin and turn to God. You may be ignorant or you may carry a Ph.D.–God makes no distinction! He simply says to those who thirst, "He that believeth and is baptized shall be saved" (Mark 16:16), and that allows the finest-clothed millionaire as well as the man in rags to come to God's fountain!

You may drive a Rolls Royce or you may herd a Ford–God welcomes all thirsty souls and invites them to come. The feast is free! There is no way you can buy it. Christ purchased our salvation by His blood. All we have to do is get to the fountain by doing what He has asked us to do.

**A FREE INVITATION**

"And whosoever will, let him take the water of life freely."

It is free! Come drink of the water of life FREELY! What a contrast between the "water of life" to which lost souls are invited by God and the fires of hell into which the devil leads his devotees!

Why die of thirst when God is inviting you to the fountain of living waters? Oh, come! Then you can shout with us: "Ho, everyone that thirsteth, come and drink of the waters freely!"[4]

---

1. A. Word's life was changed forever when a preacher, W. S. Lemmon, invited him to sing in his church at Porterville, CA.
2. A trademark of Word's personal work was his caring ministry to "down-and-outers," people other preachers and churches would not attempt to reach.
3. Not to be construed as oppostion to bus ministries. Word simply believed in "every member evangelism."
4. Isaiah 55:1

# 31

## SECRET SINS

*The Voice of Evangelism,* January 1983

"Who can discern his errors? Clear thou me from hidden faults. Keep back thy servant from presumptuous sins; let them not have dominion over me: then shall I be upright, and I shall be clear from great transgression. Let the words of my mouth and the meditation of my heart be acceptable in thy sight, O Jehovah, my rock, and my redeemer" (Psa. 19:12-14).

Self-righteousness arises partly from false pride, but mainly from ignorance of God's law. A knowledge of the deep spirituality and the stern severity of God's law would change people's minds, their thoughts, their every inner emotion. No man ever rises above his own law of life.

God's law shrivels our self-righteousness into nothingness. David, in our text, had caught a glimpse of God's law when he said, "Who can discern his errors? Clear thou me from hidden faults." After we have confessed every sin we can think of, it is good to add, "Clear thou me of hidden faults."

This sermon will deal with sins known to the sinner–but unknown to his fellowman. To you who sin secretly, or are tempted to sin secretly; to you who break God's covenant in the dark, and wear a mask of goodness in the light; to you who shut the doors, pull the curtains, shut off the light, and sin secretly; may God help you to pray this prayer of David's: "Clear thou me of hidden faults." May you give up, renounce, detest, hate, and abhor all secret sin!

Let us consider four facts about secret sin.

## THE FOLLY OF SECRET SIN

If you are a pretender–one who looks upon his outward conduct as upright, amiable, liberal, generous and Christian–but you indulge in some sin that the eye of man has not yet detected, remember: God knows it!

Perhaps it is private drunkeness. You revile the man who staggers down the street, but you secretly indulge in his sin. How foolish! Your sin will find you out–maybe very soon!

Maybe it is lust. You despise the harlots and whoremongers who practice their sin openly, but privately your mind is a den of lust! God knows it, and people may soon find out. When I was a sinner, I worked with two church members and I heard the language they used in private. Their hearts were dens of lust! What kind of literature do you read–and ENJOY? What magazines do you purchase when you are alone? "Be sure your sin will find you out!" Maybe some one knows about it right now! Your sin is not a secret, for the eyes of God have seen it!

"Thou God seest me" (Gen. 16:13). Darkness, curtains, brick walls, doors, and parked cars are all transparent to God. Do you not know, secret sinner, that "all things are naked and laid bare before the eyes of him with whom we have to do" (Heb. 4:13)? There is no secret sin–except to the fool. He has no God. Many act the part of the atheist.

See that priest as he runs the knife into the entrails of the animal to find the heart, liver, lungs, and whatever is concealed therein! So are we cut open before God! There is no secret chamber, no cellar, no blinds. Dig, dig, dig, and dig some more, as deep as the bottomless pit, and God knows the bowels of the mountains. Throw yourself into the sea, and a thousand crashing waves will tell the secret to God. Your sin is known in heaven. The deed is photographed from the sky. There it shall remain until Judgment Day!

The bank in Portland where I did business[1] had a glass cage which surrounded a nest of ants. We could see everything they were doing. This earth is like a glass ant's nest to God. Just as we looked in and saw all the secret work of these tiny creatures, so God looks down into our lives and sees ALL we think or do. "Thou God seest me." Stop! Think! Drop your stolen goods! God is looking through the clouds upon your vice. It is folly to try to hide from Him (Psa. 139:1-6).

Possibly your secret sin is a wicked temper at home. Some day you will be unveiled, and the wicked eyes of other deceivers, hypoctires, and pretenders will see you as you are. But you will all be in hell together! Your dearest family and friends, your wife or husband, your children have stumbled over your two lives–one kind of life at church and another kind of life at home. Suppose the whole church could hear you talk at home or see your actions. God, heaven, and angels see you. You are a fool to try to fool God!

Secret swearer, you do not swear before your friends. No one whom you care for has ever heard you cut loose and curse–but that oath went into the ears of God! The God of heaven heard. It is folly to continue cursing secretly. Who deserves the most respect? God or your friends? Who will be your judge?

Maybe your secret sin is evil thoughts, ungodly thinking. Suppose I should choose the holiest person in this audience and say to you, "I am in possession of photographs of every thought that has gone through your mind last week. Now I am about to show them on a screen right here, so everyone can see them." Do you know what would happen? That person would say, "Show them my ACTS, but please do not show them my thoughts!" Why? Because evil thoughts go through the minds of all of us. The sin is in keeping them there! Birds will fly over your head, but do not allow them to build a nest in your hair! Most of us would offer a bribe to stop the showing of that film or offer to buy it outright.

If you are a secret sinner, renounce the act–because it is foolishness before God. Give up your secret sin. Your sin is recorded in heaven. Some day it will be advertised on the walls of eternity – unless it is under the blood of God's propitiatory sacrifice!

**THE MISERY OF THE SECRET SINNER**

The most miserable of all sinners is the secret sinner. A drunkard in the open has his hour of pleasure and bears misery afterward. The profane swearer, who makes no claim of purity, has peace (a false peace) for awhile. But the secret sinner may be a charter member of the church, possibly walks with the preacher, is a regular attender, and tries to make a good appearance before the church while living in secret sin. What a miserable existence! It is worse than a mouse living in the family room, in constant fear of being caught. He runs out for a crumb, then back to his secret hole. How fearful they are of discovery. A slip reveals them; they recover. The next day, another slip; more cunning. They tell lie after lie to cover their actions.

*"O what a tangled web we weave,*
*when first we practice to deceive!"*

Oh, if I must be a sinner, let me be openly wicked! Let me be openly vicious as a sinner, bound for hell! Take away hypocrisy, claiming to be God's yet doing the devil's bidding secretly, always hiding! Never at peace. Oh, the misery of the secret sinner!

Men may praise you to the skies, but if they knew your secret sins, they would cast your name into hell's pit. Profession without true Christianity is merely a painted float in which to go to hell. Secret sin is like wax that melts in the sun.

No man can serve two masters. Do not try it. A woman entered a lawyer's office to sell him some books. It is not known if he purchased any books or not, but she sold him her soul. A secret room was built for her. There she lived; they were "soul mates." The lawyer had a wife and daughter who lived on the hill. For three years this continued, but one day the lawyer dropped dead–in the secret room! A doctor was called–who turned out to be the lawyer's wife's brother! The secret was out! Disgrace, sorrow, and she a suicide!

Secret sinner, if you want a foretaste of hell, just continue in secret sin. Pray this prayer with David, "Cleanse thou me from hidden faults." It will save you a lot of misery.

## THE SOLEMN GUILT OF SECRET SINS

Man's common measurement of sin is the notoriety of it–being exposed or caught. Short-changing or robbing the till is o.k., just so you are not caught. "One hand in the till is better than two in your pocket." Shoplifting, stealing auto parts, drinking, smoking, swearing, trickery in business, and writing bad checks are considered o.k., just so you are not caught. Borrowing and not returning, being a dead-beat, sneak, or poor credit risk are all right, just so you are not exposed. Being an embezzler or an absconder is o.k., just so you are not caught. But God does not judge sin that way! With God, sin is sin whether secret or public. We ought to measure sin by what God has said about it.

Secret sinners do not mind being sinners. All they fear is being exposed. Woe to the preacher who shows them up as they really are! Again, we ought to measure sin as God measures it. Secret sin is the worst sin because it is practical atheism! How? It makes your god unable to discern your thoughts and deeds. That kind of "god" is no god at all!

The secret sinner is an idolater. He thinks more of man than of God. He thinks more of his sin than he does of God. There are some who would not think of swearing, stealing, denying Christ, listening to dirty stories, smoking tobacco or pot, drinking booze, or dancing–if the PREACHER is watching them. They are idolatrous atheists! It is dishonoring God, dethroning God, making God lower than man.

God, give me the ability to preach like old Roland Hill.[2] Every person thought he was preaching to him or her. God says, "Can any man hide himself in secret places that I cannot see him?" (Jer. 23:24). "Cleanse thou me of hidden faults."

**THE DANGER OF SECRET SINS**

Secret sins betray one into public sins. You say you are going to have a little drink once in awhile, and no one needs to know? One of these days you will stagger into the streets a drunken sot, still thinking no one knows! You say, "I will read a lascivious book once in awhile. I will hide it if decent people show up." Soon your mind will be a cesspool. You say, "I will run with the worldly crowd just a little." Soon you will leave the Lord's Supper to go with the world. You might as well stick your head into a lion's mouth! You cannot regulate his jaws – and you cannot regulate your secret sin either.

Your sin will gad about, and in time you will not mind if it does. Sin kills the conscience. Sin is like a jet plane with no pilot; like a wild horse running full-speed downhill; like a runaway train or a raving maniac.

But someone says, "My sin is such a small one; please spare it." "It is the little foxes that destroy the vine. Our vines have tender roots" (Song of Solomon 2:15). Little sins are like two grown thieves who hoist a small boy up through a window so they can get in through the front door. One chipped gear ruins a transmission. One Canadian thistle breeds a thousand.

Sin is so deceptive. One man said, "A man's heart is like a cage full of unclean birds." He said that in order to excuse his own sin, but was answered, "It is the Christian's business to wring the neck of every unclean bird in his heart!" The Christian must not tolerate sin. We must not harbor sin. Our God is a jealous God.

God, give us grace to shun sin! God, give us power to overcome sin! Let me entreat you to give up your secret sin. You may be "almost persuaded" to be a Christian. You are halting between two opinions. You intend to serve God some day. You are striving to give up sin. You are finding it a hard struggle. Think it over. Will you keep your sin and be condemned forever or leave your sin and go to heaven?

Will you be honest and think straight? Will you say to Christ at the Judgment what you are saying right now? Think, friend! At the Judgment Day of God when lightning flashes and thunder shakes the foundations of the earth! Look about you! See Caiaphas? Will he pass judgment on Christ now? Will Judas kiss and betray Christ now? See if the crowd that crucified Christ will choose Barabbas now!

Secret swearer, where are your oaths on that day? Drunkard, you will finally look sober then. Infidels, you will not ridicule the Bible at judgment! Every sinner who has rejected the Lord Jesus as their Saviour will be crying for the rocks and the mountains to fall on them to cover them from the wrath of God!

My secret sinner friend, do TODAY what you will wish you had done when you at last stand bare before Him against whom you have been sinning!

---

1. The Words were now living in Gering, Nebraska.

2. A preacher in Victorian England, who even called the Queen to repentance!

MR. WORD AS SEEN BY TWO WELL-KNOWN "SONS IN THE LORD"

**By Russell E. Boatman** - To hear "A. Word preach The Word" was to hear preaching at its best. Archie Word was 14 years my senior, chronologically. Evangelistically and energetically, he was the senior of every man I have ever known. There is a phrase that follows shortly after the salutation of almost every letter written by the Apostle Paul, "I thank my God for you." Those words express my thoughts in every "remembrance and supplication of mine" in behalf of A. Word. God bless him.

**By Don DeWelt** - Everyone needs a living hero. The emphasis I have consistently placed on winning the lost and of believing if we do today what the persons in the book of Acts did, we will become what they were i.e. simple New Testament Christians, to a very large extent came from A. Word. His emphasis upon teaching has been mine - his emphasis upon the printed page has become mine. I owe a debt to A. Word I can never repay. I know he was just human - but he will always be my hero for the Lord.

"I mean business, and you had better too" (in the 1940's).

The Words in the 1950's while still in Portland.

Second Class Postage PAID at Portland, Oregon

Crossroads Church of Christ
2505 N.E. 102nd Avenue
Portland, Oregon 97220

A. Word, Evangelist "A Sinner Saved by Grace"

*Back page of tribute issue,* Crossroads Family Circle, *Nov. 23, 1988.*

## 32

# WHEN DEATH COMES

*The Voice of Evangelism,* June, 1984

"And it came to pass in those days, that she fell sick, and died..." (Acts 9:37).

In life many are prone to think of, talk about, and dwell on the bad things someone has said or done, or at least what they THINK they have said or done.

That seems to be human nature, and we have all done it. But when death comes, things change!

When death comes we then recall the departed's good points, his kind words, his helpful assistance, his neighborly deeds, his thoughtfulness of others, his love for his family and friends.

We remember his concern for the lost, his love for the Bible, his sacrifices for the ongoing of the church, his love for and his putting Christ first in his life, and his crossbearing without murmuring.

We remember his desire to see his children and grandchildren saved, his generosity with those in need, and his helpfulness to those in trouble.

We remember his generosity and prayerful support of every effort to get the "Good News" of salvation out to those who are lost.

We speak of his testimony to others and his concern for their salvation.

We remember gladly that he tried to "lay up for himself treasures in heaven."

## A BIBLICAL EXAMPLE

Consider a Bible example of this: "Now there was at Joppa a certain disciple named Tabitha, which by interpretation is called Dorcas: This woman was full of good works and almsdeeds which she did. And it came to pass in those days, that she fell sick, and died: and when they had washed her, they laid her in an upper chamber. And as Lydda was nigh unto Joppa, the disciples, hearing that Peter was there, sent two men unto him, entreating him, Delay not to come on unto us. And Peter arose and went with them. And when he was come, they brought him into the upper chamber: and all the widows stood by him weeping, and showing the coats and garments which Dorcas made, while she was with them" (Acts 9:36-39).

At a memorial service we need to remember that life will come to an end for us, just as it came for the one whom we are remembering; and that we should be getting ready for our own time of departure, because we cannot turn time back and do life over.[1]

## VOICES FROM BEYOND

Life and friendships on this earth are fleeting, short-lived. Live is passing away very swiftly. All too soon we too will be but a memory, either good or evil. I am certain if our departed friends could speak to us, they would say, "Seek the Lord and His salvation, first and always!" Your soul's salvation is the most important thing you can tend to on this earth. Everything you can see, smell, or touch, will perish!

Our departed friends would also say, "Live the life that glorifies Christ! Set your hope on things eternal!" If the departed one was a real Christian, he loved the Bible and strong preaching.

**OUR HOPE IS IN JESUS**

While you are alive and able, I want you to read Romans 3:23, "For all have sinned, and fall short of the glory of God." I want you to read Romans 6:23, "For the wages of sin is death; but the free gift of God is eternal life in Christ Jesus our Lord." I want you to read John 3:16, "For God so loved the world, that he gave his only begotten Son, that whosoever believeth on him should not perish, but have eternal life."

While you are alive and able, I want you to see that Jesus is the basis of our salvation. I want you to read Matthew 20:28, "The Son of man came...to give his life a ransom for many." I want you to read Luke 19:10, "For the Son of man came to seek and to save that which was lost." Jesus came to this earth to be our Redeemer! "But when the fulness of the time came, God sent forth his Son, born of a woman, born under the law, that he might redeem them that were under the law, that we might receive the adoption of sons" (Gal. 4:4-5).

If you were at a funeral right now, you would remember the life that the departed man lived. Let us live in such a way while we sojourn here that when our summons comes, whether by lingering and prolonged illness[2] or by some tragic accident, that we will be right with God, washed in the blood of the Lamb, be a real Christian, trusting in Him, faithful to Him, helping to get the message out to those "out of Christ," to those still lost. Let us give our lives, our time, our work, our money to do the will of the Lord we are all soon going to meet.

Let us pray that none of us be caught unprepared for death–the inevitable, unavoidable end of every person on earth. "It is appointed unto men once to die, and after this cometh the judgemnt" (Heb. 9:27). Let us all be ready, prepared in life, and have hope–expecting our demise and His reward.

When death comes, we should have lived so as to be ready to receive our reward. Let us hope for the Lord's commendation as stated in Matthew 25:23, "Well done, good and faithful servant, thou hast been faithful over a few things...enter thou into the joy of thy Lord."

I am praying that each of you friends will be remembered at your memorial service as a real Christian, having lived Christ-like and godly lives, ready by the grace of God to enter the mansion prepared for you.

This hope is very dear to His trusting ones. "Let not your heart be troubled: believe in God, believe also in me...I go to prepare a place for you. And if I go and prepare a place for you, I come again, and will receive you unto myself; that where I am, there ye may be also...I will not leave you desolate: I come unto you" (John 14:1-3, 18).

Then we can sing,

*Safe in the arms of Jesus,*
*Safe on His gentle breast.*
*There by His love o'er-shaded,*
*Sweetly my soul shall rest!*
*Jesus, my heart's dear refuge,*
*Jesus has died for me!*
*Firm on the Rock of Ages,*
*Ever my trust shall be!*[3]

1. By 1984 Word's health had weakened to the point that he was not able to hold a single revival (only the second time in 56 years of preaching that he had not been able to do so).

2. Though not known to the Words at the time, Alzheimers disease began to afflict Florence early in 1984.

3. "Safe in the Arms of Jesus" by Fanny J. Crosby.

33

# GIVE ACCOUNT OF YOUR STEWARDSHIP

A sermon preached at the Bluffview Church of Christ, Scottsbluff, Nebraska, Sunday evening, May 29, 1988, the last sermon Archie Word ever preached.

It's a privilege to be back after (voice trembles and breaks) trying to preach. (Pause). I appreciate it. And I hope I get through this service.[1]

Turn in your Scriptures tonight with me to Matthew, the twenty-fifth chapter and the fourteenth verse. This Scripture is dealing with stewardship. And I'm preaching tonight on "Give Account of Your Stewardship." That's what takes place in the twenty-fifth chapter of Matthew.

"For it is just like a man about to go on a journey, who called his own slaves, and entrusted his possessions to them. And to one he gave five talents, and to another, two, and to another, one, each according to his own ability; and he went on his journey. Immediately the one who had received five talents went and traded with them, and gained five more talents. In the same manner the one who had received the two talents gained two more. But he who received the one talent went away and dug in the ground, and hid his master's money. Now after a long time the master of those slaves came and settled accounts with them. And the one who had received the five talents came up and brought five more talents, saying, 'Master, you entrusted five talents to me; see, I have gained five more talents.' His master said to him, 'Well done, good and faithful slave; you were faithful with a few things, I will put you in charge of many things, enter into the joy of your master.' The one also who has received the two talents came up and said, 'Master, you entrusted to me two talents; see, I have gaind two more talents.' His master said to him, 'Well done, good and faithful slave; you were faithful with a few things, I will put you in charge of many things; enter into the joy of your master.' And the one also who had received the one talent came up and said, 'Master, I knew you to be a hard man, reaping where you did not sow, and gathering where you scattered no seed. And I was afraid, and went away and hid your talent in the ground; see, you have what is yours.' But his master answered and said to him, 'You WICKED AND LAZY SLAVE, you knew that I reap where I did not sow, and gather where I scattered no seed. Then you ought to have put my money in the bank, and on my arrival I would have received my money with interest. Therefore take away the talent from him, and give it to the one who has the ten talents.'"[2]

Now, this is based upon the definition of a steward. A steward is one who has charge of other people's property and he must give an account for the use of it. If you go aboard a ship to travel any distance as a passenger, you'll find they have a steward aboard that ship. And that steward is accountable for all the other stewards he has under him. Each of those stewards accountable to the chief steward, and the chief steward accountable to the owners of the ship. The stewards don't own that ship, they don't own the goods; they're simply in charge of other men's goods. And that's exactly the situtation that we are in; we don't own anything. Everything on this earth that you have, God gave it to you. Except one thing! (Long pause). Do you know what that is? Your sins! God didn't give you that. That's one of those things you got yourself. One of those "ready-made" jobs. You got out and made that yourself. But everything else, God gave to us and we're accountable to Him for how we use them.

At the accounting time, you're going to exhibit what you've been making of yourself for Christ. That's when we meet Him. More than that, it will be exposed at that time what you've been doing–that only you and God knew about–when you stand before God and give account of your stewardship. Every man will be revealed at the accounting time to be what he has been making of himself as a steward. You make it yourself. You can be a good steward or you can be a bad steward. You'll find out at the judgment whether you have been an honest steward or a crooked steward; whether you have been a faithful steward or an unfaithful steward; and it will be seen at that time whether you have been a wise steward or a fool steward; and it will be shown then whether you've been living for the present or putting your life into things that rot and are not eternal. This will all come out when we stand before God at the judgment when our stewardship is going to be judged.

But you can't get ready when that time comes. People say, "Well, I'm going to get ready on my deathbed." I want to tell you: that's a mighty dangerous thing. I'll tell you why. Do you remember the five foolish virgins? Well, they waited 'til midnight. They waited until the END to get ready. Did they get in? Well, did they?! They did NOT get in! A lot of people say, "We're just going to do this job on our deathbed." You'd better be careful. You might not make it. Those women did not get in because they were not prepared. If you're not prepared, you don't go in! And what you have done before will be exposed then–when you stand before God and give an account of your stewardship.

So, tonight, this is a simple sermon. Giving a final account of our stewardship of everything that is given into our hands. We're going to be accountable for EVERYTHING. I'm going to deal with four different things tonight—the Lord willing, if I live that long. (Coughs). Try to give it...[3]

**GIVE AN ACCOUNT OF YOUR LIFE**

In II Corinthians the fifth chapter and the tenth verse...you'll find how God talks to you about one thing that I want to talk to you about right now and that is, "Give an account of your LIFE." "For we must all appear before the judgment seat of Christ, that each one may be recompensed for his deeds in the body, according to what he has done, whether GOOD OR BAD." Now we're all going to have to give an account for our own use of our body right here on this earth. We'll have to give an accounting to God for LIFE ITSELF.

Actually, God is the giver of life and you can't get it anyplace else. When old Onassis[4] came down to the end, he couldn't buy life. He had millions of dollars, he had ships at sea (and he had lawsuits all over the world), but he couldn't buy life. When God says, "This is it!" that was it! Life was gone. God had given him that life. When Getty, one of the richest men in this nation, comes to the end of his life, he won't be able to buy life.[5] Rockefeller[6] couldn't buy life. God is the giver of life. Life belongs to God! Where else can you get it? You can't get it from anyplace else. If you're alive and conscious, you know you have life. And we know how precious it is when we somebody that we love that is dying (voice trembles)...We say, "What should we do?"[7] The doctor folds his little case and turns to the nurse. (The nurse is the one that gets the brunt—the doctor usually is gone and she has to take care of it.) Why? It's hopeless. He can't give them life. When life comes to an end he knows—and we know—that life is not our own. We can destroy it but we cannot make it.

We must give an account to God for this life that God has given to us because He is the owner of it and He will judge us for how we have used this life. We either used it for good or bad; for His profit or for His loss (and our loss). You're alive now...by the grace of God. Well, did you ever think of that? You're alive now by the grace of God! That's how we all live. Do you ever thank God for your life? Well, you ought to. Thank God for your life! Does your life praise God or does your life praise yourself? (Or does your life praise the devil?) Now we're all of us praising somebody, some way, with the life that we live that God gave us. We're using it to either praise Him, praise ourself, or praise the devil.

Many people criticize the preacher's sermon. I want to tell you folks something. You won't have to give an account for the preacher's sermon. He'll have to give an account for that. But you'll have to give an account for what you HEARD–whether you would accept instruction or not accept instruction. Your life itself is preaching a sermon and it's preaching it right here, every day that you live. It preaches when you're talking to people on the outside and it preaches when you come to church. What does your God think of your life sermon? Because it is! Your life is a sermon. How will your life–THIS day's life–look to you when you have to give an accounting to God for how you used it? HIS life! How did you use it today?

## GIVE AN ACCOUNT OF YOUR BODY

The second thing we have to give an account for is how we USED or ABUSED our bodies. Now our body belongs to God. You're just a renter! By the way, you don't even have a LEASE on life. When you lease a house they have to give you 30 days notice before they kick you out. YOU'RE A RENTER! God says, "GET OUT!" You say, "I've got 30 days!" You might not have 30 seconds! It's HIS life. And He has a right to say, "This is the end of it." Everyone of us. So we have to give an account of how we used this body God gave us. How we treated it. And there you stand, a naked soul, before God, to give an account to the God who owned your body that you lived in. (Pause). Well, do you own it?

Tomorrow a lot of people are going to go the cemetery and look at the place where we put loved ones.[8] You had to pay money to bury them in the ground. The body. Not very valuable. But God gave it to us and we have to give an account to Him for how we used that body. How did you use your's? Did you take care of the body that God gave you? It is the temple of the Holy Spirit! The Scripture tells you so in I Corinthians the sixth chapter and the nineteenth verse–the body is the temple of the Holy Spirit. We have that body from God and we are accountable for how we use the body He let us have. Did you ever loan somebody something valuable and they brought it back all covered with rust? Maybe I'm a freak but when I loan my hoe to somebody that hoe is clean when he gets it, and when he brings it back he ought to bring it back clean. Amen? Well, that's the same way with us. God gave us a body. We ought to take care of that body. It's HIS body! Did we feed it properly? Did we exercise as we should? Did we overwork it for ourselves? It's HIS body. We're just living in it, that's all. Did we overfeed it and be a glutton? Well, you can ruin your body with too much food! Did you rob His body that you're using of the sleep it should have? Every one of needs a certain amount of sleep. Find out how much sleep you need and try to get that amount. Did you poison it with tobacco or booze or with drugs?

It's been quite a while since I've visited in a Veteran's Hospital...about four years ago, in Cheyenne, Wyoming. Here's an illustration of men who did not care for the bodies God gave them! Emphysema. Men coughing up their lungs. Bad hearts. All as a result of abusing the bodies that God gave them. It's His body, loaned to us, but we'll have to give an account for how we used it. Did you keep your body in repair? Well, we're supposed to. If you have an automobile you keep it in repair.

That's your automobile. Well, this is God's body. We ought to take care of it and keep it in repair. Amen? Not much "amen" on that, is there? But we ought to! If we don't, God's going to hold us accountable.

Did you take your body to church? Or did you leave it at home? We have charge of it. But it's not your body. Did you glorify God in your body? Turn over to I Corinthians 6:19. I quoted it to you, but I want you to look at instead of taking my word for it. "Or do you not know that your body is a temple of the Holy Spirit who is in you, whom you have from God, and that you are NOT YOUR OWN?" That's what I'm talking about. Your body belongs to God. He's letting you use it. "For you have been bought with a price: therefore glorify God in your body."

In Romans 12:1 (we all know it but it's good to look at it), "I urge you therefore, brethren, by the mercies of God, to present your bodies a living and holy sacrifice, acceptable to God, which is your spiritual service of worship." Paul says that body is to be taken care of. It is God's and He has loaned it to us. We have eyes. How are you using those eyes? Summer is coming. And when summer comes, "skimpy" time comes. And the next thing you know, no clothes! And the parade of nakedness starts—how much we can get by with without being caught. So, how do you use your eyes? How do you use your ears? What do you listen to? When they turn up the radio and it's so loud it almost knocks your hair off, how do you use your ears? How do you use your HAIR? Summer is coming and you'll find some women with heads almost shaved and you'll find some men with their hair halfway down their back. They haven't read the Bible. The Bible says something about women having long hair and men having short hair. Summer is coming and people are going to be watching you to see how you live. Summer is a time when we have be careful with our bodies, from a standpoint of sin and exposure.

We are stewards! How much profit have you been to God with your body? This last four months I haven't been much profit to God with my body. But I'm thankful to the Lord for one thing: I've got 87 years to look back on–and 63 of them used in the preaching the gospel of Jesus Christ–using my body for Him. And that's kind of a comforting thing when you come down to the end time–to know that you put in some time for God, and to praise His name.

## GIVE AN ACCOUNT FOR YOUR MIND

Now the third thing that we have to give an account for as stewards is our minds. God is letting you use your mind. (Pause). And the mind is something you can't just reach out and get ahold of and put in a new nut and bolt. Your mind is something that is intangible. But I want to tell you this– when you lose it, you've lost everything. As far as this life is concerned. (Pause). It's a shame...to go up there to the hospital and see how many people have Alzheimers, old age, senility, a mind that has quit working, and there they sit. Some of them don't know their names, they don't know you, they don't the nurse, they don't know anybody. Some of them who have had a good, sweet nature are the ungodliest people you can imagine. You wouldn't think that. People who are 75, 85, and 95 years old and the only thing they can say is, "Raise Hell!" One old man, that's all he can say, "Raise Hell!" Wouldn't that be beautiful language to go and meet God? What is it? A mind that's been wrongly used. It's imprinted in his mind. And it keeps coming out his mouth. We're going to be accountable for our minds, while we have them.

When I was in college, I was a little older that most of the fellows in my class.[9] And many times the professor would say, "Word, you take charge of this group and I'll take care of this group" when we'd go on a tour of some place. We made a tour of an insane asylum (I guess that's what you'd call it, a place for people with troubled minds) in Salem, Oregon. And during our tour, they took our group of six through a section of that hospital where they had a little boy (I guess it was a little boy–you couldn't tell for sure), sitting on a stool, just sitting there, mucus running down his nose, slanted Mongol eyes, looking at you without seeing anything, an absolute blank. The lady in charge of the tour said, "That is the product of one of the smartest surgeons in the city of Portland. That's their first-born son." (Pause. Then voice begins to break). That poor kid didn't have any mind. I'D RATHER BE IN HIS SHOES AT THE JUDGMENT, than I would to be a person whom God had endowed with a good mind and to use it like an idiot! Many people use their mind less than that idiot. They don't use them at all. Two hours a week maybe for God, twenty hours with the television. Or some other kind of fun. Maybe no time at all given to God. Is that a good mind? To pull a trick like that on God? Others go to church on Sunday morning but they do no personal work of any kind to any body–they don't talk to anybody about Christ. Is that using your mind for God?

Other people study everything in the world except the Bible. You go into their homes and you find the newspaper, markets, political magazines, farm and home, etc., spending hours on being well informed on everything you can think of...except Christianity. They know more about raising chickens than raising their own children to live in righteousness. It's not an uncommon thing to find a man who will spend more money on obedience school and more time with his hunting dog than he does trying to teach his own children to be obedient and live righteously. Listen you dads and mothers. An obedient dog is valuable...but so is an obedient child. Both of them have to be taught obedience. Why am I saying this? It's a part of using your mind. Use your mind to bring your children up the way they ought to be brought up. You can't set an example that says, "This is the way to go to hell; come and follow me!" and expect them to go to heaven! We're going to give an account to God for how we used our minds.

The mind is to be developed, along with Christian abilities, to serve God. I want you to listen closely. A quotation. From me! A godly mind is of more importance than a farm, a new house, a boat, a camper, skis—either water or snow; it's more important than fishing equipment, money or bonds, a snowmobile, or a fifth-wheeler forty feet long. A mind that's right with God. We must give an account for the stewardship of our minds.

**GIVE AN ACCOUNT FOR OUR MONEY**

The last one tonight, we're going to give an account of how we have used God's money that He has entrusted in our keeping. I said that slowly so I hope you get it. Some of us are entrusted with more, some entrusted with less. In our text that we read (Matthew 25) the talent that He gave to His servants was simply the name for a piece of money. And the talent in silver was worth about a thousand dollars, determined by the price of gold and silver at that time, and the price of a gold talent was thirteen times as much as a silver one. So, if silver was worth $1000 per talent, gold would be worth $13,000 per talent. And the man that got the five talents, if he got five gold talents, would have $65,000. That's a pretty good little wad! Sixty-five thousand. Isn't it? Now if you sit down when you get home tonight and figure out how much money you've made in the last 30 years, it'll suprise you how much money went through your fists. Suppose you worked for $5 an hour. That's pretty reasonable now days, isn't it? Forty dollars a day. And you only worked five days a week. That's a pretty good little sum of money. Add that up for four weeks in the month. And then add twelve times that. And then add up your 30 years times your twelve. And you'll find out that God has entrusted you with a lot more than $65,000. If you're any age at all, more money than that has passed through your hands. You were God's stewards for that money.

Now right here, I find men all over this country who think that they are not responsible to anybody but God for their stewardship. Now they admit, readily, that they are accountible for ALL OTHER SINS, but when it comes to covetousness, they think they shouldn't be accountable for their finances. Reminds me of an illustration I heard of a preacher. The church was going to build a new building and he was trying to get people to sign up for a thousand dollars. That Sunday morning he asked for those who would sign for a $1000 note to stand, and there were mighty few people who stood up. So during the week he had an electrician come to the church and put a needle in every seat in the church and connect it with a button on the pulpit. So when he asked for the people to stand who would give a thousand dollars for the new building, everybody stood! They thought! For when they went to clean the church that week they found three dead church members! THEY'D RATHER DIE THAN GIVE!

Do you want me to tell you something? Listen to this. IF YOU DON'T GIVE, YOU DO DIE! And when you die, you'll give an accounting to God for how you used your stewardship. You're not going to miss it–every one of us. A lot of people don't know this but covetousness is dealt with in the Scripture more severely than adultery. Covetousness. You say, "What makes you say that, preacher?" Well, an illustration. Fifth chapter of the book of Acts. Ananias and Sapphira were covetous! AND GOD STRUCK THEM DEAD! In the fifth chapter of I Corinthians a man was guilty of adultery, worse than the heathens were. And the only thing they did to him was disfellowship him from the church. He was put out. He wasn't killed. Ananias and Sapphira were! For covetousness! People don't realize that the adulterer was not dealt with as harshly as the man who was covetous.

McGarvey...how many of you know who McGarvey was? Let's see your hands. Well, that shows you what happens in two generations. Two generations ago, whenever you would say, "J.

W. McGarvey," you were talking about one of the best informed and probably the best loved Bible scholar in the whole United States among churches of Christ anywhere. McGarvey preached in the Broadway church in Lexington, Kentucky, and he wrote a series of sermons called *Broadway Sermons.* And in that book, on page 277, here's what McGarvey said concerning covetousness. "Indeed, the covetous man (Word interjects: 'A covetous man is a fellow who wants stuff that belongs to somebody else for himself. If it belongs to God, you should give it to God, not yourself!') is more unlike Christ than any other wicked sinner in the world. A drunkard, who gets drunk every day, may, and often does have a good deal of kindness and good-heartedness (Word interjects: 'And that ought to belong to every Christian.'). And the man who in a passion gets mad and murders another man may sometimes be a good, kind man. But if a man is covetous, stingy, penurious, and miserly, he is further away from Christ, who gave up everything in heaven and on earth, everything that ordinary mortals consider desirable, and gave up His life for the benefit of others, while this poor wretch wants everything for himself and is not ready to give anything for others, I verily believe that the covetous man is the most wicked of men in God's sight. He is called an 'idolater,' Colossians 3:5."

Every covetous, stingy person with God, every selfish person with God, every hoarder of his own goods–leaving God out–needs to read I Corinthians 6:9-10. "Or do you not know that the unrighteous shall not inherit the kingdom of God? Do not be deceived (Word interjects: 'Now watch this.'): neither fornicators, nor idolaters, nor adulterers, nor effeminate, nor homosexuals, nor thieves (Word interjects: 'That's a pretty rotten bunch, isn't it? But notice what the next one is.'), nor *covetous*, nor drunkards, nor revilers, nor swindlers, shall inherit the kingdom of God." Now let me tell you this. It's not in the book but I'll tell it to you so you can get it. IF YOU DON'T GO TO HEAVEN, YOU'RE GOING TO GO TO HELL WITH

THAT WHOLE BUNCH! You think that over. I don't think that's worth being tight with God, do you? We ought to be a good steward, everyone of us. I'm coming down to the end of my life, so this isn't just talk with me. I know what I'm talking about. I'm facing that judgment probably a lot quicker than anybody else in this house.[10] I don't want to be found a thief from God. I don't want to be trying to two-time God.

I want to read another one in I Corinthians, 5:11-13. "But actually I wrote to you not to associate with any so-called brother, if he should be an immoral person, OR COVETOUS, or an idolater, or a reviler, or a drunkard, or a swindler..." Paul says, "Don't have anything to do with those kind of people." If you're going to be a Christian, don't have anthing to do with those kind of people–not even to EAT with such a person. "For what have I to do with judging the outsiders?" Now this was written to Christians. "Do you not judge those that are within the church?" People say, "Oh, you mustn't pass judgment." We're to JUDGE those that are within the church! Amen? That's what the Scipture teaches. But those who are outside, God judges. But then Paul says, "Remove the wicked man from among yourselves."

Now, I want to say this kindly. It is from "inexperience." (I've only been preaching 63 years.) I don't know of but one church in all my ministry that has followed this Scripture. Disfellowshipping a covetous man. Do you know of any? I know of just one.[11] A man and his wife were disfellowshipped. He came back and reconsecrated his life–after he had lost his son and his daughter to the cause of Christ. They've never come back. But the mother and father became ashamed of themselves and came back and behaved themselves. They're in the church right now unless they've died this last year.

Every preacher is a steward of God's Word and a minister to others as he sees their needs. God will call us to account if we don't see their needs. I read the other day of a preacher who was called to the deathbed of a very wealthy man in a hospital. A very covetous man. He knew the man was covetous and everybody in the community knew he was covetous and would not do his part as far as the kingdom of God was concerned. But as the preacher stood there by his bed, he asked the preacher to read the Scripture to him and have prayer. (Ever been in that kind of shape?) This preacher took out his little New Testament and opened it up to Matthew 6:19-21. It says, "Lay not up for yourselves treasures on earth, where moth and rust consume, where thieves break through and steal..." The preacher thought, "That's just a little bit inappropriate." So he took his Bible and flipped through it again. And this time it stopped at Luke 16:19. "And a certain rich man, clothed in fine linen, died and went to hell!" He thought that was a little too harsh, so he flipped the pages again and this time he stopped on I Timothy 6:9. And it says, "They that are mindful to be rich fall into temptation and a snare, and many foolish and harmful desires, which plunge men into ruin and destruction." By that time the preacher decided the Lord was trying to tell him something, so he read all three Scriptures to him. After he got through, that rich, covetous man looked at the preacher–a dying man–and his eyes met that preacher's eyes, and he said to the preacher, "Why have you (Word's voice breaks and begins to tremble here), why have you not called my attention to these Scriptures before?" What a sermon! From the lips of a dying man, a rich, covetous man headed for hell, accusing his preacher for not telling him about it.

I want to tell you this: a preacher's stewardship will include the faithful handling of the message on stewardship. And I've tried to handle this just as faithfully as I know how.

You must give account to God for your life, for your body, for your mind, and for everything on this earth that you possess. How did you use it to glorify God?

Now tonight we come to the end of this message. How's the stewardship of your life? Honestly, if God would face you right tonight, and you had to face Him, could you say, "Lord,

I've been a good steward." Or would you hear from the lips of the Lord, "Depart from Me, you wicked, lazy servant! Take away from him the talent and give it to him who has ten talents." Now, everyone of us are going to face it one of these days. Either we'll face God's commendation or God's condemnation. It's going to be one of the two. And while we're alive we can made that decision. You say, "Brother Word, you mean you ought to come down here and really straighten things out if I've been cheating God?" Just exactly that! That's what I mean. I want to tell you this: I've been preaching now for over 60 years and I've never had but ONE man, in all my ministry, that came down the aisle and admitted that he was a thief. And I know good and well that is not all the people who are guilty! That was old Bill Shoemake, a one-armed man who pitied himself, who thought that he shouldn't have to give his tithe. He was brought up in a church that didn't believe in tithing. But when he saw what the Scripture taught, old Bill came right down the aisle and he said, "I've been wrong, just as wrong as I can be, financially with God, and from here on I'm going to treat God fair." At that time he didn't have anything. He was a renter, trying to support his family, one arm. It wasn't but a short time after this that old Bill got a job as a bridge tender for the state with a good salary. Fifteen or twenty years later I met Bill and he said, "From the time that I decided to treat God fair financially, God has blessed me more than I ever have been blessed in all my life." Yet, he's the only man I've ever had come down and honestly admit that he'd been unfair with God.

I don't know what kind of way you've treated God in your finances but I know this song we're singing tonight says, "There's a great day coming." When that great day comes we're going to give an account to God for how we've used our life, how we used our mind, how we used our body, how we used our money. And if you're not using it like you ought to, you ought to come right down these aisles, just like old Bill did, and say, "God, I want to get right with You before I leave this building tonight." Let's stand and sing it together.

(Editor's note: after the sermon was over Brother Word was heard to say, "That's it. That's my last one." An open microphone, inadvertently left on, picked up the words of well-wishers and Word's responses.)

"Very, very fine, Brother Word." (Don Pinon)

"Well, I think it's the facts. And it's got to be preached. Somebody's got to preach it. A lot of preachers don't."

"Brother Word, take care." (A man)

"I'm surprised I got through it. You know what? When you preach, you use your belly muscles. And mine haven't been used much. Tell me about it."

"Isn't that a beautiful sight over there, Brother Word? That bluff?" (Don Pinon, standing in the door of the Bluffview church, looking at Scotts Bluff in the sunset)

"Yes, it is. Beautiful when the sun shines on it."

"Are you going home?" (Pinon)

"Yes. Pretty soon I'm going to put this book up."

"Good night to you, Brother Word. Good job. (A student)

"You're welcome. Practice that early in your ministry, in your life."

"I have trouble with it."

"Well, you've got to do it, that's all. You wouldn't want anyone to cheat you. You don't want to cheat God."

"I don't have any trouble tithing..."

"What's your problem?"

"Using my mind...using my time..."

"Well, you've got to use that head. You've got to develop the thing."

"I have to."

"Sure. You've had it in neutral too long."

"That's right."

"Good night, Brother" (To another man)

"How are you?"

"Good. Just fine. At least I feel better than I did when I started."

"You did an excellent job. That was a very good sermon." (A young woman)

"Well, it's the best I could do. The best I could do. I feel better now than when I started."

"Good night there, Sweetie Pie." (To a little child)

"Good night to you, Henry. BROTHER Henry. BROTHER Henry." (To a new Christian)

"Good night, Sister Word." (To another lady)

"Are you going home now?"

"Pretty soon."

"I'm not Sister Word." (Laughter)

"Yeah."

"Good night to you, Sister Hanson."

"That was a good sermon."

"Well, I hope people will put it into practice. One of these days we're going to face that Owner. We're just servants. It's getting closer all the time. Well, good night to you, Sister. Good night! Good night!"

1. Word's health took a nosedive early in 1988 after Florence was placed in a care home for Alzheimer's disease.
2. In his latter years of preaching Archie Word changed from using the American Standard Version (1901) to the more modern New American Standard Version.
3. From some comments made after the service it is clear he really did not know if he would be able to complete this message.
4. Greek shipping tycoon Aristotle Onassis, who married JFK's widow.
5. J. Paul Getty, married several times during his life, once said he would have given all his money to have had one good marriage.
6. John D. Rockefeller.
7. Here he is without a doubt thinking of his dear wife Florence.
8. This sermon was preached the evening before Memorial Day, 1988.
9. Due to his stint in the Navy in World War I, his belated graduation from high school, and three years of "raising hell" in Fresno.
10. In less than six months Word would be dead.
11. Word then named a Church in Oregon. It was not Montavilla.

34

# HOW TO PREACH TO CONVERT PEOPLE

*The Church Speaks,* April 20, 1947 (One day before his 46th birthday)

(In this "bonus" sermon, Archie Word, the man whose name was synonymous with preaching–"Hear A. Word Preach The Word"–shares 23 suggestions with fellow-preachers).

"Preach the word; be urgent in season, out of season; reprove, rebuke, exhort, with all longsuffering and teaching" (II Tim. 4:2).

Let your supreme motive, from the time you begin to prepare your sermon until the last "Amen" is spoken, be to touch some poor lost and ignorant soul for the Lord. Let your preaching be adapted to that end and no other.

Give much time to the preparation of your sermon. A sermon must have enough of the right kind of material in it to be used of God to convert a soul.[1]

Make your points distinct, and prepare your sermon with the end in mind of touching upon those conditions in your community that are disturbing issues. Only those things that are personal will stir people into action. Each man must KNOW that HE is a SINNER and in need of salvation before he will seek for it.[2]

Preach the doctrines that are true to the Bible, even though they are offensive to the carnal-minded sinner. True, they will say of you (as they did of Christ), "This is a hard saying: who can bear it?" But they will become CONVICTED–and there is no conversion nor salvation without conviction of sin! They may turn on you as they did on Paul and try to kill you, but at least you will have delivered your soul and warned them so they cannot plead ignorance on Judgment Day.[3]

Preach the spirituality of God's holy law, and keep the penalty of disobedience to it always before the mind of your hearers. This will cause the honest sinner to see his lost condition and flee from God's wrath to come.

Diagnose the disease of the sinner as SIN. And right along with it, give to him the only REMEDY God has ever given that will cure the malady. It has never failed when taken according to His divine prescription. Emphasize certain death without it, and absolute cure for all with it.

Bear down upon the lost and condemned condition of the man or woman out of Christ. Be sure that they understand what you mean by "ALL have sinned, and come short of the glory of God." And right along with it, explain what is meant by salvation by the grace of God. Make the plan of God's salvation just as firm and true as it is in the Scriptures! And just as absolutely certain!

Preach to those who are PRESENT! Preach TO sinners, not ABOUT them. Peter said, "Ye men of Israel," and "Let all the house of Israel know assuredly" while he was addressing that memorable assembly in Jerusalem, consisting of the Jews! Follow Peter's example, for it works. Make your sermon so personal that no one can go away without making a personal application of it to themselves.

Preach sermons that are searching, that probe deep into the dark and hidden recesses of every hearer's heart. Do your best to save the worldly church member that has professed to have become a "new creature," but who is living just as any other sinner outside the church is living.[4] Emphasize the awfulness of being a stumbling stone.

Do your best to remind those present of their own sinfulness, both past and present. Make every lost soul in your presence as miserable in his sin as you possibly can–for as long as men are comfortable in their sins, they will not flee from them.

Make sure that everyone present understands that God commands those who hear, to OBEY the truth–RIGHT NOW! Let this be understood: it is not YOUR command but the command of GOD ALMIGHTY. Quote the sacred Word of God to prove your every point.[5]

Let people know that you EXPECT them to do something about what you have preached; that you are not just exercising your tonsils and vocal chords, or amusing them. Emphasize that "TODAY is the day of salvation."

Make it so evident that a blind man can see it that it is not the will of God for sinners to go away in their sins to "think it over" and play around with God's time, but to get out from under the curse of God RIGHT NOW! Let every hearer know that he is a free moral agent, but that God will hold him accountable for what he does with the salvation that Jesus Christ purchased with His own blood. IT IS A SIN TO REJECT THE LORD'S SALVATION!

Show every sinner who hears you that he had better be afraid of the devil, for he is a destroyer; that he had better be afraid of hell, for it is an awful place to spend eternity. Rational fear is legitimate. That is why we put up smallpox signs and railroad signals. There is danger–and men and women should be warned! I would to God that I could get every sinner so afraid of hell that he would flee to the Lord and head for heaven!

Say so much about hell that everyone who hears you will know that you believe in it. Be sure to explain to people that Jesus loved the world enough to die for it; yet He speaks more about hell than any other Bible writer.

In converting sinners, do not forget that there is a JUSTICE side to God as well as a LOVING side of Deity. Emphasize His JUSTICE if men determine to come into His presence refusing His grace. God is good! He has done everything that even God can do to keep men out of hell, but if people determine that they will not go to heaven and will not accept God's gracious gift of salvation, then they MUST go to the place prepared for the devil and those who do his bidding.

Preach for CONVICTION OF SIN. Paul, before Felix, preached in such a way as to make old Felix tremble. The sinners on the day of Pentecost were "pricked in their hearts." Remember, there is no conversion nor salvation without conviction.

If men and women are to be converted, there must be some ONE presented that is worthy of turning to. Lay much emphasis upon the fact that following Christ is not easy nor a downhill thing to do. There is the highest law of SELF-SACRIFICE that Jesus preached to ANYONE who would be His disciple. There must be a radical change or heart, a new begetting of life from God, before the sinner is willing to leave the life of pleasing the flesh and turn to Jesus who was crucified.

Make every illustration as definetly illustrative of the point you wish to put across as words possibly can. Do not be afraid to repeat a thought that is of vital importance. Make emphatic sentences so forceful that they will raise the dead in sin and scare the daylights out of the indifferent sinner who is just coasting right into the jaws of hell, unaware of his condition![6]

Be as earnest in your preaching as if you were dealing with (and you are) LIFE AND DEATH. Do not be afraid to work at your preaching like a fireman works at saving lives from a fire. Let every listener know that you are in dead earnest about what you are saying! Address the intellect and conscience of every person within earshot.

Never forget to tell of your own experience in receiving Christ's salvation. Your experience speaks louder than anything else. If it is not good enough for you, then it is not good enough for anyone else. You can SHOW them that you have something they NEED.[7]

Let your preaching be always extremely PERSONAL. Salvation is a personal thing. No one can be saved for you. Peter said, "Let all the house of Israel know assuredly that God has made him both Lord and Christ, this Jesus whom YE HAVE CRUCIFIED." There was no evading the point. Make your sermons so no one can go home and say, "I was missed completely in that entire sermon." Let every sinner think that the sermon was prepared for him, personally![8]

Souls must be CONVERTED! People just joining the most popular church in the city means nothing. There must be conversion or there is no salvation. "Repent ye and become CONVERTED, that you sins may be blotted out..." Conversion is the product of genuine repentance–and Jesus said we must "Repent or perish!"

May the Lord help preachers not to be afraid to preach what the Lord has commanded and demand in the name of Jesus Christ, CONVERSION from all known sin to HIM. Preaching of that kind will either cause a riot or revival, and that is dead certain.

Surely it will cost you something. It cost Jesus His life! And no preacher should consider himself better than his Lord!

Paul told Timothy, "Take heed to thyself, and to thy teaching. Continue in these things; for in doing this thou shalt save both thyself and them that hear thee." The natural inference is, if we don't, we'll lose our own souls and those who look to us to lead them to heaven!

OH, WHAT A TREMENDOUS RESPONSIBILITY RESTS UPON US!

1. Word's remaining sermon outlines (some spilled into a river following a car wreck, causing one wag to say, "I'll bet the river boiled!") are carefully created masterpieces, some over 20 pages in length.
2. Don DeWelt, one of A. Word's many converts, says that all he knew after he heard Word preach the first time that he was a sinner, bound for hell! But that was enough!
3. Several attempts were made on Archie Word's life, the most notable being the attempted shooting after his sermon "21 Reasons Why I Am Not a Mormon," preached in a hotbed of Mormonism, Ontario, OR, in 1933.
4. Probably half the 3000 conversions that occurred during Word's West Coast revivals (1930- 1935) were church members who had never been converted.
5. By "quote" Archie did not mean quoting from memory. Word learned early to always read from the Bible. "I was standing by the door one night as the people went out and heard one man say to another, 'How in the h___ do we know he was quoting the Bible? He didn't have no Bible up there!'" (*Voice of Thunder,* p. 306).
6. In 1981 Word told a newspaper reporter, "I do a lot of illustrations–not for fun. If someone opens his mouth to laugh, I'll reach down his throat, grasp his liver and squeeze it. This is too important to joke about." (*Voice of Thunder,* p. 574).
7. In the early years of his ministry Archie would don his old Navy uniform and tell about the night he nearly drowned in the Atlantic, the night of his first, real prayer to God.
8. Word once heard a black fundamentalist preacher put it this way: "Bredren, don't bend 'de Book; bend 'de man!"

# APPENDIX A
# IN TRIBUTE
## Tributes to *Voice of Thunder, Heart of Tears*

*Unsolicited testimonials to the biography of Archie Word, Voice of Thunder, Heart of Tears*

Since the publication of my 643-page authorized biography of Archie James Word, *Voice of Thunder, Heart of Tears* (College Press, 1992), a good number of letters have come my way from readers who took the time to express their feelings about the book. I believe their words of testimony will prove to be a blessing to you–as they certainly were to me when I first received the following correspondence. The letters came from a wide variety of people across the nation: ministers, evangelists, elders, Bible College presidents and professors, doctors, educators, lecturers, homemakers, relatives, retirees, prisoners, mothers of prisoners, etc. I hope you will enjoy reading these 36 selected tributes to *Archie Word: Voice of Thunder, Heart of Tears.*

**Bob Chambers, Minister, Scottdale, PA** - "You should not write books like *Archie Word: Voice of Thunder, Heart of Tears*. Books like that cause the readers to neglect their responsibilities. It is too big to read in one day, but how can you lay it down and go to sleep?...The truth is, I devoured it! There are few books I have enjoyed more...You did a tremendous job. Thank you for your countless hours of research and writing."

**Ed McSpadden, Evangelist, Riverside, CA** - "Let me take this opportunity to congratulate you on a wonderful job of writing the book on Brother Word. I started reading and read until midnight; then came back the next day and finished it."

**Reva Bradley, Homemaker, Springfield, OR** - "I really enjoyed your book, *Voice of Thunder, Heart of Tears.* I stayed up late–late! several nights to finish it. You did a good job bringing out his strengths and weaknesses without being judgmental."

**Patricia Bryant, Secretary, Wentzville, MO** - "I just now finished reading your *Voice of Thunder, Heart of Tears,* and after drying my own tears, can see well enough to write to you. I loved the book! The content, the style you used to write it and the evidence of all the research that went into it truly makes it a book to remember. I found it difficult to put down. (Gary will eat peanut butter and jelly sandwiches tonight, as I didn't take time to prepare dinner!)..."

**Jennie Fagen, Homemaker, Oskaloosa, IA** - "Just a little note to let you know how much I enjoyed reading your book about Brother Word. It was well written. I found it hard to lay down. It was interesting to read how patient people were with him as he grew in the Lord...I don't think I ever heard anyone who could move people so emotionally as he did."

**K. O. Backstrand, Evangelist, Security, CO** - "Excellent...I was thrilled with the complete work...am still amazed at the detailed information you recovered on the Word family in Kentucky and the early days in California. I have never read a fairer evaluation given a great evangelist than you gave Brother Word. You soared to the heights of his lofty career and yet you didn't omit his weaknesses that appeared at times. The bomb-shell preaching joined by the tears of a man who cared if people went to hell or heaven made Brother Word one of the greatest evangelists of our time. I feel I had a choice opportunity to stand on the shoulders of a spiritual giant who laid the foundation in my life as an evangelist for the last 50 years and more...In every revival meeting I hold I look out in the congregation for some young man whom God will raise up to be a dynamic evangelist. There are still Archie Words in the world just waiting to be used. But they have to be found and challenged first."

**Russell Boatman, Retired Minister and Educator, Joplin, MO** - "I read your eagerly awaited biography in two sittings. I would likely (and would have liked to) have done it in one sitting if my eyes hadn't given out...Victor, I treasure the book...Your research was thorough and in-depth. You dealt with the man openly and honestly...Your sub-title *(Voice of Thunder, Heart of Tears)* is most apt and perceptive. Many knew him (or, more aptly stated, saw him) only as one with a voice of thunder. I knew him too as a man with a heart of tears. He shed some over me. It wasn't his preaching alone that got through to me. It was his heart of tears...God bless you. Again, thanks for the book!"

**Bryce Jessup, President, San Jose Christian College, San Jose, CA** - "I just wanted to let you know that I finished the book on Archie's life. What a great contribution this will be for years to come! I had a hard time putting the book down because I knew so many of the people who are mentioned. In fact, I read the book in about four sittings! (Not bad for a 643-page book, and a slow reader at that!) Your direct and candid style captured my attention. The varied events of his life were presented with purpose and power. It was easy to catch the goodness and patience of God manifested through Archie's life. This book offers hope to all who struggle to be used of God!...I know that I will refer to it on many occasions. It will be a treasured part of my library."

**Charles Gresham, Professor, Kentucky Christian College, Grayson, KY** - "I have finished the Archie Word biography and it was great! Your style of writing is magnificent, and the way you tied in what was happening in our American culture with what was happening in Archie's life was excellent. (I have done this somewhat in my memoirs, but not as well or consistently as you did in this volume.)."

**Rolland A. Steever, Lecturer, South Bend, IN** - "I have just finished the reading of the biography of A. Word. What an excellent job you did both in research and composition of that story! I want to purchase a copy of the biography with your authograph in the book...to be sure that my preacher-son has a copy..."

**Donald G. Hunt, Instructor, Midwestern School of Evangelism, Ottumwa, IA** - "Your painstaking care has produced not only a biography of a man, his times, his preaching, his accomplishments, and his influence, but it is a model of biographical work itself, and you have placed every appreciative reader under debt to you for your work...Thanks, Vic, in behalf of all of us for a big job well done!"

**William E. Paul, Evangelist, Seattle, WA** - "I marvel on every page at the extensive research you did...Thank you for

*Archie Word: Voice of Thunder, Heart of Tears.* I hope others will read it and come to better understand 'where we come from' as a fellowship. While I am so happy for the growth many of us have had over the years, I fear that some have tended to 'grow away' from some of the principles of dedication and commitment, especially when it comes to fervor and zeal. With the inroads of sin in virtually all the churches these days it is refreshing to be reminded of a day when people made a clean break with the world, as was evidenced during most of the years of Brother Word's ministry...This work will long outlive both of us. It is a significant contribution to the biographical literature of gospel preaching in general and the Restoration Movement in particular."

**Fred P. Miller, Evangelist, Clermont, FL** - "How deeply and favorably I am impressed by what may be looked upon as a lifetime highlight achievement! Thank you for a job well done...It is a fantastic achievement and a joy to read. Everyone of our people should have a copy. My fear that A. Word's life story might not receive the justice due him was happily unfounded. Plaudits to Victor!"

**J. Charles Dailey, Director, Northwest College of the Bible, Portland, OR** - "You have done an outstanding job on Brother Word's biography. Even thought I knew the players, or was even present at many of the events, your writing puts things in the perspective of time. Excellent! (If you wanted to expand the book to 800 pages, I can remember a few more events!)."

**Dale A. Williamson, Evangelist, Lakeland, FL** - "You have done an excellent job with your biography of A. Word–one of the best biographies I've ever read. I know you put in many hours in research, interviews, going through all kinds of material. One of the things that made the book so interesting is we knew (or knew of) so many of the people mentioned."

**A. Ralph Johnson, Evangelist, Seattle, WA** - "Just read your book on Archie Word. It was the best biography I have ever read...For a few hours I was there again. I felt Archie's commanding challenge to preach. I saw the picture of 'Uncle Word's' pointed finger saying, 'I want you.' I saw the leather zipper notebook open on the pulpit with large print in different colors. I saw the multi-colored charts hanging all around the room and the big man on the platform with the pointer, teaching about 'The Church in the Bible.' I heard the blast of the trumpet agains sin and compromise–and the break in his voice as he recounted tragic experiences or called for surrendered hearts. I remember the scores of people moving down the aisles with tears streaming down their faces–and I remembered how so many of them went on to become leaders in the great battle for souls. I was challenged anew. I was humbled. I laughed. I cried.

"Your book was superb for several reasons. It was thoroughly researched. It was impeccably objective. You let the facts speak for themselves. Those who were for Word saw the quality of the man. Those who were hostile to him saw his faults. Each of us exaggerated to his own measure what he saw. You masterfully set forth and blended his life into the struggle of the times...I especially appreciated how you brought out one of the most impressive features–his home–the the gentle feelings between Archie and Florence (What a lady!), and the strength of the two women (his mother and his wife) who had such a great part in making the man...

"One of the masterful features in handling the subject was the excellent blending of his life with international, national, and local events, along with struggles going on within the larger Restoration Movement brotherhood...With these points of reference it was easy to see where we were and know what we were doing at many points along the journey. This was not just a biography about a great man. this was a great biography about a great man..."

**Earl W. Chambers, Director, Eternal Good Tidings Productions, Sacramento, CA** - "Just finished your book about Brother Word. What a fantastic job you did–so well researched and documented. For all the many years it took–the miles you traveled and interviews you were able to get–for everything else that went to make the book the large volume that it is–I thank you! Brother Word was a giant of a man, a preacher among preachers, 'faithful unto death.' He was gifted of God far beyond most of us poor sticks, and was fearless in his stand for Christ. He had an eternal effect on countless thousands–a man of God esteemed highly."

**Ruth Howell, Teacher, Fall Creek, OR** - "I loved your Archie Word book. What a wonderful story of his life. God did a mighty work through him. How we need that revival today. There is no other hope! As I finished the book I was struck with how right Archie Word was. His concerns for the liberalism creeping into the church was prophetic. He could see the danger. We can see the results."

**Don Smith, Minister, Prineville, OR** - "I have just finished reading your biography of Archie Word. You did a masterful job of research and writing...The book had a tremendous effect on me. It was a great inspiration, but at the same time it brought me under strong conviction for not accomplishing more with my life than I have...For all his faults and sins, Archie Word was a great servant of God, and I honor him as such. And I pay tribute to you for all your work and wisdom in putting together perhaps the most memorable biography that I have ever read. Thank you so much!"

**Matt Shively, Minister to the Handicapped, Vancouver, WA** - "I have just read your book on Archie Word. By the time I got to the last few chapters, I was in tears. Partly because I was convicted, partly because I was moved, partly because I could see how God's power can work in one individual's life. I have read many motivational and inspirational books, but none like the one you wrote about Archie Word...My brother and I were just converted to Christ when A. Word came to Spokane to hold a revival meeting...I'm glad I had a chance to experience his powerful revival preaching. I wish I could travel back in time and sit in one of his meetings in the 30s...I have a great desire to preach more and, after reading this book, I now want to preach every day! Thank you for writing this book...A. Word lives on!"

**Steve Holsinger, Minister, Anchorage, AK** - "I just finished reading *Voice of Thunder, Heart of Tears.* It challenged me once again with how important preaching and evangelism are and caused me to weep–not just as I read about the deaths of these two who were an important part of my spiritual formation (I lived in their home on 95th Street during my first year in Bible College) but also in realizing how little progress the church in the Northwest has made over the years. It is sad to read about such great revivals in churches that no longer exist. You have done a masterful job in telling this story...Thanks!"

**Darrel Hall, Evangelist, New Waterford, OH** - "Enjoyed reading *Archie Word: Voice of Thunder, Heart of Tears.* It made me want to preach the Word more than ever. I laughed and I cried all the way through. Of all the books I have read in recent years, none have challenged me to keep on the firing line for

Christ like this one. I think every Bible College ought to make it required reading. I have encouraged all my preacher friends to get it and read it, and most of them have. June and I read it and hated to see the sun set on one of God's greatest servants, Brother Archie Word. What a tireless, stalwart evangelist he was! The book moved us to tears–and yet it challenged me more than ever to continue to 'preach the Word!'"

**George L. Faull, President, Summit Theological Seminary, Peru, IN** - "What a blessing the biography of Archie Word was to me. It is nolstalgic. I felt like I was in a time machine visiting almost a century of history. The letters saved by Mrs. Word and Brother Charles Crane and others made the man 'real flesh and blood.' I laughed. I cried. I was challenged, convicted, and recommitted. I intend to make this required reading in one of the courses at Summit Theological Seminary. When I read of his passion for souls, and his success in evangelism, church planting, and recruitment to the ministry, in comparison to me, I am so ashamed. Of course, I identify with him for his being criticized for openness and frankness, but I must grow to be like him in his compassion. Thank you for writing this book.

"I appreciate your picturing him 'warts and all.' I think the book is especially valuable in presenting the real hero of the story, namely Florence Word...The beautiful poems and expressions of love she had for this man shows what a great woman God placed at his side. What a couple they were! What a role model he was for preachers, and what a role model she was for Christian wives. Oh, how I pray God will raise up more harvesters like these two. Our country, our churches, yes, the world itself would be better if God had more such 'salt' and 'light' as they were! Thanks again for taking the time to write this superb book!"

**A Prisoner in Lompoc, CA (written to his wife)** - "I just finished the biography of Archie Word. It's without a doubt the best book–and most moving book–I've ever read. I cannot get over the events that touch our lives. Towards the end of Archie's life you could feel the closeness Archie and Florence shared, and how much God loved then, and they Him. I can in no way say (or would attempt to say) that our lives could match theirs–but I will say that it's my prayer and most sincere hope that our live, spiritual life and service to Christ be lived in their example and witness. I want that more than anything in the world...I've failed you so bad! I hurt for my sins against you, but if you can, please rest comfortable in knowing I will want you–and all of you–for the rest of my life...I know I've been weak in that area–but no more!...I know you put salvation first and I thank God for it. Do read the rest of the biography. You will love it...I love you so very much!"

**A Mother of a Son in Prison in New Hampshire** - "I'm really enjoying your book and have already used it as an example to see the potential and real person beyond their sins...My son became a Christian at age 8 or 9, but departed in his teen years. He accidentily caused the death of his baby daughter he loved very much and is now in prison. While there a minister led him back to the Lord...He is like Archie Word in many ways. My prayer is that he will be a preacher when he gets out of prison...Thank you and God bless you..."

**Wilma Gregory, Homemaker, Lebanon, OR** - "Please know that you deserve a Nobel prize of some sort for bringing Archie Word back to life in your book! How we have enjoyed living again the good old days! What a blessing it is! You could not have done bettter; it is a legacy you have given us all!"

**Nellie Arnold (Archie Word's sister), Brownsville, CA** "Some friends were here from Washington. The lady is one of my dear nurse friends. Her husband is a retired professor for San Jose State University and he has done a lot of writing. He started reading your book about Archie and said how well written it was...I've enjoyed reading the book...Thanks for doing such a good job of telling Archie's life."

**Anthony Hunt (Archie Word's great-grandson), Honolulu, HI** - "When I heard that you were going to write a book about my great-grandfather I remember thinking, 'What a great idea!' But as I sifted through my memories of Archie Word, I realized how little I knew about him. This led me to be all the more excited about the book's completion...When I received a copy of your 643-page book the first thing that popped into my head was, 'There's no way I'm going to be able to endure that!' This mindset changed as I began to read–and instead of 'enduring,' I found myself enjoying...Now I am on the other side of the book and feel as though I have taken a historical tour through part of my heritage...What a blessing to be able to read so clearly into my heritage! Thank you."

**Phil Davis, Doctor, Bakersfield, CA** - "I just wanted to let you know how much I enjoyed reading your new book on Archie Word. In fact, the feeling was much stronger–I loved it and could not put it down! My life is interwoven with so many of the individuals mentioned in the book...My father preached in the Lindsay church from 1951-53. We met in the building pictured in your book. As a teenage boy I pounded many nails into the new building on the corner...I knew nearly every Lindsay person mentioned in the book. Mrs. Word was often fondly mentioned by my mother...I loved Lindsay even as Archie Word did. I remember the wonderful fragrance of the orange blossoms...the hills you mentioned...the trips to Strathmore, Porterville, Tulare, Visalia and those wonderful trips to Sequoia...Again, thank you for sharing with the world your story of such a special individual as Archie Word."

**Gerry Turner, Homemaker, Vancouver, WA** - "A couple of days ago I finished reading your biography of Archie Word. What a lot of memories were brought to mind!...I grew up in Lindsay...The Words were married on my first birthday...My brothers and I were the janitors of the first church building back in 1938. Got 50 cents for doing it!...Saw Don Jessup play football when I was in Junior High...Sister Word was truly a 'lily.' Even to the end of her life whe was of a sweet dispostion. A true example of a worthy woman. I really respected and loved her...She was a jewel–and so was Maggie Word, Archie's mother, a dear saint of God...I really enjoyed the book and plan to read it agains soon. Thanks for all your work on it."

**Dawn Miner, former student under Archie Word, Kasson, MN** - "I recently read the biography of Archie Word...and just wanted you to know my impressions. First of all, I am not an avid reader. The pictures first interested me and then the first chapter led to the second and before I knew it, I was half done. I learned more history about our past than I ever did in school...My twin sister (Meredith) and I enrolled in the Gering school in the fall of 1975. The Words were most kind to us...inviting us into their home regularly for meals. I had a fair amount of fear if my lessons weren't quite up to perfection in Brother Word's classes...I wish I had know more about Archie's growing up years and what brought him to the Lord while I was in Bible college. I would have understood his tears more. I wish to thank you for your effort in collecting all the information that went into the book...Archie Word's life has surely challenged me to be faithful all of my life. And what a beautiful love story between Archie and Florence!"

**Burton W. Barber, Minister, Galax, VA** - "Your book on the life of Brother Word is superb. We have given several volumes to friends."

**L. K. Conger, Retired, Cincinnati, IA** - "I have read your book about Word. It is indeed a masterpiece. When I came to Brother Word's last words ('I will probably wake up in eternity–or, on the other hand, I may be better in the morning"), I said, 'Here is a poem.' so I wrote one. I hope you like it."

**Rick Deighton, Elder, Gresham, OR** - *"Voice of Thunder, Heart of Tears* is a powerful source of inspiration to godly living and evangelistic outreach; but that's not all–there is more. Since this book obviously involved a massive amount of research, I wondered why you took such a major 'sidetrack' from your primary thrust of promoting unity in the body of Christ. Then, about three-fourths through your book, it dawned on me what your real purpose was in this book–not a 'sidetrack' at all, but a masterful plan for clarification, edification and reunification of separated brethren. I pray God will use this book powerfully to bring greater harmony in the body of Christ."

**Reggie Thomas, Evangelist, Joplin, MO** - "I have just completed reading ALL 643 pages of your great book *Archie Word: Voice of Thunder, Heart of Tears.* I have laughed and cried and thrilled in reading Archie Word's life as told by your marvelous pen. I had the grand privilege of hearing Archie Word only once. He preached a revival in Dayton, Ohio, while I was a student at C.B.S. I was able to drive up and hear him one week night. He was powerful and made a deep impression on me. What a loss is mine to have heard him only once! But, upon reading your book, I realize why I only heard him once. All of my life I have been doing the same thing Archie did. I have traveled and traveled and preached and preached. He did it so much better than I but, it is thrilling for me to see how similar (revival meetings) our lives have been. Your book will surely bless preachers from now until Jesus comes. Oh, that every preacher might read it and learn to have the soul winner's heart and then preach God's Word with the voice of thunder and a heart of tears. Thank you, Victor, for this book."

**Richard M. Ellis, Minister, Ottumwa, IA** - "You did a marvelous job on the book. I'm sure it will bless many lives. I truly feel that God must have touched your soul and pen as you wrote this book. It helped me see more of the complete story of his life—a life that had many sad parts, but still so full of victories for Jesus. I was impressed with many things—especially Florence's faithfulness while Archie was living for the devil; and her faithfulness as a quiet wife through the years."

# APPENDIX B
# IN REVIEW
## Reviews of *Voice of Thunder, Heart of Tears*

The biography of *Archie Word: Voice of Thunder, Heart of Tears,* has received several good reviews since its release by College Press in 1992. Here are excerpts from four such book reviews.

**CHRISTIAN STANDARD, July 25, 1993. Reviewed by Bryce Jessup, President, San Jose Christian College, San Jose, CA.**

This book was written to preserve the life and ministry of Archie Word. It is directed toward Christian people who desire to understand the heart of a man fully committed to God.

Victor Knowles has made a valuable contribution to the Restoration Movement. His book is written in an interesting and colorful style. It presents the life of Archie Word from his early days, through the turbulent teenage years, on through conversion and ministry until his death. The reader will marvel at his unusual life, his boxing career, his conversion, and his significant ministry through the years.

This book is written in a candid way. It does not withhold the personal and relational problems that Brother Word encountered. The reader is made to feel the grace of God throughout its pages. The giftedness of Archie Word is illustrated in a variety of ways, including the sending of so many men into the preaching ministry. His passion for the Lord and his preaching against sin is captured within the pages of this book.

***ONE BODY*, Summer, 1993. Reviewed by Dr. Wayne Shaw, Academic Dean and Professor of Preaching, Lincoln Christian Seminary, Lincoln, IL.**

Although I never met Archie Word, I have been introduced to him through members of his family, through numerous friends who have been converted or deeply touched by his ministry, and through Victor Knowles' biography...

Knowles has given us a carefully researched account of an extra-ordinarly gifted preacher in an important era of our Restoration Movement. The era was the golden age of revival in the twentieth century when quite often revivals like his were "the only show in town" and the preacher was Archie Word, who rose to prominence from 1930 to 1935 as a traveling evangelist during that period. Over 3000 decisions were made for Christ and dozens prepared for the preaching ministry as a result of his meetings. Church divisions were healed, hardened sinners gave their lives to Christ, and many church members were converted for the first time.

Knowles traces Word's birth, his rough pre-Christian years, his conversion, education, his years as an evangelist, his ministry for a third of a century at Montavilla in Portland, and his latter years of teaching in Gering, Nebraska...Archie's method was to...stress especially hard the New Testament church, conversion, repentane and holiness, the Christian home, and Christian evidences as dramatically as he could.

Knowles works hard at being objective. He has an evident admiration for "Brother Word," but he also presents him as a man with great weaknesses as well as great strengths...(a) portrait...of the conversion, career, character, and Christian commitment of one of our Restoration Movement's great evangelists, "A. Word Preaching THE Word."

***THE VOICE OF EVANGELISM,* January 1993. Reviewed by Donald G. Hunt, Editor, *The Voice of Evangelism,* Ottumwa, IA.**

...As his son-in-law and one closely associated with him both in family and preaching, I recognized years ago that somebody should write a book on his life. But I shrank from it for two reasons: he had not saved much information that would help in relating the story and because of the time such an undertaking would involve...We rejoiced when we learned that Victor Knowles was going to do it with the authorization of College Press...

Knowles read everything Brother Word ever wrote in *The Church Speaks, Christian Standard, The Voice of Evangelism,* his several books, and correspondence with his girl friend and preachers. He wrote letters, telephoned, and made trips into several states to talk with informed people who could give him firsthand information. Such painstaking care has produced not only a biography of a man, his times, his preaching, his accomplishments, and his influence, but it is a model of biographical work itself...

I have prayed that the reading of this book will renew many in their convictions of right and wrong, that preachers will be emboldened in this weak and watered-down age to proclaim anew the forthright gospel of Christ, that some will be constrained to give up the life of sin and turn to God for mercy and forgiveness, that churches will be made to take a better stand for the Lord, and even that young men in increasing numbers will be challanged to give their lives to the preaching of the Word.

***SCOTTDALE CHURCH NEWSLETTER*, February 25, 1993. Reviewed by Bob Chambers, Evangelist, Scottdale Church of Christ, Scottdale, PA.**

It is not often that a person can relive their childhood and adolescence, and reflect upon college days and events of their adult life and ministry. Not too often can a person "see" himself once again in the audience of memorable revival meetings, or "hear" again sermons of yesteryear at large preaching rallies. You cannot read many books that retell the story of your struggle with momentous issues and the molding of your convictions. Where do you find a book that reminds you of the days when your walk with God was being impacted significantly by powerful personalities?

...Recently I have "walked" through all of these personal experiences. I have been filled with joy and anguish as I traveled memory lanes. I relived unforgettable and some forgotten experiences as I read Victor Knowles' biography of Archie Word. Brother Knowles has done a tremendous job in telling the life-story of one of the most colorful persons to touch my life. Archie Word, who has been called "America's Foremost Evangelist," was a pulpit giant, one of the most powerful preachers I ever heard. His authoratative voice made you tremble, his tender appeals broke your heart. His boldness in the pulpit and his kindness and thoughtfulness in private made you realize you were in the company of someone special.

In life, Brother Word was a very controversial man, as most strong leaders are. In death, not everyone is going to like Victor's book, for he has done an excellent job of presenting Brother Word as he really was, warts and all. (There are waves on a lake for a long time after a storm...and Archie Word was at the eye of many storms!) Some will not like the book because they thought Brother Word was exclusively "in their corner."

Victor, with his penetrating pen, reveals that Brother Word in his later years looked over some walls he helped build and saw dear brothers on the other side. Victor shows us his subject was not as narrow and dogmatic as he sometimes appeared to be.

The book makes us look at ourselves as a person's virtues are closely related to his vices. You see how the personal qualities that make one outstanding, taken to extremes, can, at times hurt. It is obvious again that the best and greatest have "feet of clay."...I am thankful for the life of Brother Word; God used him to make me, in part, what I am today. I am thankful God used Victor Knowles to tell the story of his life.

# APPENDIX C
# IN MEMORIAM
# Eulogy of Florence Belle Word

*Delivered by Victor Knowles at the Memorial Service for Florence Belle Word, February 3, 1994, Portland, Oregon*

## HAIL TO THE LILY

In the providence of God, two families back East (one in Kentucky, the other in Ohio), moved to California in the early 1900s. In Kentucky, Maggie Word was suffering from chronic bronchitis. In Ohio, Elmer Procter had a bad case of asthma. The Words moved West first, in 1906, to Lindsay, California. A year later the Procters moved to Redlands, east of Los Angeles, leaving behind two little daughters until Elmer could get work. Later Florence Procter and her sister, Evelyn, were "tagged like baggage" and sent by train to join their parents in Redlands.

In the providence of God, the Procter family moved to Lindsay when Florence was about 13. She was bright, beautiful, industrious, intelligent, athletic, and adventuresome. She enjoyed the great outdoors in the San Joaquin Valley – hiking, riding horses, swimming, playing tennis and basketball. She was also a Christian and very spiritually minded. One night, in the providence of God, the Procter family attended a revival meeting in Lindsay. It was there the dark-haired, brown-eyed beauty met a handsome young man named Archie Word.

The courtship of Florence and Archie went on for nearly 13 years. When the impulsive young man ran away from home at 17 to join the Navy during World War I, the steady young girl faithfully wrote him each week on pink stationary. She made Archie sign a Christian Endeavor "Quiet Hour" pledge to begin each day with 15 minutes of meditation and communion with God. Ske kept her pledge; he, sadly, did not.

In the Spring of 1918 Florence graduated with honors from Lindsay High School. Archie's sister, Nellie, recalls that due to a shortage of teachers during World War I, Florence passed a special exam and became a teacher. Her first school was at Springville, in the foothills southeast of Lindsay. There she boarded with a family and taught grades one through eight in a one-room school house.

Florence was glad to see Archie when he returned from the Navy in August of 1919, but it was not long until she noticed that he had become a wild and wayward young man. One of the great desires of her young heart was to be a missionary. When Archie twitted her about this she wrote, Oct. 5, 1919, in bitter disappointment: "It is an ideal I have held for years and still hold. And if it is at all possible I mean to go; alone if necessary in spite of having once known someone I would like to have had go with me." If there were ever any words that haunted Archie Word in the years to come, it must have been those words.

Finally, Archie broke off all ties with Florence, calling himself a Briar and her a Lily. She responded: "You a briar? Yes, if you want to be. No, if you do not want to be. You can make yourself just what you desire...yes, even a lily if you tried."

For three long years Florence had nothing to do with Archie – because Archie had nothing to do with God. After a car accident in 1925, in which he nearly lost his life, Archie returned to Lindsay, somewhat chastened. Florence, who was now teaching school in Strathmore, agreed to see him when he was on good behavior. When Archie went away to Bible College in Oregon, Florence wrote to him nearly every day. After his conversion to Christ in November of 1925, Archie wrote to Florence: "No one could influence a life as you have mine."

On July 7, 1926, the Briar and the Lily became one. As Charles Wesley wrote:

*Not from his head was woman took,*
*As made her husband to o'erlook;*
*Not from his feet, as one designed*
*The footstool of the stronger kind;*
*But fashioned for himself a bride;*
*An equal, taken from his side.*

Florence was under contract to teach at Strathmore, so her husband went back to Eugene alone. Florence wrote him twice a day for the next nine months. One day she received a letter from Archie which read, "No other work in the world could keep us apart for a week, let alone nine months. You've been braver than I; always looking on the brighter side of life, trying to help me to buckle up and look the world in the face" (March 21, 1927).

Finally, in June of 1927, Florence was able to join her husband in his work as director of music and youth in the church at Dallas, Oregon. During the next three years she set up homes in Dallas, Eugene, Crabtree, and Toledo before they decided to go on the road in revivals – right in the middle of the Great Depression! Those were hard times. The roads were mainly dirt or gravel, and dust would filter into the trailer where Florence covered the girls with blankets. For the next five years Florence learned to live in other people's homes: doing her family's cooking, washing, ironing, raising three small children, seeing to their schooling (Margaret attended seven different schools in three states during her first year of school!).

The Word Revival Team was just that – a team of three: God, Archie, and Florence. She would often call with the preacher's wife, teach special ladies classes, help Archie in the afternoon Booster Club (sometimes attended by as many as 300 children), bring special music and help with the song services. Minnie Mick (now married to Woody Phillips) was converted in 1934, during one of the Word's revivals in Pomona. She says, "Mrs. Word led the singing each evening and was loved by all."

In a revival at Lindsay, where 136 people were converted to Christ, the people still talk about the influence of the Words. Alpha Engleking said, "We were so hungry for the Word. Archie helped bring us to Christ, but Billy (Florence's nickname in Lindsay) fed us in her Bible studies."

Harry Chapin, "The Smiling Singer" (Archie's song evangelist in those years) said, "Florence was as devoted to as was Archie, and she stood by him in all his work. She was a most humble and gracious lady."

Archie's own sister, Nellie Arnold, said, "A book about Archie would surely not be complete without much said about his wife Billy...Billy was a great lover of children. She was a wonderful story teller and children in her neighborhood frequently wanted to know when she was going to iron because she would tell stories as she ironed. I sincerely believe my sister-in- law was the very best a preacher could have for a wife. When Billy would pack his suitcase for his trips, she would write little notes and tuck them in his clothing."

When the Words finally left the field of full-time evangelism and settled in Portland in 1935, Florence was so tired that she didn't even hang curtains in the house on Glisan Street for over a year. But the first night in her very own home she instructed Margaret and Barbara to thank the Lord for their room and beds. Their bedroom, however, was soon dubbed the "guess" room because the Words opened the door of their home to many people in the coming years. Warren Bell was only one of scores who found refuge, haven, and a little bit of heaven in the house on Glisan Street. I'm sure that all who tasted of Florence's hospitality would agree with Sir Walter Scott's definition of woman: " A ministering angel thou!"

It has been said, "The woman who creates and sustains a home, and under whose hands children grow up to be strong and pure men and women, is a creator second only to God." Florence Word was that kind of woman.

Margaret learned to sing while wiping the dishes. After putting up hundreds of jars of strawberries and peaches one summer, Barbara said, "We learned many lessons and responsibilities in those tender years. How thankful we are now–but not then!" Jenelle and Esther remember their mother ironing in the kitchen, making up "Mischief Elf" stories as she pressed the family clothes. Arch recalls a nostalgic moment sitting by the old wood stove in his parent's bedroom. "The stove would glow cherry red. Mom would sew and I would sit by the stove." Warm memories, all of these. Anna Jean's memories include sitting on the back porch churning butter or sitting on the kitchen counter drying dishes. "There was a love and tenderness that pervaded our home such as is rarely found today. Many of my early childhood memories are dominated by my Mother's life because Daddy was gone extensively (sometimes six months at a time) in revival meetings. Mother lived each moment in anticipation of his return."

Once, when Archie was in Alaska for a long revival meeting in 1946, Florence put the children to bed and wrote a poem which she was feeling so keenly in her heart that lonely night.

**Just Missing You**

*Sure 'tis funny how we miss the muss*
*Of someone who is gone:*
*No newspaper in the bedroom*
*At night when day is done.*

*No shirt collars to be cold starched*
*When the ironings tucked away.*
*No old work pants in the corner*
*Bits of sand and wisps of hay.*

*No necktie on the bed post*
*Dirty socks upon the floor.*
*No bits of crumpled paper*
*Where he'd looked the days mail o'er.*

*Some would say, "Must be convenient,*
*That much less work to be done."*
*I must answer, "Foolish person!*
*Work for loved ones is just fun."*

*True, we miss these little duties*
*But the "miss" no pleasure is*
*For we also miss the blessing*
*Of the smiling face of his.*

*Miss the whistle in the doorway*
*When the meal time brings him in,*
*Miss the happy squeal of children*
*Welc'ming him with quite a din.*

*Miss his presence, miss his loving,*
*Miss him all the long day through.*
*But are happy for, though far away,*
*We know he's always true.*

*Yes, we miss the mess of someone*
*Who is gone–but so much more*
*We'll be happy when he's home again*
*And coming in the door.*

It has been said, "If the time should ever come when women are not Christians and houses are not homes, then we shall have lost the chief cornerstones on which civilizations rest." Florence Word was the real cornerstone in the home on Glisan Street.

It must have been difficult for the First Lady of Montavilla to leave her home of 33 years when Archie resigned from the church in the summer of 1968. Like Sarah of old she divided many of her earthly goods with family and friends and set off with her husband in their Silver Streak trailer, to wherever the Lord would call them. After a year or so they settled in Gering, Nebraska. From 1969 to 1984 Florence kept a daily diary. Her entries, always neat (except when Archie hit a pothole) reflect the great love she had for her husband – whom she always called "Daddy" – her children, grandchildren, and great-grandchildren. She described their 50th Wedding Anniversary as "the greatest event in our lives" because they were together with all their children and old friends. A pleasant June day in 1979, when the Words spent a day in California with old friends Bill and Carrie Jessup, Lewis and Minnie Mick, Nellie Word, Dorothy Shaw, Hal and Evelyn Martin, was described as "a glorious, precious afternoon."

Throughout her life Florence had been a deeply devout woman. She loved the Lord, she loved the church for which Christ died, she loved the Lord's Day, and she had a special love for prayer meeting night. Whenever the Words were on the road they would always stop for prayer meeting, wherever they were. One of the most heart-touching entries in her diaries is when Alzheimers disease had begun to affect her so that she could not think to pray. One night, coming home from prayer meeting, she wrote, "When it was my turn to pray I could not speak. I felt very bad, ashamed, chagrined...How I wish I could pray as others do."

When Tom Burgess called the other night, informing me of Florence's death, I hung up the phone and looked at the calendar. Wednesday. Prayer meeting night. How fitting. Then the words of the old hymn came to mind:

*Sweet hour of prayer, sweet hour of prayer,*
*May I thy consolation share,*
*Till, from Mount Pisgah's lofty height,*
*I view my home, and take my flight:*
*This robe of flesh I'll drop, and rise*
*To seize the everlasting prize;*
*And shout, while passing through the air,*
*"Farewell, farewell, sweet hour of prayer!"*

I am convinced that is precisely what happened on prayer meeting night, Wednesday, January 29, 1992, to dear Florence Word. To paraphrase something Florence once wrote:

*Yes, we'll miss the life of someone*
*Who is gone–but so much more*
*We'll be happy when we see her*
*Standing in the open door!*

Author's note: Florence Word was laid to rest by her beloved husband in Willamette National Cemetery Portland, Oregon, a briar and a lily lovingly placed in her hands.